RHETORIC IN DEBT

RSA·STR

THE RSA SERIES IN TRANSDISCIPLINARY RHETORIC

Edited by
Michael Bernard-Donals *(University of Wisconsin)* and
Leah Ceccarelli *(University of Washington)*

Editorial Board:
Diane Davis, The University of Texas at Austin
Cara Finnegan, University of Illinois at Urbana-Champaign
Debra Hawhee, The Pennsylvania State University
John Lynch, University of Cincinnati
Steven Mailloux, Loyola Marymount University
Kendall Phillips, Syracuse University
Thomas Rickert, Purdue University

The RSA Series in Transdisciplinary Rhetoric is a collaboration with the Rhetoric Society of America to publish innovative and rigorously argued scholarship on the tremendous disciplinary breadth of rhetoric. Books in the series take a variety of approaches, including theoretical, historical, interpretive, critical, or ethnographic, and examine rhetorical action in a way that appeals, first, to scholars in communication studies and English or writing, and, second, to at least one other discipline or subject area.

Other titles in this series:

Nathan Stormer, *Sign of Pathology: U.S. Medical Rhetoric on Abortion, 1800s–1960s*

Mark Longaker, *Rhetorical Style and Bourgeois Virtue: Capitalism and Civil Society in the British Enlightenment*

Robin E. Jensen, *Infertility: A Rhetorical History*

Steven Mailloux, *Rhetoric's Pragmatism: Essays in Rhetorical Hermeneutics*

M. Elizabeth Weiser, *Museum Rhetoric: Building Civic Identity in National Spaces*

Chris Mays, Nathaniel A. Rivers and Kellie Sharp-Hoskins, eds., *Kenneth Burke + The Posthuman*

Amy Koerber, *From Hysteria to Hormones: A Rhetorical History*

Elizabeth C. Britt, *Reimagining Advocacy: Rhetorical Education in the Legal Clinic*

Ian E. J. Hill, *Advocating Weapons, War, and Terrorism: Technological and Rhetorical Paradox*

Kelly Pender, *Being at Genetic Risk: Toward a Rhetoric of Care*

James L. Cherney, *Ableist Rhetoric: How We Know, Value, and See Disability*

Susan Wells, *Robert Burton's Rhetoric: An Anatomy of Early Modern Knowledge*

Ralph Cintron, *Democracy as Fetish*

Maggie M. Werner, *Stripped: Reading the Erotic Body*

Timothy Johnson, *Rhetoric, Inc.: Ford's Filmmaking and the Rise of Corporatism*

James Wynn and G. Mitchell Reyes, eds., *Arguing with Numbers: The Intersections of Rhetoric and Mathematics*

Ashely Rose Mehlenbacher, *On Expertise: Cultivating Character, Goodwill, and Practical Wisdom*

Stuart J. Murray, *The Living from the Dead: Disaffirming Biopolitics*

G. Mitchell Reyes, *The Evolution of Mathematics: A Rhetorical Approach*

Jenell Johnson, *Every Living Thing: The Politics of Life in Common*

Kellie Sharp-Hoskins

RHETORIC IN DEBT

THE PENNSYLVANIA STATE UNIVERSITY PRESS
UNIVERSITY PARK, PENNSYLVANIA

This book is freely available in an open access edition with
the generous support of The Pennsylvania State University
Libraries. Digital copies are available for download through
the Pennsylvania State University Press website.

Library of Congress Cataloging-in-Publication Data

Names: Sharp-Hoskins, Kellie, 1982– author.
Title: Rhetoric in debt / Kellie Sharp-Hoskins.
Other titles: RSA series in transdisciplinary rhetoric.
Description: University Park, Pennsylvania : The Pennsylvania
   State University Press, [2023] | Series: The RSA series in
   transdisciplinary rhetoric | Includes bibliographical
   references and index.
Summary: "Examines the relationship between rhetoric and
   debt, arguing that they are fundamentally entangled in
   producing and disciplining who is deemed worthy of credit
   and how debt materializes differentially: as a credit to some
   and condemnation of others"—Provided by publisher.
Identifiers: LCCN 2023005029 | ISBN 9780271095301
   (hardback) | ISBN 9780271095295 (paper)
Subjects: LCSH: Debt—Social aspects. | Rhetoric.
Classification: LCC HG3701 .S437 2023 | DDC 336.3/4—
   dc23/eng/20230421
LC record available at https://lccn.loc.gov/2023005029

Copyright © 2023 Kellie Sharp-Hoskins
All rights reserved
Printed in the United States of America
Published by The Pennsylvania State University Press,
University Park, PA 16802–1003

Copyright © The Rhetoric Society of America, 2023

The Pennsylvania State University Press is a member of the
Association of University Presses.

It is the policy of The Pennsylvania State University Press to
use acid-free paper. Publications on uncoated stock satisfy the
minimum requirements of American National Standard for
Information Sciences—Permanence of Paper for Printed
Library Material, ANSI Z39.48–1992.

Contents

Acknowledgments | vii

Introduction: Imagining Rhetoric in Debt | 1

1 Accounting for Rhetoric in Debt | 24

2 Economic Crisis, Financial Literacy, and Accounting for Student Loan Debt | 54

3 "Dividuals," Community Development, and Accounting for Municipal Bond Debt | 89

4 Community Risk, Actuarial Remainders, and Accounting for Medical Debt | 124

Conclusion: Rhetorical Futures in Debt | 156

Notes | 167

Works Cited | 173

Index | 187

Acknowledgments

In another project, my advisor-turned-collaborator Julie Jung and I argued that *how* something comes to matter *matters*. I don't know if or how this project will matter to others, but I know how it came to exist and matter for me—as an effect of people and relationships that have trained and sustained me, to each of whom I am indebted.

I am indebted, in particular, to Julie, who combines daunting brilliance, intellectual generosity, and kindness in perfect proportion. I learned from her how to ask big questions and pursue their answers. I learned how to consider complexity and when to use simplicity, when to speed up and how to slow down, the parts and the wholes of scholarly and intellectual work. I learned in classes and through feedback, in coffee shops and on "pizza Monday," from her scholarship and as we collaborated on multiple projects. In fairness, I am still learning these things—from the best teacher.

Other teachers and mentors who profoundly influenced me and this project include Angela M. Haas, Amy E. Robillard, and Lynn Worsham, each of whom served on my dissertation committee. What a gift to work with and learn from the scholars who most inspire me. I can't—and don't have to—imagine my work without Angela's commitment to interrupting colonial, racialized, and gendered power dynamics and her keen sense of methodology, Amy's insistence on tracing out the logics and effects of rhetoric (and her unbounded joy in and delight with dogs), or Lynn Worsham's field-changing attention to power, violence, affect, and embodiment.

Other scholars who inspire me started out as graduate-school friends: Erin Feld, Kyle Jensen, Marie Moeller, Erin Clark Frost, Kathleen Daly Weisse, and Chris Mays. Erin Feld's devotion to friendship and desserts as we navigated our MA program (and in the nearly twenty years since) introduced me to the joy of friends who share academic interests. Kyle offered to read my work first and has continued to make that offer for fifteen years. His generosity and belief in me are palpable in every conversation we have. In Marie, I have found a true kindred spirit. She is wicked smart and hilarious, and she cares deeply about doing good (and being awesome). She daily models interrupting power dynamics, always looking out for the ways everyday practices might be harming those who are unseen and building more equitable systems in their place. Erin Clark Frost introduced me to a whole new world within academia—accomplishment without fanfare, work without whining, impact without ego. I look up to her as a scholar and a person. I want to be like her when I grow up—and to room with her at every conference until then. Kathleen rounds out the Fem(s)Quad with Marie, Erin, and me. Her brilliance and wit would be intimidating if it weren't packaged with such warmth and fun. Finally, Chris is the friend who has most impacted my thinking, not only because we have shared interests but because he truly listens and makes space for me to work through ideas. Chris's kindness and enthusiasm emerge in encouragement and affirmation. I have been lucky to present and publish with him but more so to call him a friend.

Although I didn't start my PhD program at the same time as any of these friends, I found intellectual kinship with each through years of conversations—about our work, about our feelings, and about our lives. I hope to continue these conversations for decades to come.

My current and former colleagues at New Mexico State University make my work possible by contributing to a context where I can *do* my work—where pizza nights and sandwich afternoons are frequent and necessary rejoinders to the grind of university positions. I am grateful, in particular, to Justine Wells, who generously offered feedback on an early draft of what proved to be a critical juncture of this project, to Patti Wojahn for her unmatched enthusiasm, to Anthony Stagliano for his intellectual curiosity, and to Kerry Banazek for daily problem-solving, feelings-sharing, and plans-making. I am indebted, too, to Ryan Cull, Tyson Stolte, and Megan Bell, whose friendship has been nothing short of sustaining. The project also emerged as the direct result of a yearlong sabbatical through the College of Arts & Sciences at NMSU.

Conversations that definitely were *not* about this project also allowed it to emerge: frequent chats with my siblings—Tiffany, Jamie, Andy, Becky, and Kylie—and check-ins from loving parents, Chris and Bob Sharp. Without quite knowing what I am up to or why, they each support me. Frankie Sharp-Hoskins, the best dog in the world, also doesn't know quite what I am up to, but she has been my daily companion in research and writing for fourteen years. A soundtrack of this project would surely be set to her snores.

Finally, I need to save my biggest and loudest thanks for Mike Hoskins, whose expertise in accounting and finance allowed me to make interdisciplinary connections that would otherwise have been unavailable. Indeed, I can trace the origin of this book both to one specific conversation in which we compared disciplinary definitions of materiality and to the hundreds of conversations since. But this was not just an intellectual partnership: he is also truly my partner. Plus, we share *all* our debt.

Introduction | Imagining Rhetoric in Debt

In 2019, a string of news stories across the United States reported on how school districts manage "school lunch debt"—money owed to public schools that provide meals on credit to students who do not qualify for free school lunch and without cash on hand—revealing policies designed to differentiate students who are unable to pay for meals from those who are able to do so. From serving only cold food to punitive measures that include denying access to field trips or prom, such policies mark the debt by marking students as debtors ineligible to participate as equals alongside their peers (Fu). Students who cannot pay for lunch are posited as undeserving: they do not deserve a hot lunch, a learning experience off campus, or a rite of passage. Those experiences are reserved for students who have met their financial obligations. Moreover, students who cannot pay for lunch must be held accountable: if they eat on credit, they have incurred a debt. And debts must be paid. Or punished.

While not every school "owed" money for school lunches turns to punitive measures, CNN reports that a significant majority must contend with this issue, insofar as "75% of US school districts report student meal debt" (Lou). Interestingly—and despite contemporary economic and cultural logics that underwrite and authorize this type of reasoning, in which individuals are held accountable for their debts—the emergence of these stories as *news* suggests some discomfort with *who* is being held to account and *how* they are made accountable. By exposing these practices and their differentiating effects, news stories implicitly question the culpability and punishment of the students themselves, minors who are not generally considered accountable economic actors. Indeed, in a US context that aligns childhood with innocence, who can blame a child for being unable to pay for lunch? And how does punishing these students do anything more than shame or stigmatize them?

In addition to inviting critique, stories of student lunch debt have also invited philanthropic responses from individuals and organizations willing to *pay off* these debts on behalf of economic innocents. Thus, stories of benefactors circulate alongside stories of specific punitive policies in the public imagination. The philanthropic response is lauded for its simultaneous ability to meet the fiscal obligation of the debt (keeping schools solvent) while protecting students from hunger or differentiation. Because the debt is paid, no punishment is necessary. What is more, individuals and organizations that intercede in student debt signify their upstanding moral character as they use their own money to ensure equitable access and treatment for children.

The school policies in question and mediation by specific benefactors seem to invite straightforward epideixis. Punishing, shaming, or stigmatizing students with food insecurity is reprehensible; interceding in food insecurity is praiseworthy. Rather than evaluate such actions in terms of praise or blame, however, I begin with this brief description of the contemporary public discourse of student lunch debt in the United States as an example of the deep imbrication of debt logics in shaping our rhetorical imagination of accountability, morality, and social worthiness (or credit) broadly conceived. That is, rather than take for granted the actions or ethos of policy makers, enforcers, or benefactors of school lunch debt, I question how logics of debt so readily and rhetorically map the situation and stick to bodies, eager to assign praise and blame to individuals who can—or cannot—pay their debts. Ostensibly acute in significance, this introduction allows me to posit rhetorics of student lunch debt as symptomatic of how debt materializes and organizes social and cultural relations under the rubric of simple, individual, and calculable economic obligation. In the case of student lunches, even the presence of children—who are characterized as innocent or in need of protection—does not undermine the persuasive appeal of debt to narrate what is owed and what is due and to allocate morality in individual, fiscal terms.

Although, as I demonstrate throughout this book, debt makes considerable rhetorical appeals, this project is not limited to an analysis of the rhetoric *of* debt, insofar as such a prepositional relationship figures rhetoric and debt as discrete and extant, rhetoric merely a useful analytic tool to scrutinize debt. Rather, *Rhetoric in Debt* considers rhetoric *and* debt as constitutively entangled, materializing in relation. This is crucial to understanding how debt—both in general and in specific cases—comes to matter, differentially impacting bodies, lives, and futures such that debt is both incentivized and pathologized, rewarded and penalized, enabling and destructive.

An emphasis on materialization does not deny debt what the critical accounting scholar Miranda Joseph calls "the constitutive social *fact*" of debt (x, emphasis added). Indeed, conceptualizing rhetoric in debt builds on scholarship across economic, social, and critical theory that posits debt as, in the words of the debt scholar and Occupy Movement founder David Graeber, "the lifeblood of our economy" and "central issue of international politics" (5) or, following Joseph, "*the determining economic and thus social relation, superseding relations of production or consumption as the socially formative economic dynamic*" (ix). Far from economic determinism, however, this scholarship centers debt in the production, distribution, and valuation of social relations and tracks its complex functioning at multiple levels of scale: hailing and disciplining individuals through affective, moral imperatives; taxonomizing haves and have-nots; indenturing communities and cultures through interest rates and austerity measures; organizing military and political relationships among nation-states; and controlling our (rhetorical) imagination and allocation of value, worth, and worthiness. As the critical debt theorist Maurizio Lazzarato explains, "What is expropriated by credit/debt is not only wealth, knowledge, and the 'future,' but more fundamentally the *possible*" (*Governing* 23, emphasis added).

Postulating rhetoric in debt, then, considers the rhetorical, material, and political economic conditions of possibility through which debt emerges and takes shape, so successfully *becoming* "the determining economic and social relation" that it seems to always already exist as a social fact, describing a preexisting, economic reality. As Lazzarato makes clear, the stakes of the ascendance of debt cannot be overstated: "reconfiguring sovereign, disciplinary, and biopolitical power, the debt economy fulfills at once political, productive, and distributive functions" (*Making* 104). Such reconfiguration emerges through what David Harvey terms "the financialization of everything" (33), where financialization might be understood, following Greta R. Krippner, as "a broad-based transformation in which financial activities (rather than services generally) have become increasingly dominant in the U.S. economy over the last several decades" (2). That is, whereas finance itself might be understood in simple terms of providing funding or managing money, financialization describes how those acts infect and inflect daily life, describing "how credit and debt are lived" and depending "as much upon exclusion as inclusion" (Martin vii, 6). Configuring power around inclusion and exclusion, debt not only bifurcates haves from have-nots but maps such boundaries geopolitically and bodily, not replacing but enlivening and exacerbating historical inequities. In the words of John N. Robinson III, "Modern debt relations continue to reflect the racial history of debt and capitalism. The struggles of debtors around the world are not solely about regaining economic agency, but also inextricably embedded in the broader struggle for racial justice." Or, as succinctly articulated by Gargi Bhattacharyya in *Rethinking Racial Capitalism*, "Indebtedness itself is a highly variegated condition" (175).

Whereas scholars from a variety of critical traditions have thus centered debt as crucial to understanding social, cultural, political, and economic relations, explicit *rhetorical* attention to debt has been limited (as exceptions, see Herring, "Rhetoric"; Merskin). This might be attributed, in part, to Rodney Herring and Mark Garrett Longaker's broader critique that "rhetoricians discuss economics in ways limited and contained" (236) or to Christopher M. Duerringer's more recent claim that "rhetoricians have not paid much attention to the field of economics" (284). Limited attention also indicates a tacit acceptance of debt as an economic issue and economics as something independent or bounded. As Wendy Brown explains in *Undoing the Demos*, however, conceptualizing the economy as something discrete "may have been a brief twentieth-century event," whereby it was "cast as a self-contained structure, one in which wealth generation becomes its own autonomous sphere" (82). But bounding economic—and specifically financial—activity in scientific (as opposed to rhetorical) terms, as Rodney Herring argues, has significant consequences, undermining the possibility for intervention in its terms of articulation ("Neither Pistols" 159) and relegating discussion of economics to a question of truth or "economic correctness" (Aune, *Selling*). Following the communication scholar Joshua S. Hanan, it becomes possible to conceptualize economics in terms of an "economic imaginary," acknowledging their constitutive power and complex rhetorical and material interanimations (88). In other words, economics are better understood in relation to other forms of life, *homo politicus* always in relation to *homo economicus* (Brown 86), the latter of which Lazzarato (re)defines as not only economic man but "the indebted man" (*Making* 30).[1]

Responding to the implicit invitation of Herring and Longaker, and aligned with rhetorical scholarship devoted to the entanglements of rhetoric and economics that Brown implicitly marks (Chaput; Greene, "Rhetoric"; Hanan and Hayward; Herring, "Rhetoric"), I propose that rhetoric is uniquely situated to explore debt's *emergence* as "a constitutive social fact" and thus specifically obligated to expose and intervene in its differential violence—how it not only produces indebted subjects but, in doing so, contributes to gross inequities in wealth, health, and livability. Accordingly, *Rhetoric in Debt* theorizes and mobilizes a rhetorical methodology capable of exploring, exposing, and intervening in the "social fact" of debt by calling attention to the emergence of its individuating premises and complex, differential effects.

I begin this work in the remainder of this introduction by exploring how the seeming *fact* of debt, its function as *"the* determining economic and thus social relation" (Joseph ix), might be better understood as the conclusion to an enthymeme, whereby suppressed premises sponsor its reputation as a matter of fact. In this chapter, I thus conduct enthymematic analysis—identifying the unstated premises that support widely held conclusions about the fact(s) of debt—but not as an end in itself. Rather, I use such analysis in order to lay bare the complexities that are embedded in the seeming fact of debt. Surfacing the premises of debt through enthymematic analysis, as I do in this chapter, reveals that rhetoricians must look beyond discourses *of* debt (and thus beyond existing analytical methods) and toward financial instruments themselves as rhetorical devices that constitute subjects (differentially). Enjoining critical interdisciplinary scholarship concerned with the function and effects of debt to manage bodies, lives, subjectivities, futures, and the possible itself in the enthymematic analysis, I propose the need for additional rhetorical coinvestigation of debt capable of considering how it materializes across temporal and spatial levels of scale. Such materializations of debt manage its complexity and underwrite its violence by reducing our rhetorical imagination of debt to something individual and quantifiable, moral and calculable. I conclude the chapter by introducing the chapters that follow, which first articulate and then mobilize a methodology capable of accounting for rhetoric in debt.

Debt Exists

As indicated by increasing, interdisciplinary critical attention as well as public and media accounts, debt is everywhere. Moreover, circulating under a variety of names (credit, loans, finance, bonds, securities) and attached to the variety of bodies and entities (consumers, students, car owners, home owners, health care patients, inmates, small businesses, cities, nations), debt is everywhere *up*. This is corroborated by historical accounts of debt as well as by contemporary statistics about its magnitude.[2] Reported as matters of fact, histories and statistics point to a seemingly benign conclusion: debt exists. Or, more specifically, debt denotes and describes a literal, material relationship of exchange in which *something* (money, time, expertise) has been given away with the understanding that it will be returned, refunded, or otherwise repaid in the future. Of course, terminologically, "debt," and "indebtedness" in particular, can be used to denote relationships outside of financial transactions (see, for example, Sharp-Hoskins; Vealey and Layne; and this book's conclusion), but a history of colonization, capital, and property, combined with the contemporary reach of neoliberal policies, practices, and technologies on a global scale, gives the economic connotations of the word unprecedented power to define its terms and ethics. In vernacular and public discourses, "debt" is used to indicate fiscal obligations and situations, which are, increasingly, circumscribed by *finance* and thus bind the extension of credit to and use of debt by individuals to a much larger system of monetary exchange and capital markets. As Lazzarato argues, finance is not a feature of but "*the politics* of capital," such that creditor-debtor relations have fundamentally displaced capital-labor relations as the "center of economic, social, and political life" (*Governing* 13, emphasis in original). In other words, when we consider the history of the concept coupled with its role in legislating and regulating the daily lives and futures of most people within a global neoliberal system, monetary or financial debt is the most common referent of the term, and, importantly, it infiltrates and organizes the term's other uses.[3]

In addition to facts or statistics about rising debt, then, evidence of its existence is also manifest in lived, embodied experiences, affecting relationships, regulating daily and long-term decision-making (about employment, education, housing, and medical care), and producing affective and emotion-based orientations to the world. Indeed, often described as a possession or object, something someone *has*, debt is also qualified in terms of its force or weight: it can be suffocating or crushing. Meanwhile, prepositional relations for expressing debt figure it as a container (Lakoff and Johnson), context, or circumstance that likewise overwhelms bodily capacities: "I am *in* debt," or "I'll never get *out* of debt." In addition to these rhetorical framings that bespeak its relationships to the body, debt has also been linked with stress, anxiety, depression, and suicidal ideation—it is bodily lived (Turunen and Hiilamo).

Though evidence for debt's effects (and affects) abound, however, the simple existence of debt can also be understood as the conclusion to an enthymeme, which relies on accepting unstated premises that elide its complex rhetorical function. As I argue for and evidence shortly, these premises include (1) that debt is individual, volitional, and moral and (2) that debt is numerically and mathematically calculable and quantifiable. Often surreptitious, these premises work together to establish debt as an ahistorical, arhetorical fact: it exists. In the following sections, I thus draw on Matthew Jackson's conceptualization of enthymeme and enthymematic analysis to unpack these premises in turn before showing how they work together to sponsor the conclusion that debt *exists* and the consequences of this conclusion. More specifically, I use Jackson's definition of enthymeme as an informal syllogism that circulates in "everyday discourses," in which premises and conclusions "are not laid out so neatly for us" and "we often only catch one of the premises or the conclusion floating by, a piece of drifting discourse as it were" (605).

Identifying these suppressed premises and their rhetorical impacts grounds the work that follows: an argument for a methodology of accounting for rhetoric *in* debt that not only exhumes unstated premises but examines how they ground our rhetorical imagination, writ large. But beginning with enthymematic analysis is not merely an inconsequential means to an end. Rather, it gestures toward the scalar emergence of rhetoric in terms more familiar to rhetoricians. By unpacking the (unstated) premises that lead to conclusions, enthymematic analysis tacitly confirms the temporal and spatial scales of rhetoric: conclusions *do not* just exist. They *emerge* as the consequence of—and always in relation to—a series of premises, a history and field of other conclusions. Enthymematic analysis thus uniquely paves the way for me to introduce a methodology that is more explicitly attuned to debt's scalar emergence and effects, which I argue for in the conclusion of this chapter and theorize in chapter 1.

Debt as Individual, Moral, and Volitional

A significant premise that leads to the conclusion that debt exists can be identified by turning to its colloquial, prepositional usage and is confirmed by scholarship in a range of fields: in public discourses in the West, debt principally signifies as an economic relation between and a responsibility of individuals. As Graeber points out, however, the idea that "debts must be repaid" is an individual and moral, rather than economic, understanding of debt, which emerges from a "mythic past" that naturalizes community relations as always already economic. He argues that the effect of this truism about debt is "moral confusion," wherein debt in its current global and financialized forms is equated with an imagined past of individual barter and trade (ostensibly characterized by clear accounts of what was owed, what was due, and by whom) (4). Tacitly corroborating this assessment of false equivalency, Alexander X. Douglas argues that complex cases of debt are rationalized and moralized through comparison to those more "close-to-home," resulting in "the careless bundling together of very different situations under a single concept" (xiii, xii), and pairing his work with Graeber's helps to explain how debt-as-individual becomes an accepted, acceptable premise: it is used to describe histories of exchange, validated by daily, individual experiences and relationships, and then extended to evaluate appropriate (moral) action in diverse contexts. Thus, even though debt functions in distinct ways at different levels of scale (Krugman), it is nonetheless haunted by rhetorical echoes of individuality and morality across its many contexts.[4]

These echoes and rhetorical slippage are evident in representations of the US national debt that not only visually figure the total debt as a constantly increasing number—as represented by USdebtclock.org, for example—but divide it by the number of residents in the United States, suggesting that each individual is equally responsible for their "share" of the total debt. Accordingly, individuals are invited to donate to pay down the national debt through treasury.gov via check, PayPal, debit, or, ironically, credit card. Although this website may not yield many returns, the implication that individuals are responsible for national debt is deeply entrenched in individual morality as a basis for neoliberal reasoning.[5] As Lazzarato explains, "Debt represents a mnemotechnics integral to the construction of a (bad) conscience and guilt. These are the subjective conditions necessary for keeping the 'collective' promise of reimbursement, a promise state debts implicitly make. The state, technocratic governments, and the media must therefore invest considerable energy to ensure a population's guilt for debt into which it has never entered and, therefore, its responsibility for faults it has never committed" (*Governing* 42). The guilt for debt is distributed by accounts of debt and deficit crises, used to threaten morality and economy alike. Returning to Douglas's terms, we might say the guilt that arises in "close-to-home" cases is leveraged to shape the subjectivities necessary for large-scale economic practices. Further, national debt itself is terministically framed as "sovereign debt," equating national economies in their complexity with the figure of an individual who can make intentional decisions that reduce debt and secure morality. This equation helps explain why national debt that nears default levels is met with calls for austerity measures: sovereign countries are expected—like individuals *in* debt—to tighten their belts, to cut spending and benefits and other so-called entitlements and luxuries, to pay off debt and right their (moral) relationship with their lenders. In a US political economic context, this equation also fuels anxiety about the debt ceiling, which becomes a rhetorical pawn in assessing fiscal responsibility, mapped, as it is, by close-to-home logics of and moralization about debt.

The fault lines at work in mapping individual logic onto much more complex cases of debt are stark. Whereas the moral expectation of repaying a neighbor seems universal, the same expectations would radically undermine the global debt economy because, as noted by Andrew Ross, "our creditors don't want us to pay off our debts entirely," which would undermine the profits associated with servicing the debt (i.e., interest payments): "The goal is to keep us on the hook until we die, and even beyond the grave in the case of student debts that are co-signed by parents or grandparents" (216). Given that repayment in full compromises the ability of lenders to (literally) capitalize on debt, Lazzarato's description of the necessity for individualized guilt is clarified. Guilt does not secure repayment but subjectivity. The *feeling* of individual, moral obligation of repayment—rather than only the action of repayment—fuels the debt economy. This connection between individual guilt and the function of debt within the global economy is not incidental but central to neoliberal capitalism, premised on the guarantee of the "freedom" for individuals to consume (Harvey 2).

Imagining debt as individual and moral not only affectively invites particular financial behaviors but simultaneously offers rhetorical cover for its emergence in racialized and colonial histories and effects on intergenerational relationships.[6] In *Black Wealth / White Wealth*, Melvin L. Oliver and Thomas M. Shapiro argue that common economic indicators (including income, employment, and education) elide the significance of intergenerational wealth in shaping economic possibilities and futures, which not only follow but fundamentally sponsor racial inequality (2). Although Oliver and Shapiro do not explicitly study debt, their attention to intergenerational wealth disrupts the capitalist commonplace that financial holdings or obligations are individually held; it further contextualizes wealth generation in its histories, revealing significant and structural racialized differences in opportunities for and barriers to investment as well as "the sedimentation of racial inequality" (50).[7]

Identifying the contextualizing factors that sponsor and deny wealth accumulation and (I would include) the availability of credit and debt likewise reveals the impact of such contexts on the intergenerational accrual and practice of *financial literacies*, a term that can serve as a euphemism for racialized disparities in wealth. Assumed and represented as a cognitive or behavioral skill that individuals learn and demonstrate, financial literacy indicates normative economic practices that are neither equally available nor equitably assessed.

Whereas histories of inclusion in financial markets and policies might invite trust and investment as indicators of financial literacy, for example, related histories of radical, racialized exclusions (on which the inclusions depend) sponsor quite different literacies.[8] Moreover, markers of financial literacy also indicate that having, owing, and repaying debt (or not) is rational and volitional: individuals are assumed to make rational and literate (read: normative) choices about whether they will live up to the moral obligation of debt. What is more, the assumption that debt and repayment are individual choices affirms their morality. This assumption is further valorized when patterns of debt accumulation are not contextualized in relation to colonial and racialized patterns; debt signifies as a choice about the future and a choice without history. By this logic, it is because debts are chosen by (financially literate) individuals that they can be used to measure the morality of those individuals, who are presumed to *decide* whether to use debt and whether to repay it. Individuals who decide to use credit cards (and accrue credit card debt) or take out student loans (and accrue student loan debt), for example, are not only evaluated with regard to their likelihood to repay (i.e., how much economic credit they merit), but the likelihood to repay is linked to their moral standing (i.e., their credit a metonym of their credibility). Tied to individuality and morality, such assumptions also move across levels of scale, such that students, drivers, home owners, companies, states, and whole countries are assumed to draw on a universal literacy to make sovereign choices about whether they will repay a debt. These assumptions redact racialized and colonial histories, eliding their participation in how—and for whom—debt emerges, and invite methodologies capable of surfacing the differential impact of these histories and relations on those who live them.

As I discuss in more detail in the chapters that follow, financial literacy, like debt, is not a predefined or static attribute of an individual but something that emerges in specific contexts as the boundary condition and marker for normative economic practices *and* embodiments. Moreover, the language or rhetoric used to *describe* financial literacy overwrites its tacit rhetorical appeals to individual or market rationality, itself coded language for white and Western logics. Darrick Hamilton and William A. Darity Jr. begin to demystify this code in their exposé of the language of debt, which bifurcates "good" versus "bad" debt in the US imaginary. Used in disciplinary discourses of accounting and insurance to indicate whether a debt is deemed payable or not in ostensibly neutral terms, qualifying debt as "good" or "bad" further moralizes the term in public and popular discourse. As Hamilton and Darity explain, what "we traditionally perceive as good and bad debt has different implications once we consider the following factors: race, the prevailing framework of targeting unprivileged racial groups with inferior housing and educational products, predatory finance, and ongoing housing and labor market discrimination. These factors limit the choice set and rates of returns to homeownership and a college degree, all based on race and ethnicity" (62). Whereas financial practices are presumed to be individual, Hamilton and Darity implicate their significance in rhetorical economies of racialized meaning, which limits *and* codes individual "choices" about debt. Such an economy of meaning for debt in the United States—and worldwide—fundamentally rests on its colonial histories and reliance on chattel slavery, in which land was claimed without financial compensation to its occupants at the same time that enslaved peoples were conceptualized as property that could be bought and sold, considered an asset rather than a human. Investigating laws and cultural practices that protect the accumulation and continuation of white wealth shows that they are historically matched by laws divesting Indigenous peoples of their lands while inviting ongoing debts of enslaved peoples and their descendants.[9]

Such patterns suggest, as Graeber argues in more general terms, that neither capitalism nor debt can be disarticulated from their entanglement in violent histories: "It is the secret scandal of capitalism that at no point has it been organized primarily around free labor. The conquest of the Americas began with mass enslavement, then gradually settled into various forms of debt peonage, African slavery, and 'indentured service'... recruited largely from among people who were already debtors" (350). In other words, debt is not a coincidental feature of the history of the United States but structures its articulation and relations from its inception, underwriting the terms by which the Americas were claimed and colonized (see Chakravartty and Ferreira da Silva; Rosenthal). These debts and their afterlives—including the rhetorical ascendance to debt as individual, volitional morality—thus must be understood as a form of colonial amnesia: "the inability (or unwillingness) of the colonizer to recall the past oppression that they have perpetuated on the colonized ... due to a long history of covering up or minimizing such events" or "a strategy to prevent the public accounting of crimes and unfair treatment against Indigenous Peoples" (Bird 282). The "forgetting," in this case, takes the form of history in which economics and debt are radically disarticulated from the colonial and racial terms of their emergence and thus not only successfully signify as individual but actually *go without saying*, serving as an unstated premise in service of the neutralized conclusion that debt simply exists.

Debt as Quantifiable, Mathematical, and Self-Evident

Another way to understand moralizations of debt is to track the concept beyond its significance within financial exchange or a contemporary "debt economy" and to consider its less transactional connotations, in which debt indicates interpersonal rather than fiscal relationships. Indeed, figures of debt and indebtedness are widely invoked to represent nonmonetary relationships. But, while terministically debt can be articulated in terms of social obligations or favors—as in, "a friend invited me to dinner so I should invite her back" or "I am deeply indebted to my academic mentors"—under the global auspices of neoliberalism, it most often invokes calculations of value, exchange, and futures that can be metonymically figured as numbers (see Engels). "Neoliberalism has meant," as David Harvey explains, "the financialization of everything" (33). As referenced earlier, this includes the financialization of "daily life," which is not only a "proposal for how to get ahead, but also a medium for the expansive movements of body and soul" (Martin 3). In addition to being overwritten by the language of finance and neoliberalism, as Graeber contends, the history of debt "is necessarily a history of money," because "money and debt appear on the scene at exactly the same time": "the difference between a debt and an obligation is that debt can be precisely quantified. This requires money" (21). Rather than scapegoat money itself, however, Graeber suggests that it is the calculation and equivalency practices that problematically position debt from its inception and, I would add, ground it in additional unstated premises: "The difference between owing someone a favor and owing someone a debt is that the amount of debt can be precisely calculated. Calculation demands equivalence" (386).

Two correlated premises that underwrite this calculation and equivalency (and very existence) of debt are seemingly benign: quantities are numerical or mathematical, and they are self-evident. While this rings true on a micro scale or, again, in "close-to-home" cases—as individuals use specific, numeric values to represent and evaluate financial obligations (loans, debts, payments)—it also characterizes larger scales, as complex algorithms determine rates of acceptable risk, appropriate interest, and the timelines at which a debt can be repaid (for anything from microfinance loans to impoverished people to federal student loans in the United States to acceptable debt holdings of the entire nation of Greece). The numerical foundation of Western math allows it to signify as concrete, the so-called universal language; or, in other words, numeracy and mathematical calculation are understood to accurately and neutrally represent relationships between creditors and debtors, reflecting what is owed and what is due, what has been lent and thus what must be repaid. Graeber echoes Marx to point out that such equivalencies are hardly neutral: "equivalence—especially when it involves equivalence between human beings (and it always seems to start that way, because at first, human beings are the ultimate values)—only seems to occur when people have been forcibly severed from their contexts, so much so that they can be treated as identical to something else" (386). In this context, they demand a critical, rhetorical accounting.

While Graeber ties the problematics of quantification and equivalence to the definition of debt, I propose that they are also embedded in practices and technologies that *account* for debt, which offer the means and methods by which equivalencies are calculated, including human equivalencies. When such practices and technologies are taken for granted, they appear, again, factually and neutrally to represent transactions and relations. The stakes of this supposed neutrality, as Steven Katz argues in writing about the Third Reich in Germany, however, are no less than dehumanization. Studying the representation practices of the Nazi program, in which technical—including numeric—equivalencies structured their "cold-blooded method" (265), Katz forcefully argues that a focus on objectivity and detachment not only precipitated but fundamentally sponsored its capacity for genocide. Using a seemingly mundane memo as exemplary of the type of technical writing at work in the regime, Katz shows how people were reduced to "cargo" and suffering was reduced to a calculable problem of load capacity, under the guise of expediency.

What Katz terms the "technological ethos" of the documents he analyzes resonates with the broader Nazi accounting system used to identify and mark Jewish and other abjected persons, who were tattooed with numbers in place of names, metonymically representing their denied humanity. Such systems were not radically particular to the Nazi regime, however, but, as Cynthia Haynes notes, integral to "the history of computing, which is at once both the (innocuous) history of human accounting and the (noxious) counting of humans as nonexistent" (43). Although the Nazi regime was neither specifically capitalist nor neoliberal in its economic practices, it drew on specific and shared accounting technologies and practices to generate economic capital necessary to sponsor its political (genocidal) campaigns, the heirs of which persist in modern-day accounting and computer technologies.

Likewise precise and appalling, the accounting practices of the transatlantic slave trade relied on representing people as cargo. As Christina Sharpe shows in *In the Wake: On Blackness and Being*, enslaved persons transported by ship were not identified by name but as "'Negro man' or 'Negro woman' at the top of the ledger and the account book followed by 'ditto' all down the page" (M. NourbeSe Philip, qtd. in Sharpe 52). Although not technically recording individuals as numbers, this accounting system nonetheless prioritizes *quantity* as an indication of value. Whereas during the Holocaust numeric substitution authorized and supported mass extermination, transatlantic ledgers—as argued by Sharpe—relied on such substitutions to track the "value" of cargo in order for slave traders to be properly compensated and to justify insurance claims, indicating how "a crude human calculus had evolved at the heart of the slave trade and was accepted by all involved" (James Walvin, qtd. in Sharpe 36).[10] This type of accounting, as Caitlin Rosenthal argues, rested on "no ordinary balance sheet: it was denominated in the units of human life" (9).

Not specifically focused on accounting or debt, Katz and Sharpe attest to the ethics embedded in accounting practices, valued for their accuracy and precision. Rosenthal, for her part, directly takes up the relationship in *Accounting for Slavery*, identifying "a balance sheet of life and death" (9) that served as the ground for the transatlantic slave trade and practices of slavery at micro and macro levels of scale. What Sharpe refers to as a "crude human calculus" can be linked to the history of the modern fact itself, whereby facts came to "reflect things that actually exist" vis-à-vis historical technologies of equivalency, including double-entry bookkeeping (DEB; Poovey 29). Miranda Joseph confirms that accounting does not merely record or report facts but rhetorically creates them by equating "formal precision" and "empirical particulars" with accuracy (27), and James Alfred Aho corroborates that accounting—including double-entry bookkeeping—and the calculations and equivalencies it relies on do not exist outside of moral systems but, instead, encode and codify them. Indeed, "instead of arguing that DEB was originally devised to serve exclusively information or theoretical ends," Aho "suggests that its purpose was largely rhetorical—that is, to justify an activity about which there existed in medieval Christian Europe a considerable suspicion: namely, commerce itself" ("Rhetoric" 22).[11]

For Bruce G. Carruthers and Wendy Nelson Espeland, double-entry bookkeeping emerged as not only technically superior to other forms of accounting but paramount to rationality itself (33), playing both a technical and "crucial rhetorical role in legitimating an expanding capitalist economic system" by "altering the conceptual categories used to interpret business and to make decisions" (64). Despite the profound rhetorical effects of double-entry bookkeeping, Carruthers and Espeland remind us that it is not usually understood rhetorically but instead "considered a form of neutral, technical information" (35). It is this reputation of neutrality and technical measurement that paves the way for the contemporary economic stronghold of neoliberalism, which disarticulates accounting practices from specific histories and invokes precision and equivalency to persuade subjects of its rationality and inevitability. Insofar as double-entry bookkeeping is imagined as *arhetorical*, colonial economics could enlist it to account for slavery, and neoliberal economics can enlist it to account for the numeric "facts" of finance and debt. But as Joseph argues, speaking of the latter, "Life under neoliberalism has been shaped by the intertwined accounting practices through which these regimes of accumulation and governmentality have been implemented. These two domains of accounting are really inseparable" (xi). In short, neoliberalism "requires us all to manage our own lives through financial accounting practices" (xi). In this current, neoliberal moment, of course, accounting practices remain grounded in a double-entry system but simultaneously rely on more complex statistical practices and algorithmic calculations (xi), all of which take cover under the self-evident ethos of numbers.

Critical and interdisciplinary studies of the practices of accounting not only historicize how numbers came to stand in for more complex relations of lending, credit, and business relationships but also resonate with recent interdisciplinary literature on the social, cultural, and economic work of numbers and math *themselves* that exposes their rhetorical emergence and differential effects. That is, while critical accounting scholarship identifies how accounting practices and technologies visually *create* equivalencies between credits and debits and represent such as ontologically extant and factually neutral, recently math itself has been scrutinized as participating in—rather than transparently representing—value and disparity, encoding bias into the technologies that govern our daily lives (see, for example, Chaput and Colombini; Eubanks; Weisse et al.; Noble; O'Neil; Wynn and Reyes). Assumed to be universal, mathematics themselves emerge culturally, reflecting specific paradigms, epistemologies, and logics. This is evident in the historical emergence of a specific type of numeracy in the colonial Americas (Cohen) as well as in the significantly different mathematical practices of Indigenous peoples (Raju, "Decolonising Mathematics"). Rather than exclude math from culpability or bias, then, quantifying debt vis-à-vis math—or a mathematical premise of debt—implicates it in cultural practices of representation, equivalence, and differentiation, adjudicating worth and risk on the basis of mathematical approximations of ideological assessment.

The work of math to neutralize questions of differential value under the sign of a neutral—for example, by assigned creditworthiness vis-à-vis a numerical "score"—has also been critiqued as a Western colonial project.[12] The decolonial mathematics scholar Chandra Kant Raju explains, "Present-day mathematics rests on formal proof, which varies with logic, but logic varies with time beliefs and culture. So mathematical theorems are no more than cultural proofs" ("New Mathematics"). As Raju shows, it is Western math's separation from empirical proof—critiqued for *its* fallibility—and insistence on formal, deductive reasoning that allow it to retain its reputation. But such a reputation ignores how validity itself is constructed in cultural terms. Raju explains in an interview about his approach to decolonizing mathematics, "Empirical proof is rejected by Western mathematics on the grounds that empirical proof is fallible. Our senses might mislead us. To use a classical example from Indian philosophy: I might mistake a rope for a snake or a snake for a rope. But deductive proof too is fallible: one may easily mistake an invalid deductive proof for a valid one" ("Decolonising Mathematics"). In short, the self-evidence of Western mathematics is based on a premise that, itself, can be contested. The reputation of Western math as infallible is a cultural proposition. From a rhetorical perspective, of course, a cultural premise or proof is *expected* for reasoning, and proofs are not measured in zero-sum validities so much as effects. Rather than assume that mathematics have lost their validity once they are situated as cultural proofs, then, I propose that it is the *effects* of Western mathematical reasoning to substantiate debt that invite rhetorical investigation insofar as they position mathematical calculations as neutral arbiters of cost, benefit, value, and human life itself.

Implicitly highlighting this rhetorical exigence, Safiya Umoja Noble asserts that "the near-ubiquitous use of algorithmically driven software, both visible and invisible to everyday people, demands a closer inspection of what values are prioritized in such automated decision-making systems" (1). When algorithms are created, for example, to assess the risk associated with lending money to women in low-income countries, they seem to be *more valid* or *accurate* when they take into account women's health, education, and autonomy measured by

Western standards (Karim). And such assessment is persuasive under a rubric of predicative capability. Perhaps more insidiously, the *effects* of the loans are narrated without attention to their cultural implications or differential effects. Loans are considered successful insofar as they provide women with means to earn money, which elides how the loans simultaneously entangle them in complex asymmetries that are often met with family and communication backlash, including violence.[13] As economic research reveals, loans are offered, debts incurred, and ideological and financial colonization secured when the (Western) math is deemed precise.

The existence of debt as premised on numerical quantification and mathematical calculation further belies the *circulation* of debt that gives it its (rhetorical) force: when we believe debt can be calculated and represented numerically, we miss or ignore the ways it *moves*, allocating value to some *at the expense of* others, articulating debt as opportunity for some and as shame for others. Circulation itself also relies on mathematics to calculate parity across currencies and evaluate risk comparatively, but it is rhetorically subsumed under the *fact* of debt. The debt exists; it must be (re)paid.

Enthymematic Reasoning: Individual and Moral + Quantifiable and Mathematical

To combine the premises of debt exposed and explored in this chapter, the individual morality of debtors can be measured, assessed, and legislated in mathematical terms. It is when debt is calculated as a specific percentage of gross domestic product, for example, that the concern for default of sovereign nations can trigger austerity measures. The trigger, of course, is set up in colonial histories that sponsor staggeringly different concerns: colonizers are afforded significantly more credit and debt than the historically colonized are (see, for example, Christina Sharpe's analysis of Haiti's ongoing indebtedness to France in *In the Wake*). On another level of scale, a credit score is an algorithmic rendering of how much debt an individual can be trusted to borrow and pay back, how big a risk they pose to the lender. The widely used credit rating company FICO, for example, uses five categories to determine this score—new credit, length of credit history, credit max, payment history, and amounts owed—but explicitly acknowledges that their importance can vary. Ostensibly based on numbers as fair arbiters—where a one-year credit history, for example, seems to be objectively less time than a ten-year history or where a credit-to-debt ratio seems to be objectively represented through concrete numbers—credit scores codify and conceal their participation in affirming (or denying) economic credibility on the basis of histories that circulate and accrue credit differentially. An unemployed young person whose parents open credit in their name and pay their bills, for instance, may have a much higher score than an employed person with recent credit who pays their own bills or a recent immigrant (who must establish credit anew no matter their credit history elsewhere). Put another way, as explained by FICO, "Your FICO Scores are unique, just like you. They are calculated based on the five categories referenced above, but for some people, the importance of these categories can be different. For example, scores for people who have not been using credit long will be calculated differently than those with a longer credit history." Superficially alleviating fears that a FICO score is *impersonal* or that individuals are being treated *only* algorithmically, this explanation surreptitiously confirms the normative bias built into numerical renderings of credit (and creditworthiness).

The assessment of credit or how much debt an individual can be assumed to repay synthesizes the premises of mathematical reasoning and individual morality. That is, mathematical calculations attempt to predict individual behavior by aggregating data about groups of people with long versus short credit histories, people with high versus low credit availability, people with outstanding balances, and so forth and to forecast risk accordingly. Despite this context of numerical assessment through calculation based on statistical inference and premise-based forecasting, which tabulates new credit and significant debt and demarcates the terms of defaulting on a loan or declaring bankruptcy, it is the individual who is ultimately understood as failing to make good on a promise, who merits individual credit, credibility, and morality or guilt and shame. As I explore in detail in the chapters that follow, these affects "stick" risk to individuals in the context of neoliberal financial systems built on both the value of riskiness to investors and also (denied) colonial and racialized histories. Further, the individual, volitional premise of debt—that it exists as a function of individuals making choices and accepting responsibility, an indication of financial literacy—moralizes any consequences for "failure" to repay. Hunger, poverty, bankruptcy, repossession, eviction, and austerity become the moral reckoning for individuals (as well as companies, municipalities, and sovereign nations) who do not repay their debts. Ultimately, premises of individual, calculable debt ignore how debt emerges and individuates, distributing wealth and credit differentially, participating in conditions of possibility for who emerges as a (worthwhile) risk.

Surfacing Premises, Surfacing (Rhetorical) Opportunities

Surfacing unstated premises as I do in the preceding section vis-à-vis enthymematic analysis, which identifies how they are carried by commonplaces and fragments of discourse that pass without critique, can begin to reveal our complicity and participation in their function. That is, paying close attention to what goes *unsaid* or *without saying* when we consider debt is a vital analytical tool for unpacking its rhetorical constitution and consequences. Public discourses of student lunch debt, for example, which often take the form of a news story or report, retain rhetorical fragments that point to the unremarked and individuating, mathematical premises on which logics of debt rest. Indeed, "student lunch debt" itself is a noun phrase, which neatly packages debt in terms of not only who *owes* it or even *owns* it (better reflected, perhaps, with a possessive construction, as in "students' lunch debt") but an existing thing, an uncontestable fact, where the debt is synonymous with the student who owns it. Identifying this phrasing as a "fragment of discourse"—to invoke Jackson's terminology—assists us in recognizing the larger logics on which it is built, making visible the ways that unstated premises (debt is individual, debt is owned) ground uncontested conclusions (debt exists).

Building on the affordances of such enthymematic analysis, I propose that to better understand and intervene in the work of debt, which apportions morality, legibility, and livability and invests in colonization, white supremacy, and racism, we can move on from studying the rhetorics *of* debt—which uses rhetoric as a tool to analyze how debt is (re)presented—to conceptualizing and critiquing rhetoric *in* debt, which to is say, as complicit in its structural maintenance of privilege and oppression. To do so requires identifying the significant premises on which logics and discourses of debt rest (as demonstrated earlier), but it further invites a methodology capable of accounting for how debt emerges, circulates, and sticks to different bodies and subjects in asymmetrical, patterned ways. It invites us to ask, for example, how "student loan debt" became a thing, a matter of fact. This not only requires attention to how debt functions in technical or theoretical terms as described by financial specialists but to how it is daily described and lived, how it moves and to whom it sticks. As the Nobel Prize–winning economist Robert J. Shiller argues, "to understand a complex economy, we have to take into account many conflicting popular narratives and ideas relevant to economic decisions, whether the ideas are valid or fallacious" (xv). Rather than cast debt in terms of validities or fallacies, then, a methodology of accounting for rhetoric *in* debt considers how debt materializes in relation to both specialized and vernacular rhetorics, apportioning credit, risk, livability, and futures. Indeed, while politicians and op-ed pieces alike decry the administration of forgiveness programs and inequitable effects of these debts or praise microloans programs for their ability to save women and girls, they have yet to question the accounting practices and technologies through which debt is calculated and its assignment to individuals who "take out a loan." In this case and others, as I show in the chapters that follow, the terms of debt and forgiveness cannot be captured by money owed and repaid—the extant methodologies of financial accounting. They are also insufficiently accounted for by rhetorical methodologies that focus on textual representations of debt without paying attention to its materialization and materiality. Accounting for debt thus requires representation and analysis that shifts from a double-entry system (which flattens relations of debt to numeric, mathematical entries or calculations) and the practices, technologies, and institutions built on that system to a system that accounts for the emergence and effects of debt across temporal and spatial scales.

To this end, and in order to build a methodology capable of accounting for rhetoric in debt, in chapter 1, I turn to recent work that rhetorically theorizes affect and risk, concepts that are integral to drawing together issues of economics, materiality, and differential livability and are thus crucial to this project. Moreover, I center scholarship that prioritizes attention to *how* rhetorics move across contexts as well as across levels of scale, producing and disciplining subjects as they attach to bodies in highly local ways. Taking cues from Rebecca Dingo's articulation of her "transnational feminist rhetorical analytic," such work has the capacity to track "how complex networks of relationships affect rhetorical meaning" (*Networking Arguments* 14). It is further influenced by Dingo, Rachel Riedner, and Jennifer Wingard, when they insist that a thin notion of "the global" is insufficient to conceptualize the complexity of transnational rhetorical movements (of policy, people, and violence) across levels of scale. I also invoke transnational feminist scholarship more broadly in order to, following Inderpal Grewal and Caren Caplan, "advocate a mode of study that adopts a more complicated model of transnational relations in which power structures, asymmetries, and inequalities become the conditions of possibility of new subjects" (673). Although my own case studies—in chapters 2, 3, and 4—are articulated at a national level of scale and based in the United States, I propose that this emphasis on rhetoric as entangled across multiple levels of scale is critical to understanding its differential work. Motivated by feminist commitments, this work, like the transnational feminist rhetorics with which it resonates, seeks to "draw attention to power relations as well as the political and material consequences of rhetorical circulation" (Dingo, *Networking Arguments* 17).

In a study of debt, these joint emphases on movement and asymmetry allow me to disambiguate its premises, showing how debt's circulations secure differential subjectivities, doling out debt as credit and risk, leverage and liability. Or, in other words, enlisting a feminist rhetorical approach to investigating and accounting for rhetoric in debt not only emphasizes its productive capacity but accounts for the differential politics of productivity that allow debt and indebted subjects to surface and signify in multiple, even competing, ways. Moreover, this work with debt reveals how the concept carries and rhetorically distributes precariousness across contexts, undermining representations of the different forms, allocations, and representations of economic vulnerability and indebtedness. Indeed, it asks, following the anthropologist Janet Roitman, "What is the difference between debt that disturbs and what one might call socially sanctioned debt? How is it that some forms of wealth are socially sanctioned in spite of their origins in debt relations while others are denounced quite flatly as 'debt,' portrayed as a negative economic indicator, a disruption in the order of production and exchange? And in what contexts does debt mark out not negative space in the social imaginary but rather a critical and perhaps strategic stance?" (73). With the affordances of contemporary rhetorical theory, this project considers not only differences between types of debt—as if they exist outside systems of interpretation, meaning, and materiality—but differences in the rhetorical emergence of debt: *how* it emerges, I show, is central to its individuating and differential work.

Organization of *Rhetoric in Debt*

The centrality of debt in public life and daily lived experience and the transdisciplinary critical, theoretical attention it attracts combine to invite more sustained rhetorical inquiry. More than an opportunity to map the rhetoric *of* debt as yet another application of rhetoric as the architectonic art, however, this project implicates rhetoric in debt, exposing and accounting for their relation, coconstitution, and insidious, differential effects. I propose that this requires identifying the significant premises on which our logics and discourses of debt rest (as demonstrated earlier) as well as the redacted histories from which they emerge in particular forms. Accordingly, in chapter 1, I theorize a rhetorical methodology capable of tracking the emergence and effects of debt. By combining interdisciplinary critical debt scholarship and rhetorical economic inquiry with rhetorical uptakes of affect, risk, and scale, I propose a methodology of accounting for rhetoric in debt that moves beyond numerical or transactional representations of debt to foreground *how* risk surfaces and to *whom* it attaches, leveraging perspective on how credit, risk, futures, and livability adhere (or not) to specific bodies and groups in a contemporary neoliberal economy.

In chapters 2, 3, and 4, I mobilize this methodology of accounting for rhetoric in debt in three case studies, dramatizing the entanglements of rhetoric and debt and the affordances of a methodology that exposes their differential emergence and work. In chapter 2, I focus on student loan debt in the United States, which signifies in popular and academic discourses as a looming crisis that threatens individual livelihoods and futures as well as national economic stability. However threatening in its breadth and scope, I argue that numerical assessments or statistical representations of student loan debt are insufficient to account for its differential work. Drawing on a methodology for accounting for rhetoric *in* debt, I trace the emergence of student loans and debt to complex colonial, racialized, and gendered histories of wealth accumulation and denial, showing that student loans rhetorically misrecognize grossly inequitable histories under the banner of offering equal opportunity, all the while interpellating and moralizing minoritized and gendered bodies under the banner of "financial literacy." I further show how the "choice" to take on, take out, or use student loan debt is not individual or moral but normative, itself emerging within radically asymmetrical histories of access to financial markets and credit.

In chapter 3, I turn my attention to municipal bond debt in the United States, which receives significantly less attention in popular rhetorics of economics than do individual or consumer debts. Municipal bonds nonetheless signify in explicitly moralized terms: when they pay *off*, they serve as evidence of financial literacy or fiscal savvy for individual investors who use them to grow or protect wealth. When municipal bonds, which finance public works and community development, do *not* pay off (when municipalities cannot repay creditors according to the terms of the debt), however, the consequences are meted out on the most vulnerable—those who require public services for basic needs. By invoking a methodology of accounting for rhetoric *in* debt, I show how municipal bonds sponsor inequalities (in community development) when they are both successful *and* unsuccessful vis-à-vis what Lazzarato calls "social" and "machinic subjection," the latter of which hails "dividuals" (rather than individuals) into technological, bureaucratic processes and practices by rote participation. At odds with the reputation of debt as an individual, rational choice, the case of municipal bonds again interrupts any simple conclusion that debt merely exists. Indeed, the case of municipal debt demonstrates how its discursive and material forms are paramount to its emergence and rhetorical functions.

As a final case study that exposes the imbrications of rhetoric and debt, in chapter 4, I turn to medical debt, which I articulate as the remainder of a health care calculus built on accounting and actuarial technologies that recast collective and community risk in individual, financial, and literate terms. Addressing health insurance policies in their historical and political emergence, I show how their rhetorical terms of possibility distribute differential effects across the insured, uninsured, and underinsured on the basis of geopolitical patterns. Unlike the seemingly volitional debt of student loans and municipal bonds, medical debt is rhetorically framed as the consequence of unforeseen circumstances and urgent medical care. Despite this framing, however, individuals assume the responsibility for risk assessment unaccounted for by insurance options or for which insurance companies are unwilling to take accountability, effectively living out the truism that "the indebted man must pay because no other possibilities exist" (Lazzarato, *Governing* 23).

The conclusion of *Rhetoric in Debt* returns to the question of how—and to what ends—rhetorical inquiry can offer needed perspectives on and interventions into critical debt studies. In addition to disarticulating debt from its ahistoricizing premises and identifying and exposing its emergence, I propose that rhetoric is uniquely situated to collate interdisciplinary scholarship dedicated to redressing its differential effects. It is only when we imagine rhetoric in debt, I argue, that we can imagine rhetoric *and* debt differently.

1

Accounting for Rhetoric in Debt

As I argued in the introduction, positing the existence or fact of debt as the conclusion of an enthymeme renders it in terms of concealed logics that deny its emergence and relations across space and time. These include practices of property ownership and exchange that sponsored imperialism, colonization, and chattel slavery, as well as ongoing disparities in access to and accumulation of wealth and recognition of literacies. Accordingly, I unpacked two related clusters of unstated premises—debt as individual, moral, and volitional and debt as mathematically quantifiable and calculable—not only identifying them *as* unstated but considering their emergence within histories of violence and asymmetrical power and their differential effects.

In this chapter, I argue that rhetorical attention to debt must not end with enthymematic analysis and its focus on rhetorics *of* debt. Though such analysis usefully reveals the logics (and practices) of debt, unpacking the unstated and unspoken premises on which it rests and directing attention to how it is talked about and even to its uneven effects, it does not account for their conditions of possibility. Debt remains a conclusion, a rhetorical fact. By contrast, a methodology of accounting for rhetoric *in* debt, as I argue for and theorize in this chapter, makes it possible to consider rhetoric *and* debt as concomitant and coemergent, collaborators in ongoing production of differential materiality—where bodies and debts always matter *in* complex rhetorical relations. Indeed, as scholars working at the intersections of rhetoric and economics argue, economics (and, I argue, debts) do not exist independently, and thus rhetoric does not merely report or represent them (Hanan and Hayward; Greene, "Rhetoric"), or, in other words, "no rhetorical articulation of economic value can exist outside the contingency of its own social and institutional production" (Hanan 88).

Accounting for rhetoric *in* debt thus requires rhetorical attention adequate to its complexity, configured across multiple levels of scale—both temporal and spatial—and adequate to exposing how, and with what effects, rhetoric is immanently entangled with how debt emerges and is allocated, evaluated, and lived, how it matters. Accordingly, in this chapter, I propose and build an original methodology capable of accounting for rhetoric in debt. More specifically, I enjoin feminist articulations of bricolage to collect and collate rhetorical theories of economics, affect, literacy, risk, and relations, layering them together to conduct rhetorical accounting sensitive to scalar emergence and effects and committed to differential embodiment and the complexities of materiality. This methodology, I contend, is particularly poised to intervene in how and for whom debt materializes, how and for whom it matters.

Before articulating this mode of rhetorical accounting vis-à-vis bricolage, however, I first situate it within two interdisciplinary scholarly conversations—rhetoric and economics and critical debt and accounting studies—both of which help me identify the transdisciplinary need for a methodology of accounting for rhetoric *in* debt. Thereafter, I contribute to these conversations by drawing on bricolage as an approach to building methodology capable of considering the material, affective, and scalar dynamics critical to imagining debt in its complexity. This chapter thus (1) situates this project within existing transdisciplinary scholarship, (2) affirms the necessity of including rhetorical perspectives in the ongoing work of demystifying debt, and, most critically, (3) theorizes a methodology adequate to intervening in the differential work of debt. I conclude the chapter by suggesting how it can be used methodically to examine specific cases of rhetoric in debt, a method I practice in the chapters that follow.

Accounting Methodologies

Before introducing a methodological bricolage capable of accounting for rhetoric *in* debt (as I do in the latter half of this chapter), it is important to acknowledge extant perspectives on accounting methodologies that contextualize my own. As reviewed in the introduction to this volume, contemporary (financial) accounting practices and technologies are neither ahistorical nor arhetorical but emerge in specific places, times, and moral milieus (Aho, *Bookkeeping*; Poovey; Quattrone; Rosenthal), embedding rationalities based on representation and equivalency in visual and textual modes that redact any traces of their values. Recording debt in terms of credits and debits elides the differences in the ways debt is lived, the differential impacts it has when it interfaces with different histories and economies of meaning. Thus, numerical representations of debt might be best understood, to borrow a phrase from Matthew J. Newcomb, as "vulgar numbers," which he defines in terms of "the roles of statistics in causing and inhibiting affective responses and feelings" (177), or what Miranda Joseph draws from Angela Y. Davis and Lauren Berlant to claim as "the fetishizing function" of "numerical representations" (31). Tying this phenomenon to accounting technologies, Joseph acknowledges that although the "deployment of counting and accounting to mark injustices is a nearly inevitable rhetorical strategy for those who seek justice" (30), there are significant limits to how numbers or statistics can represent the social processes of debt. Indeed, returning to Newcomb (who investigates numbers as wholly inadequate to represent atrocities like the Rwandan genocide), we see how numbers can inadvertently overwhelm rhetorical sense making, undermining the conditions of possibility for empathy via prodigious abstraction.

Despite popular connotations of accounting as a self-evident record of transactions or exchange (debits on the left, credits on the right), where accounting entries merely *reflect* material holdings and debts, however, financial accounting guidelines and critical accounting scholarship alike propose a more complicated relationship between what *exists* and what *matters* in accounting. That is, within accounting scholarship and studies of accounting across disciplines, the double-entry system and the systems of Western accounting that rest on it— including how it represents debt—already attract critical attention, whereby accounting experts acknowledge the limits of accounting practices in representing the financial transactions in a complex and interconnected neoliberal context. In addition to interdisciplinary scholarship that tracks the historical emergence and ascendance of double-entry bookkeeping (as discussed in the introduction), disciplinary attention within the growing field of critical accounting studies likewise calls into question the premises and effects of financial accounting. As expressed by the editorial board of the international journal *Critical Perspectives on Accounting* when articulating its purpose, for example, "conventional theory and practice is ill-suited to the challenges of the modern environment, and . . . accounting practices and corporate behavior are inextricably connected with many allocative, distributive, social, and ecological problems of our era."

A critical perspective on accounting complicates a more vernacular understanding of debt by reminding us that accounting policies, practices, technologies, and methodologies *materialize* debt, making it visible, making it matter. Indeed, despite what I have articulated as the commonplace understanding of debt as *existing* (and disarticulated from its premises), within financial accounting, debt is marked and comes to matter when it meets threshold conditions, which are neither uniform nor universal. "Information is material," according to the International Accounting Standards Board (IASB), "if omitting, misstating or obscuring it could reasonably be expected to influence the decisions that the primary users of general purpose financial statements make on the basis of those financial statements, which provide financial information about a specific reporting entity" (IFRS). But as explained by MaterialityTracker.net, a consulting service that collates and applies international research about materiality in accounting to help companies better understand and frame their own practices, "Standard international guidance on calculating materiality, considering agreed thresholds, does not exist. Individual auditing firms provide guidance to their managers on what thresholds to apply." Acknowledging the impact of governing bodies like GAAP (Generally Accepted Accounting Principles), which is used in the United States as well as for companies traded on the New York Stock Exchange, or IFRS (International Financial Reporting Standards), used in many contexts outside the United States, the service nonetheless suggests that the judgment of preparers tends "to be influenced by factors such as whether their industry is more exposed to litigation. The closer the reporting organization is to break-even results (small profit/loss), the more sensitive the threshold applied becomes. At stake therefore is not just the absolute magnitude of the event involved but also the severity of its implications, the positive/negative nature (direction) of the information, the sensitivity of the firm's equity returns to the information (the stock price reaction), and the impact of the information on the firm's default risk (importance to debt-holders)" (MaterialityTracker.net). Whereas stereotypes of and public and popular discourses about accounting position it as a mathematical and hence value-free appraisal of debt that merely *reflects* it, then, financial accounting literature itself reveals such a reflection—and here I invoke Kenneth Burke's terministic screens—as a simultaneous *selection* and *deflection* of other possibilities for representing debt. Debt does not just *exist*; it emerges and comes to matter when it meets specific, shifting, and contextual threshold conditions.

Critical accounting scholars not only acknowledge materiality as paramount for accounting practices but increasingly question the acceptance of accounting principles as neutral arbiters of vastly different cultures and economies.

Elisavet Mantzari and Omiros Georgiou, for example, question the IFRS's wide acceptance as "de facto global accounting standards," contending that there is no empirical evidence that its use leads to "improving information and comparability, reducing the cost of capital, or leading to a better allocation of resources in capital markets" (70). Despite the standards lacking empirical support, however, Mantzari and Georgiou argue that they are "widely presented as a rational, exhaustive, and internally consistent technology to account for financial transactions" (70). Though limited, the type of scholarly attention to the cultural emergence and effects of materiality demonstrated by Mantzari and Georgiou suggests a rhetorical sensibility that belies the need for methodologies that explicitly cast debt in rhetorical terms. Insofar as accounting policies and guidance admit that *how* debt is represented is inextricably tied to contingent values and metrics, they seem already attuned to the rhetoricity of debt. I propose, however, that methodological attention to materiality itself (within accounting practices or rhetorical inquiry) is *not* sufficient to account for its emergence and differential effects. Although accounting standards carefully repudiate "material misstatements," they articulate such in terms of the "primary users of general purpose financial statements" who might be impacted, eliding differences in impact or how specific, embodied debtors might be affected quite differently. Moreover, the conditions through which materiality *emerges* is subsumed by its statement, which is evaluated in terms of hit or miss, corroborating the reputation of accounting in simple terms of accuracy.

Building on the analysis modeled by Mantzari and Georgiou via explicit and tacit rhetoric commitments, I propose that we can both better contend with the rhetorical appeal of standards (like IFRS) and attend to how standards and accounting practices and technologies alike (as well as values associated with each) *emerge*—or materialize—as such in complex historical, cultural, political, material, and highly rhetorical relations. A methodology attuned not only to a statement of materiality but to *differential* materiality, I propose, invokes rhetoric to better account for how materiality emerges relationally, effecting not only "primary users" in unilateral ways but indebted subjects in myriad and differential ways. I begin to respond to this invocation in the following section by considering how scholarship at the intersection of rhetoric and economics paves the way for this rhetorical accounting, before moving on to build a methodology through purposeful, feminist bricolage of specific concepts and theories adequate to accounting for rhetoric *in* debt.

Invitation to Rhetorical Accounting

Scholarship at the intersection of rhetoric and economics has laid much of the groundwork for what we might call a rhetorical accounting practice. That is, even with limited attention to debt itself (as exceptions, see Herring, "Neither Pistols"; Herring, "Rhetoric"), economic terminology, tropes, and premises saturate rhetorical inquiry and methodology, evidencing not only metaphorical uptake of economic concepts but tacit agreement with William Rodney Herring and Mark Garrett Longaker's claim that "economics again sits center stage in US public discourse, presenting an opportune moment to revisit its relationship to rhetoric, to entertain more citizen bravery and less academic timidity" (236). Indeed, as James Arnt Aune succinctly puts it before reviewing a long history of the entanglements of rhetoric and economics, "There is nothing new about the connection between rhetoric and economics" (*Selling* 15). Despite this long connection, disciplinary boundaries successfully disarticulated the fields until, Aune argues, the classically trained economist Deidre N. McCloskey somewhat scandalously invoked rhetoric to consider how the science of economics is nonetheless relayed via (human) argument: "Science," she argued, "is an instance of writing with intent, the intent to persuade other scientists, such as economic scientists" (*Rhetoric of Economics* 4). So situated and aimed at persuasion, McCloskey's work identified key possibilities for rhetorical attention to—or methodology for the study of—economics: "to understand it, to admire it, to debunk it, to set it beside other works of persuasion in science, to see that science is not a new dogma but is thoroughly and respectably part of the old culture" (19). For McCloskey, economics must be submitted to rhetorical analysis because it emerges through rhetoric—through the metaphors, tropes, and figures economists use as they advance and counter theories—and rhetorical analysis can lead to better economic writing and argumentation.

The impact of McCloskey's work within economics has been at once significant and incendiary, alternately praised and heavily critiqued for its methodological possibilities (Klamer et al. vii; Duerringer 287). Within rhetoric (and communication studies in particular), on the other hand, there is the limited but increasing attention paid to McCloskey's work in particular—which ranges from extending its application to critiquing its methods as superficial—amid a more general blossoming of contemporary rhetorical scholarship at the intersection of rhetoric and economics. This spans casual mentions of neoliberalism or economies of meaning to more sustained investigations and critiques of, for example, rhetoric and capitalism (Cloud, "Book Review"; Greene, "Rhetoric and Capitalism"; Riedner, *Writing*; Wingard), rhetoric and political economy (Aune, "Historical Materialist Theory"; Chaput et al.; Colombini; Hanan and Hayward), the political economies of rhetoric and composition (Abraham; Edwards and Reyman; Sano-Franchini; Villanueva), and rhetoric and labor (Mountford; Bousquet et al.; Enoch; Lindquist; Riedner, "Where Are the Women?"; Schell, *Gypsy Academics*). These scholarly trends in the contemporary field build on half a century of rhetorical grappling with materialism (see, for example, Aune, "Historical Materialist Theory"; McGee; Charland; McKerrow; Greene, "Another Materialist Rhetoric"; Cloud, "Book Review"; Hanan and Chaput) and, more recently, rhetorical inquiry into "financial incentives" and their "influences on the behavior of economic actors," as well as "financial transactions" and "the role and operation of finance in our economy" (Herring, "Neither Pistols" 148, 157; see also Ohlsson; McCloskey, "Rhetoric of Finance"). Of course, the latter category is particularly relevant to understanding economics in their neoliberal forms and "the financialization of daily life" (Martin).

Rhetorical investigations of materialism articulate explicit and tacit relationships to contemporary heterodox economics in particular, which diverges from mainstream—or orthodox—reliance on methodologies, methods, and metrics substantiated by positivist premises (i.e., where mathematics, statistics, and algorithms calculate and represent human behaviors, relationships, and risk in attempts to identify and isolate causes and effects) to employ intellectual traditions and research methods more attuned to the imbrication of economic activity and consequences in larger systems of power. Insofar as orthodox economics are rooted in a conceptualization of *homo economicus* as "the rational actor calculating utility in a given case" (Aune, *Selling* 20), they cannot account for larger systems of belief and meaning that circumscribe rationality, action, calculation, and utility. Heterodox economics, by contrast, most often consider economics *in relation* to larger systems—historical, cultural, ideological, and otherwise normative. Though hardly unified in purpose or approach, heterodox economics cohere under the rubric of questioning, disrupting, and challenging received logics and commonplaces of the larger, orthodox field, which emphasizes "scarcity, equilibrium, and rationality" as well as individualism (Mearman 494).

Whereas orthodox economics and rhetorical inquiry might be understood to be at conceptual and methodological cross-purposes, respectively affirming and disrupting the ability of economic measures (or measurability) to exist independently from rhetorical discourses, various articulations of heterodox economics resonate with the contemporary field, centering issues of power, affect, discourse, and systems.[1] Accordingly, rhetorical studies evidence consistent engagement with heterodox economics, especially those influenced by Marx and Foucault (see, for example, McGee; McKerrow; Hanan and Chaput; Hanan and Hayward; Chaput; Cloud, *Reality Bites*; Greene, "Another Materialist Rhetoric"), keen to account for what McGee observes as a commonplace—that "human beings in collectivity behave and think differently than human beings in isolation" (2)—and to reject rhetorics of "economic correctness" that elide the *impact* of economic rhetoric *on* bodies, livelihoods, and lives (Aune, *Selling*).

Less represented in rhetoric and economics proper is a sustained engagement with "racial capitalism," a term coined by Cedric Robinson to reflect the premise that "the historical development of world capitalism was influenced in a most fundamental way by the particularistic forces of racism and nationalism" (9). Or, rather, whereas various subfields within rhetoric acknowledge the imbrication of rhetorical patterns and possibilities with racial histories and ongoing relations (see, for example, Flores, *Deportable*; Siegfried; Codagnone et al.), these have yet to find real purchase within explicit conversations about rhetoric and economics. As one of several exceptions to this generalization, Ronald Walter Greene acknowledges the need for more focused attention on the interrelations of race, nation, and economics in his critiques of well-known rhetoric and economics scholarship (which might be articulated as symptomatic of larger disciplinary patterns) and calls for more sensitivity "to how the division of labor is itself organized around race, gender, and nationality" as well as how "the cultural elements of domination (racism, sexism) are not so easy to disentangle from an 'economic' emphasis on exploitation" ("Rhetoric" 193).[2]

Ironically, the tendency to avoid issues of difference might itself be attributable to the flattening effects of neoliberalism. Tacitly invoking Wendy Brown's insistence that "neoliberal rationality disseminates the model of the market to all domains and activities" (*Undoing* 31), the communication scholar Robert Asen argues that "neoliberalism imposes a homogeneity on market actors, ascribing to them uniform motivations and goals" whereby "the market treats all actors equally; differences of race, gender, ethnicity, class, sexual orientation, and more presumably play no role in the behavior of market actors and their successes and failures" (330–31). When the same patterns of treating—or eliding—difference become apparent in rhetorical economic inquiry and theory, it might be posited that the same neoliberal rhetorics that circulate to "make inequality invisible" on a broad scale (Asen 331) inflect even its most cogent critiques.

In addition to centering complex issues of race, gender, and nation following the advice of Greene, rhetoric and economics scholarship—what we might also refer to as its methodologies of accounting—would also benefit from shifting citational practices to include economic and political economic theories beyond their major canons, because, as Siddhant Issar argues in the journal *Contemporary Political Theory*, the "most influential accounts of neoliberalism in critical political theory ... theorize race and racial domination ... as epiphenomenal to the structure and logic of contemporary capitalism" (49). Or, put otherwise by Arun Kundnani, "Prevailing scholarship on neoliberalism fails to recognize that it generates its own distinctive forms of racial domination" (51). Accounting for relationships among rhetoric and economics that are attuned to race and racial domination thus requires a more capacious lineage of (rhetorical) economic inquiry. Although a full genealogy of scholarship devoted to theorizing and demystifying racial capitalism in relation to rhetoric is beyond the scope of this project, imagining rhetoric *in* debt, as I demonstrate in the chapters that follow, centers issues of differential, including racialized, mattering. This offers a key theoretical and disciplinary contribution to studies of the constitutive relationship between rhetoric and economics: rhetoric is *in* debt not only because it entangles with economics but because it cannot be disarticulated from histories of racialized exclusion and exploitation. In the words of Lisa Flores, rhetorical criticism that elides race "is incomplete, partial, and irresponsible" ("Between Abundance" 6). Or, as forcefully argued by Darrel Wanzer-Serrano, "rhetoric studies (as a 'field') has a race problem" (466–67).

Somewhat better accounted for in rhetoric scholarship is the constitutive work of gender in economic practices, which, as argued by Lynn Worsham in her landmark essay "Going Postal: Pedagogic Violence and the Schooling of Emotion," is bound to the violent work of dominant discourse to discipline and secure subjectivity as "an integral part of ... the sex/affective production system of advanced capitalism" (216). In this vein, feminist rhetoricians center the bodies, lives, and experiences of women as conditionally accepted economic actors (see, for example, Dingo, *Networking Arguments*; Riedner, *Writing*; Schell, "Gender"). Moreover, centering affect in studies of the relationships between rhetoric and economics offers many rhetoricians a methodology for understanding how economic rhetorics *work* on bodies.[3] Catherine Chaput, explicitly engaging with orthodox and heterodox economic theories specifically but without considering gender itself in her analysis, investigates historical economic debates to identify how the market "is an affective force that influences rhetorical action by linking bodily receptivities to economic persuasion" (2). Chaput's specific analytic focus grounds a larger argument about the significance of affect in understanding the relationships between rhetoric and economics, where rhetoric is critical to understanding how and why specific theories of economics have been—and continue to be—so persuasive in the public imaginary. Affect, she argues, echoing Worsham, is an underscrutinized aspect of the rhetorical successes of economic arguments.

This rhetorical emphasis on affect in economic rhetorics extends the truism offered by Herring and Longaker that "linguistic and economic assumptions" ground both economics and rhetoric in the twenty-first century, such that both "incline toward a belief that value depends on future fungibility" (250, 249). Whereas Herring and Longaker affirm rhetoric and economics as inextricable, however, Worsham, Chaput, and others direct specific attention to their affective function and functioning. By considering rhetoric as both symbolic and material, as a matter of circulation and transmission of affect, energy, and sensation as much as language and representation, these scholars fundamentally reconfigure rhetorical economic inquiry. As Chaput suggests of the effect of affect, "My speculation is that it challenges and expands the traditional rhetorical repertoire, making biopolitical production part of its invention strategies and repositions the *ethos-pathos-logos* triangulation from the symbolic onto the bodily" (4). This focus on bodies and biopolitical production redirects rhetorical attention from materiality as an economic indicator—as in material conditions of production and reproduction (in the vein of Marx)—to materiality as embodied and embodied differently, and it brings with it the potential to reject or recast the flattening effects of neoliberalism.

Rhetorico-Affective Accounting

An emphasis on affect, biopolitical production, and embodiment is vital to the project of accounting for the *differential* work of debt or, in other words, to identifying how debt secures subjectivity (Lazzarato, *Making*), or what Chaput might refer to as "rhetorical dispositions" (4), in vastly different ways and with massively inequitable results. To be sure, the affective resonance of economics and debt is not an entirely new idea or reality, nor is it disciplinarily specific.[4]

And both rhetoricians and critical debt scholars alike often cite a similar theoretical genealogy of affect, subjectivity, and biopolitics, especially work by Jacques Derrida, Gilles Deleuze and Félix Guattari, and Michel Foucault and, more recently, Sara Ahmed, Lauren Berlant, Patricia Clough, Brian Massumi, and Kathleen Stewart. Drawing heavily from Deleuze and Guattari, for example, Lazzarato articulates a specific relationship between neoliberalism, subjectivity, and affect necessary to understand debt as it functions in the contemporary geopolitical moment.[5] With book-length essays dedicated to theorizing "the making of the indebted man" and "governing by debt," however, Lazzarato nonetheless claims that "we currently lack the theoretical tools to analyze the entire scope of the relation between creditor and debtor and the different functions of debt" (*Making* 32). This is truer still when we consider the glaring absence of racialized and gendered histories and rhetorical relations of debt.

Rhetoric in Debt is itself indebted to Lazzarato's work and the intellectual and scholarly genealogies from which it emerges, and it is with this provocation that this book draws on rhetoric more explicitly (than does Lazzarato) to track the emergence, work, and effects of debt, both invoking and straying from the scholarship named earlier to account for the conditions of possibility through which debt emerges and takes shape differently and differentially. That is, while affect theory does contribute to the methodology I build (as I discuss shortly), I prioritize scholarship that, following Joseph, is capable of accounting for the "stark differences in whether and how differently situated subjects are held accountable for their failures" (19). Accordingly, I invoke theories and concepts that prioritize complex, differential relationships between bodies and political economies to materialize and manage subjectivities, possibilities, and rhetorical futures.

Accounting for Methodology and Method via Feminist Bricolage

In order to articulate a methodology and method capable of accounting for rhetoric in debt and attentive to its differentiating work, I take cues from feminist rhetoricians who use "bricolage" as a guiding metaphor to represent the need to *build* methodologies and methods sensitive to the multidirectional demands of positions, relations, and subject matter (Schell and Rawson).[6] The decolonial feminist rhetoricians Erin A. Frost and Angela M. Haas define "bricolage" in terms of "the feminist postmodern understanding of 'making do' by bringing together seemingly disparate elements of materials at hand to work toward feminist agendas" (90). Their definition and model, like much feminist rhetorical scholarship, resonates with Jacqueline Jones Royster's recounting of her attempts to create a methodology "adequate to the task" of her subject matter (Black women's historical rhetoric and literacy practices), with many resources but without a guide (252). Rather than decry this lack of guidance, feminist rhetoricians use it as an opportunity to theorize methodology that is sensitive to the complexities of their subject matter (which are ignored or flattened by more conventional and patriarchal methodologies) and framed by explicit, ethical commitments to equity and social justice (see also Schell, Introduction; Calafell).

Like these and other feminist rhetoricians, I seek a methodology that is dynamic and flexible, capable of interrogation and revision, study and recovery, investigation and contribution (Frost and Haas 92).[7] In the context of accounting for rhetoric in debt, I propose that such a methodology must prioritize specific values and concepts—and their relationships—that rhetorically secure and manage the differential work of debt. Such concepts include affect, complexity, and scale, as well as subjectivity, circulation, and risk.[8] As I demonstrate in the following sections, the concepts themselves are not wholly discrete; they must be considered in relation. Thus, while I introduce each in turn, each tends to return, adding nuance at *each* turn. The effect is a methodology that is more cyclical than linear: each concept that is folded invites renewed attention to those already addressed. This approach itself thus aligns with that of Miranda Joseph, who explains, "rather than approach debt as an origin or cause or crisis to be analyzed, I posit debts, and credits, as components of complex performative representational practices that I refer to collectively as *accounting*" (x). Imagining accounting as complex, performative, and representational requires Joseph, as it does me, to draw on and draw in the theories and concepts from multiple traditions to better understand how debt emerges differentially, how it lives in the world, and with what effects. In the sections that follow, I review each in turn, layering them together in an explicit act of bricolage, which I propose as necessary to account for rhetoric *in* debt.

Accounting for Economics and Affect

A first critical contribution to a bricolaged methodology is scholarship that considers the necessary, often unexamined, relationship between economics, affect, and rhetoric. As reviewed in the introduction of this book, interdisciplinary critical debt scholarship identifies affect as essential to the production of Maurizio Lazzarato's definition of *homo economicus* as the "indebted man [*sic*]." This can be attributed, in part, to emotion's role in the persuasive force of economic narratives because, in the words of Robert J. Shiller, "the economy is composed of conscious living people, who view their actions in light of stories with emotions and ideas attached" (12). Not explicitly rhetorical, Shiller's focus on emotion and attachment to economic narratives parallels contemporary rhetorical studies of political economy, directing attention to the fundamental role of the circulation and materiality of affect in the persuasive capacity of narrative. Jennifer Wingard's work, for example, investigates how "terms work together to affectively produce the material conditions under which branding becomes a central rhetorical technology of neoliberalism" (1), while Rachel Riedner invokes the affective theory of Sara Ahmed to consider how human-interest stories "align readers with the feelings, sentiments, and actions available within a neoliberal moment, conserving a political settlement where the activities of responsible, self-reliant individuals are provided the 'available means' to act and feel" (*Writing* 8). Both projects performatively enact Chaput's call to account for "what the market is and how it cajoles so invisibly, effortlessly, and yet authoritatively" by way of "the energetic power of affect, which invisibly compels our instinctual ways of being, thinking, and acting" (2, 29). Chaput's analysis of historical economic theories itself reveals how the terms by which economics are articulated (what Shiller might call its "narratives" or Wingard its "brands" but also includes professional and public discourses as well as the technologies, networks, and practices through which narratives circulate) do not exist independently from affect, which she defines as "a physical energy" that "moves into signs, spaces, and bodies" (31).

Pursuing the relationship between rhetoric, affect, and economics further, Sara Ahmed's work is particularly relevant here. That is, although her work is not explicitly situated in rhetorical inquiry, she explains the intimate connections between language and culture that are critical to contemporary rhetorical thinking. Explaining the movement of affect that Chaput identifies, Ahmed argues that affect "does not reside positively in the sign or commodity, but is produced as an effect of its circulation"; moreover, "signs increase in affective values as an effect of the movement between signs: the more signs circulate, the more affective they become" (*Cultural Politics* 45). Applying this reasoning to debt reveals how it accrues and distributes differential meanings and significance, "sticky"—as Ahmed suggests—with the affect that accumulates through circulation. Accordingly, circulation is not under the control or direction of any specific institution or entity; it nevertheless follows histories of use, sticking affect to bodies and managing their feelings and futures.

Without citing Ahmed specifically, Jenny Edbauer enjoins this thinking to call for a rhetorical framework of affective ecologies—which "recontextualizes rhetorics in their temporal, historical, and lived fluxes"—to allow the field "to more fully theorize rhetoric as a public(s) creation" (9). It is the stickiness of affect—the patterns of "connections . . . lived as the most intense or intimate, as being closer to the skin" (Ahmed, *Cultural Politics* 54)—that sponsors subjectivity, creating norms, expectations, and judgments within complex ecologies of meaning and signification. Or, as Ahmed further argues, "What moves us, what makes us feel, is also that which holds us in place, or gives us a dwelling place" (*Cultural Politics* 13). Dwelling places are thus the effect of the circulation of affect *sticking* to signs, bodies, and objects in patterned ways and narrated through cultural norms and relations, including economic relations, that allocate meaning(s) to the patterns.

Drawing these insights into a methodology of accounting for rhetoric *in* debt offers a distinct departure from an individual or positivist account (as discussed in the introduction); it does not, however, elide the highly personal and psychological *effects* of the circulation and stickiness of debt and its affects. As proposed by Stephen E. G. Lea, Avril J. Mewse, and Wendy Wrapson, "The psychological causes of debt are real, but probably minor compared with the economic and social causes. The psychological *consequences* of debt are much more obvious, and the social constructions such as the feeling of stigma can have significant effects on future economic behavior" (164). Brian Knutson and Gregory R. Samanez-Larkin confirm that "emotion influences immediate choices," and, "as it does so repeatedly and consistently over time, it might have a significant cumulative impact on life financial outcomes such as debt" (169). Framed in terms of of decision-making and emotion, the conclusions offered by these psychology scholars are productively complicated when rhetorically reframed in terms of the circulation and sticky work of affect as it circulates and emerges through materio-discursive ecologies and relations, but the psychological consequences of debt nonetheless reveal its uneven work: securing and disciplining identities, well-being, and behaviors vis-à-vis normed, neoliberal economic practices.

Using the concepts of affect and circulation, then, shifts accounts away from specific persons as literate, rational economic actors understood to be *in* debt or having *chosen* debt to consider how debt *sticks*, creating dwelling places in patterned ways. Laziness, incompetence, and irresponsibility, for example, stick to the bodies and identities of those who seek public assistance as narratives of individual morality and agency circulate alongside and circumscribe unemployment, underemployment, or food and housing insecurity (as well as the discourses, processes, practices, and technologies that produce them). We can see the affordances of this analytic shift in an example from Lazzarato's work, when he describes his research with beneficiaries of a specific public-assistance program in France to illustrate Nietzsche's argument that "the main purpose of debt lies in its construction of a subject and a conscience, a self that believes in its specific individual and that stands as guarantor of its actions, its way of life (and not only employment) and takes responsibility for them" (*Making* 134). Lazzarato describes the mandatory monthly interview required of would-be "beneficiaries" of public assistance, wherein they are made to "talk about themselves (or make a show of themselves) and justify what they are doing with their lives and their time" in order to receive public assistance (135). Beyond articulating a relationship to employment, these interviews admonish participants to articulate a "self" worthy of economic benefit, or worth the risk of investment. Importantly, though public assistance is here understood in terms of economic debt—what is *owed* the state—repayment is "made not in money but through the debtor's constant efforts to maximize his employability." Lazzarato continues: "Debt repayment is part of a standardization of behavior that requires conformity to the life norms dictated by the institution" (135).

Statements of self in a monthly public-assistance interview are symptomatic of the way "debt is administered by evaluating 'morality' and involves the individual as well as the work on the self which the individual must undertake" (Lazzarato, *Making* 131). But with respect to Ahmed's conceptualization of affect and its uptake in rhetorical inquiry, it becomes evident that such morality is regulated not only formally or institutionally, by the distribution or withholding of assistance, for example, but rhetorically and affectively, marking morality and social worthiness as affect circulates and sticks to specific bodies, branding them by "evacuating them of meaning and circulating their images as representative of otherness and exception" (Wingard 9). A debtor who "repays" the state through work on the self is morally upright, worthy of assistance, worth the risk. One who does not performatively repay the debt is marked not only risky or lazy but ineligible for social recognition or material support (life itself). Complicating a simple equation of debt with moral failure as it is often marked in public discourse (i.e., someone *in* debt is not living up to their economic and thus moral obligations), recipients of public assistance evidence eligibility *for* debt as an indication of social recognition. Accordingly, "debt operates not only in the manipulation of enormous quantities of money, in sophisticated financial and monetary policies; it informs and configures techniques for control of users' existence, without which the economy would not have control on subjectivity" (Lazzarato, *Making* 137).

While this performance of worthiness for debt undoubtedly affects and sticks to all who seek public assistance, all are not affected equally because the affects of debt interface with complex histories, subjectivities, environments, and embodiments. Affects of debt are not, however, radically idiosyncratic or pathological because, as Chaput explains, although affect, "as a physical entity, moves through all matter" and is thus "open to an indeterminate range of potential response, . . . in a given political economic context, those responses remain narrowly predictable" (4). Such predictable responses emerge in contexts that include, Ahmed emphasizes, the repetitive circuits of racialization, as affect circulates within histories of racism and violence and sticks fear, disgust, and hatred to Black and Brown bodies and the spaces in which they circulate and live.[9] Thus, the "affective charge" of repeated encounters not only lives differently on the skin of people of color than on that of white bodies but marks each as such, producing the boundaries between them; in Ahmed's words, "emotions create the very effect of the surfaces and boundaries that allow us to distinguish an inside and an outside in the first place" (*Cultural Politics* 12). Repeated encounters likewise characterize spaces, which "obtain their descriptions as good/bad sites from the affective and embodied experiences that circulate: feelings of fear or comfort, for instance" (Edbauer 11). These insights are critical to considering rhetoric *in* debt as one of the conditions of possibility of rhetoric *of* debt. Whereas a rhetoric of debt positions individuals as preexisting the terms of their indebtedness, making choices and meriting the effects of those choices by using, for example, normative financial literacies to conduct cost-benefit analysis, Ahmed's work here alerts us to the faultiness of such thinking and directs attention, instead, to how individuals become identifiable as specific sorts of subjects within a broader "economy of emotion."

Alongside Ahmed's analyses of the differentially subjectivizing work of fear, disgust, and hatred, she also analyzes how shame marks the boundary between self and other, which "consumes the subject and burns on the surface of bodies that are presented to others" (*Cultural Politics* 104). We can see how debt emerges and sticks differentially through shame by way of the infamous example of the "Welfare Queen" invoked by US President Ronald Reagan in introduction to his conservative fiscal policy, which also invites attention to the intersectional work of race and gender on materializing debt differentially. Narrated as taking gross advantage of social programs (by collecting undeserved monies and support) to fund lavish, illicit lifestyles (of drug use and supposedly immoral sexual activity), this description not only *sticks* shame to Black women but produces Black women as unworthy social debtors. Just as important to understanding the rhetorical work of debt, it simultaneously produces worthy social creditors: taken-advantage-of taxpayers, the hardworking (white) people (men) who do not expect "handouts." Although shame is lived as highly personal, then, Ahmed explains it as individuating rather than individual: "The individuation of shame—the way it turns the self against and towards the self—can be linked precisely to the inter-corporeality and sociality of shame experiences" (*Cultural Politics* 105). Indeed, the figure of the "Welfare Queen" circulates shame to specific debts and debtors to mark boundaries of legitimate and illegitimate economic and social relations.

Only alluded to by Lazzarato in terms of individuation, Ahmed's discussion of shame elucidates how the circulating, sticky work of affect might participate in the rhetorical production of differentially indebted subjectivities. That is, her work with affect illuminates how the failure to repay a debt does not unilaterally burn on the skin of the indebted. Rather, shame *sticks* to certain bodies on the basis of its histories and patterns, constituting them as, for example, financial illiterates or unnecessary risk takers. Someone on public assistance, for example, *feels* the shame of debt when monthly required to perform creditworthiness and *ask* for (public) assistance. Ritually circulating alongside other embodied realities, including unemployment or food or housing insecurity but also gendered and racialized histories and narratives of citizenship or ethnicity, this request for credit becomes shameful. The shame sticks more effectively when repetition continuously allocates it to brand specific bodies. Moreover, the repetition corroborates the boundaries by which those bodies are identifiable, continuously marking which bodies are worthy of social credit and which should be shamed for their debts.

This dynamic might be further evidenced by the 2019 change by the US Food and Drug Administration (USDA) to the Supplemental Nutrition Assistance Program (SNAP), wherein benefits were "extended only to households that have sufficiently demonstrated eligibility" (Food and Nutrition Service). By aligning eligibility with "sufficient demonstration" and, later, "self-sufficiency," the proposal questions the validity of SNAP requests and the worthiness of recipients while simultaneously requiring them to present themselves for inspection. Moreover, it does so along normative lines, as these rules explicitly apply to "able-bodied adults" and disproportionately affect people of color. By questioning the worthiness of these recipients, the proposal affirms such populations as questionable or worth investment and reinscribes gender, race, and ability as markers of (eligibility for) social debt. As suggested by the Oregon congressional representative Suzanne Bonamici and reported by NPR, the changes also stand to eliminate "automatic enrollment of close to a million children in the school lunch program," specifically affecting schools that "provide free lunches to all of their students—regardless of income—because so many are poor" (National Public Radio). By requiring "sufficient demonstration," the changes to SNAP require marking eligibility for food assistance, affirming school lunch as a debt that must be applied for, extended, and repaid. In so doing, it metes out eligibility on the skin of children, who signify as social debtors required to evidence their worthiness for credit (read: lunch).

We can further see the sticky work of affect to differentiate social credit and debt at work in Rebecca Dingo's analysis of "the empowered third world girl" narrative, which, she argues, circulates the stories of recipients of monetary or education loans from Western nongovernmental organizations ("Re-evaluating" 137). The circulation of these stories, Dingo contends, holds together "Western liberal feminism *and* financial logics" (144, emphasis added) under the rubric of empowerment, such that the stories affirm the intentions and politics of donors and elide the relational and affective consequences for the girls themselves, which include "increased gender stratification within the home (and often violence), more hours of formal and informal labor, and thus exhaustion and fear of debt and lack of employment opportunities once they are educated" (137). In this case, empowerment *sticks* to the "third world girl" as a benevolent gift from first-world donors, who understand the girl as a victim of a global economy who can escape her circumstances with the right financial literacies. The girls thus demonstrate worthiness for the program through the performance of Western gender politics: they are worthy of financial credit (debt) insofar as they embody sympathetic victims of a global economy. Like recipients of SNAP benefits, the "third world girl" is assessed in terms of what Dingo elsewhere calls "fitness," or "fitting women into a global capitalist economy by changing their behaviors" (*Networking Arguments* 67).

This example also surfaces entanglements of highly gendered rhetorics with debt, evident in the application of Western assumptions about the relationships between girls, victims, and financial fitness and empowerment. The "third world girl" does not emerge as a worthy debtor independent of histories of gendered access to exchange and other economic practices. Rather, it is in the context of economic exclusion that practices of inclusion can rescue and empower such a girl. Such inclusion is based on the girl's normative economic behaviors and performance of eligibility and fitness in the context of economies of meaning, including the meaning(s) of debt, which emerge in long (and short) histories of empire, colonization, and globalization. Indeed, terms of recognition of the girls are themselves colonial, only allowing the girls to emerge as subjects when they materialize in terms set by Western economics (Coultard).

Importantly, while public assistance as debt (and in myriad other circumstances) invites the repeated performance of eligibility and accrues the adhesive capacity of shame, eligibility checks for debt in other contexts do *not* necessarily invite shame, corroborating its differentiating effects. Requesting (debt for) a mortgage, for example, requires a performance of eligibility: a specific combination of credit score, bank statements, and employment history presented to a loan officer who calculates and assesses their worth(iness) for debt. When successful, this performance might be celebrated by the would-be debtor and their creditors—a sign of maturity or stability indicating a shrewd investment in the future. Likewise, shareholders of companies might encourage debt, framed by the terminology and acceptability of financing, to grow profits and offer the higher potential return on investment.[10] While not all mortgage seekers or companies are praised for their debts, they nonetheless evidence the broad discrepancies between how and to whom debt sticks. In other words, individuals and companies not only have debt or are in debt but relationally emerge with debt and its sticky affects.

Accounting for "Financial Literacy"

This focus on the constitutive work of affect to secure and stick economic narratives to individual, individuated bodies and subjects on the basis of differential histories and circuits of meaning requires another layer of theoretical attention that is sensitive to rhetorical discourses that produce debt not only *for* individuals but *as* individual. Accordingly, an equally vital part of the proposed bricolaged methodology of accounting for rhetoric in debt comes from critical literacy scholarship that disarticulates literacy from its reputation as an individual skill or performance and reinvests it in its contexts of emergence. Or, in other words, considering the sticky, emergent affects of debt (as discussed in the previous section) productively underwrites a departure from interpretations of debt in terms of individual "financial literacy" that frame disparate debtors in polar terms—savvy or not, risky or not, literate or not—and debt management as a problem of education. Claess Ohlsson uses a classical definition of "ethos" to explain the problem with an interpretive scheme that posits financial literacy as the possession of an individual. Whereas "ethos," he posits, must be understood to be *both* situated and derived, negotiated between actors and contexts, financial literacy programs imagine it as static—"based on official authority and/or professional expertise in various fields of finance"; these include "banking in both national and commercial domains, education on many levels and also supervising bodies for all kinds of finance markets." This specific and singular possibility for appealing to ethos denies the many "possible rhetoric situations where financial literacy is promoted" as well as the "different categories" of "actors involved" (66). Put otherwise, we might say that the concept of financial literacy is used to justify and evaluate financial actors and their actions in normative terms, measuring decisions of credibility (and creditworthiness) using standards of professional finance that cannot begin to account for the many contexts in which finance—including debt—is implicated and debtors constituted.

From a critical accounting perspective, Charlotta Bay, Bino Catasús, and Gustav Johed explain how financial literacy is not only individualized by such organizations as the International Organization of Securities Commissions, the World Bank, and the European Commission, which all conclude that "the level of financial knowledge needs to be raised so that non-professional investors can act in a financially responsible manner" (36–37), but further corroborated by traditions of research *about* financial literacy, which (1) "measure the level of financial literacy in different demographic areas," (2) "investigate the effects of financial literacy on financial decisions," and (3) "study the effects of financial education" (37). Financial organizations and scholarship alike, Bay, Catasús, and Johed show, assume literacy to be an individual capacity that, "when gained, automatically affects people's financial practices" (37). Contesting this premise, the authors draw on new literacy studies to propose, instead, a "context-bound meaning for financial literacy that is *not* primarily about possessing the skills to interpret accounting and financial information" (37, emphasis added), one that accounts for "how, when and toward whom the literacy event is directed" (38). Emphasizing the "toward whom" of literacy events is particularly important in building a methodology that surfaces the differential work of debt to reveal how financial practices are evaluated in the colonial, racialized contexts in which they occur. As discussed previously, what might be considered a savvy investment for a white, middle-class financial actor—buying a home in a so-called up-and-coming neighborhood, for example—might be evaluated quite differently for a racially marked actor (whose investment itself potentially reduces the neighborhood's characterization as "up-and-coming"). Directing attention to discourses of financial literacy here helps us understand how evaluations of literacy are not predetermined but emerge in contexts that include colonial attitudes (who deserves to occupy neighborhoods) and racialized paradigms.

The importance of considering financial literacy programs to understand the work of producing debtors along differential lines is alluded to in the work of Crystal Broch Colombini, who, citing Wendy Brown, explains, "If neoliberal capitalism is adept at conscripting individuals into difficulty then charging them to resolve it for themselves, it does so through the allocation of communicative burdens.... It creates 'responsibilized' subjects, who 'are required to provide for themselves in the context of powers and contingencies radically limiting their ability to do so'" (241).[11] Considering this burden in relation to the ways responsibility and morality *stick* to debt, we can further shift our understanding of financial literacy from its definition as static or a priori to itself emergent: financial literacy surfaces and marks normate embodiments and relations to financial systems, managing subjectivities and possibilities for those who can perform it.

The mark and affective securing of financial literacy for some people and the denial of financial literacy to others does not exist or emerge in separate or even parallel circulatory systems. Or, put otherwise, the "possible rhetoric situations where financial literacy is promoted" are not discrete (Ohlsson 66). This was dramatized on a global scale in 2008 with the subprime mortgage crisis, during which the effects of legislation deregulating investment practices landed more often, and with more impact, on Black and Brown borrowers, who, "lacking property and stocks passed on through generations and burdened by greater reliance on consumer credit, ... were less able to weather the sudden decline in home values" (Chakravartty and Ferreira da Silva 362). In this context, such borrowers' increased use of consumer credit took shape within an assessment of the morality of borrowers rather than the morality of lenders, producing *both* in the process (362). Whereas lenders were financially incentivized to offer more and riskier loans by the demand of investors capitalizing on changed financial regulations and thus explicitly targeted so-called risky neighborhoods and borrowers (Rothstein), it was the borrowers to whom shame and stigma stuck. As Paula Chakravartty and Denise Ferreira da Silva suggest, unlike the interest rates charged to "prime borrowers" (those deemed a safe bet), whose debt and repayment signify in ostensibly neutral economic terms, "references to law and morality, expectedly, prevail in condemnations of those served with 'subprime' loans, who are construed as intellectually (illiterate) and morally (greedy) unfit" (362).

Accounting for (Differential) Risk

As the subprime mortgage and prior examples suggest, critical attention to risk and its production and circulation is a needed component of a methodology of accounting for rhetoric *in* debt. Indeed, the terms "credit" and "debt" themselves have different sticky attachments, or connotations, when circulating alongside different bodies. While each debt (or line of credit) is ostensibly extended based on an individualized, mathematical determination of economic risk of default, calculations reflect social and cultural norms of risk as calibrated by Western individual, mathematical, and neoliberal standards (see the introduction). A third layer of this bricolaged methodology is thus required—one capable of accounting for the interplay of risk within a sticky affective milieu of financial literacy and economic fitness.

Linking so-called mathematical calculations to risk assessment, the social theorist and risk scholar Joost Van Loon confirms that "the wide appropriation of the mathematical and statistical concepts of 'probability' illustrates that the notion of risk has been endemic not only in modern western technoscience, but also in the very institutional infrastructures of twentieth-century capitalist social formations" (5). He takes up the germinal work of Ulrich Beck, who defines risk as "the modern approach to foresee and control the future consequences of human action, the various unintended consequences of radicalized modernization" (*World Risk Society* 3). Beck further argues that scientific and mathematical attempts to anticipate and mediate future harms or hazards by calculating risk fundamentally *reshape society as a whole*, influencing systemic possibilities, individual actions, and the relationships between them. "Consequences that at first affect individuals," he explains, "become 'risks,' that is, systemic, statistically describable and hence 'calculable' event types that can be subsumed under supra-individual compensation and avoidance rules" (*World at Risk* 7). Health risks related to lifestyle, for example, are calculated by insurance agencies through actuarial technologies and statistical evaluation of large data sets, which prescribe and interpret individual behaviors and actions based on probabilities. Individual behaviors and actions are seen as high or low risk on the basis of statistical probability of their resulting in compromising health (see chapter 4).

Rhetorically articulated in terms of statistical probability and calculability, risk does not merely *describe* potential hazard or harm but participates in their emergence; accordingly, as Van Loon argues, "risks have been taken up by a form of technological culture in which risk aversion provides the predominant 'ethical' imperative" (4). He continues, "The logic of practice of engaging with risks is mainly driven by a managerial approach to regulate these undesired 'bads' and transform them, whenever possible, into 'opportunities'" (4). Both Beck and Van Loon affirm that the grounding of risk in statistical probability—and its attendant mandate for decision-making—invites individuals into a new relationship with hazard and harm. Individuals not only are hailed to used probabilistic thinking and calculation to seek "goods" and avoid "bads" but are ethicized in relation to their outcomes. This relation to forecasting probability, as Beck proposes, is not universal but the specific feature of a "risk society." Van Loon further explains vis-à-vis Peter Bernstein that "what distinguishes modern 'man' from 'his' predecessors is the way in which hazards are being handled. For modern 'man,' hazards have to be controlled by 'himself,' through systematic application of science and technology, most of all mathematics. That is, modern 'man' turns hazards into risks" (2). Importantly, though not explicitly addressed by either Beck or Van Loon, the systematic application of technologies and mathematics *necessarily* includes financial accounting and its regulation. Though financial accounting predates—by a significant period—the markers of what Beck terms a "world risk society," it (and its regulation) serves as the technology through which credit and debt become numerical facts subject to calculable interpretations of risk (Poovey).

Whereas Van Loon asserts a condition for "man" in general—who "turns hazards into risks"—rather than setting up expectations for differentiated groups or individuals, Beck is unambiguous in his assessment of the effects of a risk society *on* individuals, arguing that "the impenetrability, omnipresence and undecidability of systemic risks are foisted onto the individual" (*World at Risk* 6). But he is also careful to note the asymmetry of systemic risks or how they—we might say following Ahmed—*stick* differentially: "The globality of risk does not, of course, mean a global equality of risk. The opposite is true: the first law of environmental risk is: *pollution follows the poor*" (*World Risk Society* 6). He continues by exposing this same logic for financial risk, suggesting that "like the global ecological risks, the global financial risks cannot be 'kept on one side' but flood and transform themselves into social and political risks, that is, risks for the middle class, the poor or the political elites" (*World Risk Society* 7).

Given that assessments of debt or creditworthiness are calculated as assessments of risk, J. Blake Scott's rhetorical study of risk and riskiness as it attaches to and becomes synonymous with specific bodies is also instructive here, especially as it articulates how risk attaches to some bodies *in relation* to others. Studying the rhetorics and cultural practices of AIDS and HIV testing in the United States specifically, Scott identifies how "risk is located in deviant 'others' who must be detected and avoided. Risk is furthermore represented as a fixed, essential part of these others. There are clean, safe people, and then there are infected, risky people" (*Risky Rhetoric* 100). Given the specific context and rhetorical objects of Scott's study, it would be inappropriate to suggest that the risk associated with debt and the risk associated with HIV or AIDS are synonymous. They are not, however, wholly separate. Indeed, the concept of "preexisting condition" that is so significant in the calculation of medical insurance and the cost of medical care in the United States directly contributes to who is deemed worth the risk of medical credit (insurance) and who is destined for significant medical debt (the subject of chapter 4).

As Scott's research elucidates, risk is rhetorically situated to describe bodies and subjects: they become defined by risk rather than understood to be engaged in risky behavior or taking a risk. Importantly, this metonymic slide is made in cultural terms, following cultural norms. It is the "deviant"—especially here in relation to heteronorms but also in relation to how such norms interface with race, class, and citizenship—that frames specific subjects as themselves risky rather than any specific sexual practices. Scott's analysis here reframes how risk is "foisted" onto individuals: not as a disinterested, statistical calculation but following cultural constructions and attendant perceptions of risk. Indeed, the technical communication scholars Jeffrey T. Grabill and W. Michelle Simmons affirm that risk and risk assessment *must* be understood as socially constructed within a framework that includes "social, political, and economic factors" (425). Following Chaput and Ahmed, we can also add to this list the material and affective factors that shape how—and to whom—risk attaches and gets narrated; social, political, and economic factors emerge as meaningful and impactful in different ways, for different subjects, such that risk attaches more readily to specific bodies when those bodies are already imagined risky. Moreover, as Beck reminds us, "Risk and *responsibility* are intrinsically connected, as are risk and *trust*, risk and *security* (insurance and safety)" (*World Risk Society* 6). Not only, then, does risk attach differently but, in so doing, it inversely attaches (or denies) responsibility, trust, and security. Moreover, risk is not a stable or set marker but shifts in relation to economic and cultural reasoning and norms as well as in relation to material networks and technologies (Scott, "Tracking" 32).

In drawing out the logics and rhetorical functions of risk articulated by Van Loon, Beck, and Scott to understand debt, it becomes clear how debt and indebtedness get attached to specific bodies and subjects not as a consequence of discrete practices or decisions made by individuals, or even a demonstration of individual financial literacies, but based on the significance of their bodies and practices within cultural, political economies of meaning. Accordingly, the credit score, spending habits, and amount of debt for the economically and socially precarious "live on the skin" (Ahmed) differently than they do for people with stable social recognition (whether it be economic, racial, or otherwise normative). Debt is considered risky as it attaches to specific bodies already imagined as a risk. As Scott argues, these differences make risk "difficult to track," tied as they are to cultural perceptions that make them "function differently in different locales," which "ultimately have no discrete boundaries or destination" ("Tracking" 30). But this difficulty, he continues, mandates a rhetorical sensibility and methodology, not only because "risks are constructs," and rhetoric "plays a crucial form in their forms, functions, and effects," but because risks produce "actual material harm" (30). A methodology capable of rhetorically tracking risk must therefore, following Scott, "involve capturing the movement and transformation of risks and their effects across a web of local and global contexts and actors . . . and might also involve examining how the local-global publics who deploy and respond to risks shift and transform" (30).

To Lazzarato's point that neoliberalism and global capitalism invite us to define subjectivity itself in terms of *homo economicus* as always already indebted, then, scholarship from Ahmed and Scott helps articulate *how* "economicus" is lived differentially—as affect circulates, sticks, and comes to define subjects, allocating rhetorical meaning and social credit and risk in radically inequitable ways. Rhetoric and cultural studies scholars working under the conceptual umbrella of precariousness and precarity further clarify how a universal statement of being-in-relation must nonetheless be understood with respect to its differential work. As Judith Butler explains, although all lives are definitionally precarious, "precarity designates that politically induced condition in which certain populations suffer from failing social and economic networks of support and become differentially exposed to injury, violence, and death. Such populations are at heightened risk of disease, poverty, starvation, displacement, and of exposure to violence with protection" (25–26). As articulated by Butler, whose definition grounds much interdisciplinary, including rhetorical, attention to the concept, precarity emerges in political, social, and economic relations, marking out which and how specific populations and bodies are valued or made vulnerable. While precariousness considers how all bodies are vulnerable to toxins, for example, precarity allows specific populations and bodies to be housed near toxic waste (Pezzullo), to work with toxic materials (Neilson and Rossiter), or to suffer the consequences of toxic exposure without adequate medical care (Taylor). Kathleen Stewart adds to this definition in the context of her own study of precarity's forms, which, she argues, "register the tactility and significance of something coming into form through an assemblage of affects, routes, conditions, sensibilities, and habits" ("Precarity's Forms" 518). Centering precarity, then, turns attention not only to the politics of precariousness but to the material and affective circuits that sponsor and corroborate those politics. In the words of Wendy S. Hesford, Adela C. Licona, and Christa Teston in their introduction to *Precarious Rhetorics*, "precarity has become a key concept in scholarly work devoted to the affective, relational, and material conditions and structuring logics of inequality" (2).

These definitions of precarity align with Miranda Joseph's proposal that "*debt* should be understood as a 'form of appearance' . . . of the broader social processes of exploitation and dispossession, an immanent component of social relations rather than external imposition" (2). That is, contra debt's reputation as extant, volitional, and calculable, as a choice made by an individual, Joseph asserts that it must be understood to *produce* social relations and subjectivity (2). The conceptual importance of precarity to the possibility of accounting for rhetoric in debt, then, lies in its ability to address the "affective, relational, and material conditions and structuring logics of inequality" that Hesford, Licona, and Teston articulate, to which debt not only contributes but fundamentally sponsors. Moreover, the concept of precarity is also conceptually useful to reject binary logics of debt. Rather than posit a neat division between haves and have-nots of debt (of capitalism more broadly) or reinstating such divisions as "liberal personhood/rights, inclusion/exclusion, victimization/agency, vulnerability/resistance, and human/nonhuman," the concept of precarity can, according to Hesford, Licona, and Teston, "recalibrate" them. More specially, they argue, "a rhetorical approach to these divisions reconfigures them such that they can be understood as *relational* rather than as simply oppositional" (3, emphasis added).

Accounting for Relations, Surfacing Scales

A final contribution to this bricolaged methodology comes from scholarship capable of accounting for the complex relations that serve as the conditions of possibility for debt. That is, collating the scholarship presented in this chapter leverages a perspective on debt that foregrounds affective circulations and relationality, disarticulating it from commonplaces and taken-for-granted reasoning that deny its emergences and effects. Ahmed corroborates the value of methodologies that focus on the relational, which move attention away from unilateral attention to *what* surfaces and instead foregrounds "how things surface." This shift from *what* to *how*, she argues, simultaneously acts as "a critique of what recedes" (*On Being Included* 185). Writing in the context of accounting for diversity in institutions, she argues explicitly that "to account for what recedes is to offer a different kind of account" (185). In building a rhetorical methodology capable of accounting for rhetoric in debt, we can consider how debt surfaces and sticks—its premises and conclusions, its causes and effects, its technologies and practices—in the context of critique of what recedes: economic, geopolitical, racialized, gendered, and colonial relations that indebt specific bodies in patterned, violent ways. We can investigate, for example, when and for whom debt is articulated as a risk factor and when it is understood as an investment. We can investigate the colonial histories of countries that require austerity measures before they are "bailed out." We can examine the new rhetoric of forgiveness that surrounds student loans and how it sticks differentially to generational financial commonplaces. We can consider the historical relations of racialized labor and exploitation that are reproduced under the signs of finance capitalism. We can track how local bond measures indebt community members in differential ways to community development projects and infrastructure. In short, rather than surface or examine only the numbers that predict risk within specific situations, this methodology interrogates how those numbers are chosen and at what, and whose, expense.

Importantly, these affordances of accounting for debt as it surfaces *in relation* invite methodological attention not only to disparate rhetorics of debt (variously articulated as loans, bonds, credit) and their effects but to the scales at which they are articulated. As Julie Jung argues in her meticulous rendering of the rhetorical possibilities and limits that accompany different systems theories—which likewise prioritize relations and emergent causality above "mechanical modes of analysis" (Connolly 179)—"a complex system cannot be understood by reducing it to its component parts, since it's the *interaction* among parts and not the sum of their individual properties that produces macrolevel behaviors attributable to the system as a whole" (Jung). She continues, "To begin to understand a complex system, then, one needs to generate descriptions of localized interaction occurring at different levels within the system."[12] This focus on scalar descriptions likewise resonates with transnational feminist rhetorical analysis, which, as articulated by Dingo, "is necessary to show how . . . rhetorical acts relate to one another and how they shift and change as they cross national and developmental boundaries" (*Networking Arguments* 15).

To be sure, debt studies across disciplines (from critical accounting studies to social and cultural theory) investigate debt within and across scales. These range from considering the effects of national or international loans on individuals, families, and communities (Zaloom; Karim) to the history and function of sovereign debt for particular nations (Bohoslavsky and Raffer, *Sovereign Debt Crises*; Donovan and Murphy; Papaconstaninou) and the global work of finance and debt in a neoliberal economy (Antoniades and Panizza; Bateman et al.; Lazzarato, *Governing*). And it is by articulating specific scales—or analytic boundaries predicated on defined geopolitical spatiality and temporality—that such work can offer meaningful contributions to furthering our understanding of debt and its effects. Building on this implicitly scalar work, then, a methodology to account for rhetoric *in* debt more explicitly surfaces the scales of debt.

Attention to the scales and scalar contexts in which debt emerges, I argue, not only offers a sense of the scope and differential work of debt within and across scales but also creates necessary boundaries through which rhetoric and debt can be studied. Of course, scales do not preexist their rhetorical articulation any more than does debt, and thus positing named scales—institutional, local, regional, national or historical, contemporary, and so forth—risks reinscribing commonplaces of spatiality and temporality that misrecognize their own rhetorical emergence and conditions of recognition as well as the political and ethical impacts of that naming work. Starting analysis of student loan debt on a "national" scale, as I do in chapter 2, for example, risks privileging hegemonies; overwriting subaltern or marginalized perspectives; disregarding the complexity of Indigeneity, migration, and citizenship; or naturalizing colonization. Rather than posit scales as a priori, however, following Jung and Dingo, we can see how they *participate* in the construction of the meaning of debt and can thus be leveraged to understand rhetoric *in* debt. In other words, by naming scales in the chapters that follow, I "generate descriptions of localized interaction" (Jung), rendering an account of debt's complexity otherwise unavailable. This is not to suggest that such scalar naming and analysis can—or seeks to—produce a totalizing account of rhetorics in debt but instead, as articulated by Kyle P. Vealey and Alex Layne, "understands scholarly work as a series of practices that constitute, rather than reflect, ontologies" (53).

Ultimately, then, accounting for rhetoric in debt invites description of rhetorics *of* debt and their differential effects within particular scalar contexts as well as its emergence and movement across scales or contexts. This accounting work thus explicitly follows cues from Wendy S. Hesford, who describes her methodology of "intercontextual analysis" in terms of its ability to "foreground both the textual and contextual dimensions of representational practices" and to "complicate analytics that focus solely on scale (such as nation-to-nation analysis) by foregrounding how meaning is produced, materialized, and experienced between and among multiple, ever-shifting contexts" (10). Importantly, as Hesford suggests of her own work in the context of human rights rhetoric, "an intercontextual analytic . . . does not invalidate geopolitical categories, especially given the mobilization of such categories such as the West and the non-West in the field of human rights internationalism by both its proponents and adversaries" (10). Likewise, accounting for rhetoric in debt does not ignore geopolitical—or other named scalar—categories but attends to their participation in the rhetorical work of debt. Indeed, I propose that it is only by considering how rhetorics *of* debt emerge in specific geopolitical contexts, at particular levels of scale, and by tracking their diffuse work *across* scales that we can account for rhetoric *in* debt.

Moving to Method

As indicated earlier, the purpose of using bricolage to theorize a methodology of accounting for rhetoric in debt is to offer a rejoinder to accounting practices that flatten debt's representation, allowing it to signify as an individual, volitional, and moral agreement that is easily calculated numerically. By considering the scalar emergence of debt and its rhetorics by way of material and affective circulations and patterns, however, debt can be disarticulated from its commonplace enthymematic conclusion (that it merely exists) and understood in relation to its differential effects.

In order to illustrate the potential of this methodology, in the following chapters, I mobilize it as a method to investigate student loan debt (in chapter 2), municipal bond debt (in chapter 3), and medical debt (in chapter 4). Simultaneously focused on debt that emerges within US histories, policies, and practices, and thus less paradigmatic than symptomatic of the complexity of debt of a global scale, each of these cases demonstrates the need for methodologies capable of surfacing rhetoric in debt capable of leveraging perspective on how, and with what effects, it so stealthily, so successfully, and so differentially manages lives and futures. Indeed, though such cases are ostensibly premised on comparable (national) scales, accounting for each through its temporal and spatial (scalar) emergence demonstrates the necessary work of tracking debt in its specific articulations. Whereas student loan debt, municipal bond debt, and medical debt may heretofore signify in the public imagination as similar—each demarcating financial literacy, each requiring repayment—they circulate and stick in patterns and with effects that demand investigation prior to attempts at intervention.

2

Economic Crisis, Financial Literacy, and Accounting for Student Loan Debt

As discussed in the previous chapters, coordinated neoliberal premises lead to the seemingly benign conclusion that debt exists: it denotes a mathematical calculation of credibility predicated on agented individuals who assume moral and contractual responsibility for the financial credit they are extended. The significant difference between the forms debt takes—transnational microfinance, national treasury bonds, mortgages, payday loans, credit cards, home equity loans, small business loans, and bail bonds, to name a few—are rhetorically organized by a shared morality. Debt does not signify unilaterally as *immoral*. It is warranted, in part, when present cost is weighed against future benefit and the latter is deemed worthy. Thus, specific debts can signify as *investments* in the future, while others indicate poor decision-making, faulty cost-benefit analysis, irresponsibility, or outright recklessness. Importantly, the financial cost-benefit is bulwarked by moral cost-benefit, such that those who make "wise" decisions about debt are framed not only as more worthy of credit but as more credible. Meanwhile, those who use debt on so-called nonessentials, extravagances, or whims are understood not only to undertake unnecessary risk but—invoking the terminology of J. Blake Scott—to be themselves risky. These assessments of costs and benefits, creditability and risk, need and want, are not made in a vacuum, nor do they operate as absolutes. They emerge, circulate, and stick differentially within what Sara Ahmed calls a "cultural politics of emotion," wherein histories and patterns of circulation ready bodies and subjects for assessment of their worth and worthiness. Presented as a mathematical (which is to say rational and neutral) calculation, debt is considered to *belong* to individuals, but such a calculation does not factor in how debt emerges within colonial, racialized, and gendered histories of value and morality across different levels of scale.

Whereas accounting for debt in financial terms invites complicated financial accounting practices and technologies, its reputation as self-evident and extant belies complex relations that sponsor its emergence and differential effects. To account for rhetoric in debt beyond the balance sheet, then, in chapter 1, I proposed a methodology adequate to this complexity, which takes into account *how* debt materializes, for whom, and with what consequences. To demonstrate the affordances of this methodology, I now turn to my first of three case studies of debt—student loans—by tracking its rhetorical emergence and significance through multiple articulations of scale, both temporal and spatial. More specifically, in this chapter, I consider the rhetorical significance of student loans at a national level of scale by considering how they emerge as a "crisis" only when they meet threshold conditions of mattering, calculated and accounted for through ratios and averages. I then turn attention to how such conditions and calculations elide histories of radical exclusion by attaching loans (and loan crises) to individual economic actors who demonstrate financial literacy (or not) as measured by rubrics of dominant, public pedagogy of debt. By prioritizing attention to a specific scalar emergence and resonance of debt, I do not aim to discount the impact of other scales but to illustrate, more acutely, how a politics of attention shapes possibilities for how debts emerge. That is, by shifting to accounts that contextualize the differential emergence and effects of debt and in naming my own practices of accounting, I acknowledge how rhetoric itself emerges *in* debt, participating in its conditions of possibility, party to its differential work. Rather than disavow the entanglement of scales themselves, then, I show how rhetorical practices can leverage perspective on which and how debts matter.

Student Loan Crisis?

Currently in the United States there is unprecedented public and political attention to student loan debt, as it surpasses and outpaces all other forms of individual debt aside from mortgage debt. Indeed, the "crisis" of student loan debt is often invoked to characterize its significance and economic impact. This crisis rhetoric accords with other debt crises and economic crisis rhetoric more broadly, especially following the increased attention to and media coverage of "sovereign debt crises" that have become a consistent feature of international economics since the 1980s (Bohoslavsky and Raffer, "Introduction" 1). Though distinct in their histories and forms, the crises alluded to by Juan Pablo Bohoslavsky and Kunibert Raffer and studied by the contributors to their collection *Sovereign Debt Crises: What Have We Learned?*, can also be characterized in terms of "common trends and challenges" ("Introduction" 6): massive defaults, political and social upheaval, austerity measures, poverty, and decades-long recovery. Invoking the term "crisis" to describe the impact of student debt in the United States draws on these connotations. Of course, in US public discourse, crisis is also invoked to create or describe exigent matters of economics, health, and public safety: the oil crisis of the 1970s, the savings and loans crisis of the 1980s and '90s, the subprime mortgage crisis of the 2000s, the opioid crisis, the refugee crisis, and the climate crisis, to name a few.

Circulating along and drawing from the connotations of these other crises, which name existential threats to health and livelihood, student loan debt has recently taken on the qualifier in media discourse—a turning point from its perceived role in sponsoring sound, smart economic opportunities to threatening them. Looking closely at representative artifacts that center debt in public, political, and popular discourses reveals a cluster of terms through which crisis emerges—"recession," "inflation," and "financial ruination"—but "crisis" itself has become the preferred rhetorical descriptor. While some economists decry this description (as I discuss in more detail shortly), suggesting a distinct rift between the rhetoric and reality of student debt (Akers and Chingos; Baum), in the past two decades, student loan debt has exploded in material and political significance, both essential to underwriting college education and central to political economic debate in the United States.

At the time of this writing (March 2022), student loans in the United States total $1.76 trillion (US Debt Clock.org). Ow(n)ed by fifty million people, the total amount, rate of increase over the past twenty years, and effects on the lives of those with loans explicitly mark this a crisis, with news reports and analysis daily addressing its economic impact and long-term tenability. But attention is not limited to its size or scope alone. Increasingly, political and media attention and economic analysis speculate on the validity of student loan debt, as indicated by reports on lawsuits against for-profit universities and political candidates' proposals to cancel or expunge student loan debt and make college free.

Moreover, while the standards and strictures of student loan forgiveness programs have come under scrutiny for being too restrictive, disqualifying otherwise-eligible debtors on technicalities, and prompting the Biden administration to recalibrate such programs, the former education secretary Betsy DeVos, with the approval of Donald Trump, proposed canceling such programs altogether (Friedman). Notably, political interest in student loan forgiveness only sharpened during the outbreak of COVID-19 in the United States. While Trump initially suggested that he would suspend *interest* on federal student loans during the pandemic—a move later determined to be at once outside the scope of his executive powers as well as nominal in effect (as payees would still be required to make full payments that would go toward principal)—ultimately, the first aid package (introduced by the Senate, revised by the House of Representatives, and signed by then-President Trump) allowed certain federal student loan recipients to defer payment for six months (Federal Student Aid). Additional proposals authored by a variety of congresspeople included canceling student debt for health care first responders, protracting student loan repayments for longer than the initial six months, and canceling debt altogether. This "pause" or "freeze" has since been extended multiple times, and each time it is set to expire, "crisis" is invoked again as the rejoinder to such a decision. Correlating the ability of former students to repay loans with the ongoing financial consequences of the pandemic rhetorically entangles the issues in a shared financial world and logic, such that the crisis of each is exacerbated by the other and relief from each is alleviated by the other. During a national emergency, then, the significance of student loan debt is (re)asserted as paramount in its importance—both in national discourse and to the daily, lived experiences of debtors—and its acknowledgment in the relief package suggests that it is not of peripheral concern, either politically or experientially, but centered in the politics, policies, and anxieties of a nation in health and economic crisis.[1]

As historicized by Caitlin Zaloom in her book-length study of the role of finance to underwrite college for middle-class families and futures, student loans emerged as de rigueur over the course of the last several decades of twentieth-century policy change in the United States. These included a shift to government backing of private student loans (in the 1970s) and political acceptance of a more limited role for government to fund public education (in the 1980s), which paved the way in the 1990s for an agreement between the federal government and banks regarding the necessity and appropriateness of debt to fund (Zaloom 13). As Zaloom argues, however, it is not only the stark rises in costs to attend college—the average costs of tuition, even adjusted for inflation, have more than doubled since the mid-1980s (National Center for Education Statistics)—that have directed students (and their families) toward student loans but the insistent middle-class narrative since the 1960s that college education offers "economic security and reasons to feel confident about the future" (1).

Building on Zaloom's important work exposing the effects of this narrative on middle-class individuals, families, and relationships, in this chapter, I explore the emergence of this narrative and its differential work, considering, too, its heightened national exposure in the context of crisis rhetoric and a global pandemic. To be sure, whereas education, including higher education, has always been differently and asymmetrically accessible in the United States, the rhetoric of student loans did not ascend to crisis until it began effecting white, middle-class Americans categorically. Moreover, those who discredit crisis rhetoric do so citing data about its manageability for *most* people, indicating an accepted rate of harm for the effects of student loan debt on the *few*. And in the acute context of the outbreak and proposed responses to managing the economic fallout of COVID-19, this critical status only intensified. As I argue in this chapter, the crisis rhetoric of debt itself serves to flatten the uneven effects and affects of debt, reinvesting it in moral commonplaces of individual responsibility and calculable risk assessment and corroborating white, middle-class values.

Of course, one way to explore the available narratives of student debt (and their effects) is to conduct close textual analysis, which could expose the cluster of terms and cases through which student loan debt is described as a "crisis." This could include enthymematic unpacking of "fragments of discourse" (Jackson) or ideographic analysis (McGee), for example, of federal student loan policy or regulatory documents or news reports or op-eds about the presence and impact of student loans. It could include synchronic or diachronic maps of the terms that have and do circulate alongside "student loan debt" or "student loan crisis" (McKerrow; Rice). It could also take the form of qualitative analysis that rhetorically documents and codes the presence, patterns, and frequency of crisis terminology. These and other options for close textual work would offer critical, granular insight into how student loan debt is represented, how it appeals to different audiences and ideologies (and with what effects), and how it participates in constituting a rhetorical imaginary of debt.

But acknowledging rhetoric *in* debt, as I propose to do in this work, requires rhetorical attention that moves beyond textual analysis toward methodologies that not only situate such texts in place and time but acknowledge rhetoric as entangled in material relations that allow it to emerge as persuasive. This is rhetoric *in* debt. By tracking the rhetorical emergence of student loan debt through its discourses, institutions, and material relations across spatial and temporal scales, then, I surface its differential work and expose possibilities for intervening in the reproduction of debt's differential mattering.

National Discourses of Need for Student Debt

The scale at which I consider the emergence, effects, and affects of student loans is national—indicated by the policies and public discourses that sponsor and secure the story of student loans in broad, normative ways in the United States. This scale is circumscribed historically and temporally, emerging in relation to generations of politics, policies, and trends that rhetorically and affectively secure commonplaces about and lived experience with debt. That said, a comprehensive diachronic history of the emergence of debt at this national level of scale is beyond the scope of this study: not only, as discussed in chapter 1, can discourses of debt be traced back to the nation's beginnings, but the idea of the United States itself is one that emerges *in* debt. This is evidenced, for example, by the establishment of specific colonies as debtor's prisons and a national bank to underwrite state debt (Lepore), the use of credit by colonial merchants to conduct transatlantic trade based on seasonal agrarian exports (Flynn), and public political argument about the use of debt to secure the nation (Herring, "Rhetoric"). It is also evident in the continued citation of and national lore about the Boston Tea Party, for example, wherein taxes levied by the British Crown were rejected as an unjust debt. Less cited but no less relevant to the establishment of the United States was rising debt in the United States immediately following the Civil War. Rather than canceling fiscal relationships between European nations and the new republic, the war sparked astronomical (for the times) debts, which peaked at $120 million four decades after "independence" (Debt.org, "Timeline"). Of course, as discussed in the introduction to this book, the imbrication of debt in the US imaginary must also be traced to the conceptualization of enslaved persons as property, accounted for as such in ledgers equating people with the market value of their lifelong labor and exploitation, as well as with the trade agreements with Indigenous peoples premised on European and colonial understandings of individual property and debt. These unpaid debts of colonization and slavery both funded and continue to underwrite US economics and culture. In short, the story of the United States is a story of debt (see also Bruner).

The long history of debt in the United States gives way to specific and polar articulations and rhetorics of debt in particular moments. For example, the debts of war are largely untaxed in public memory—either forgotten or justified through rhetorics of crisis, security, or self-preservation. But such debts have also historically contributed to unprecedented national economic growth through the highly entangled military-industrial complex. Deficit spending during World War II, for example, reached an all-time high of $57 billion ("Deficit Spending"), but such credit-based investment in weapons and technology (including atomic weapons) is narrated as a worthy price to pay not only to defend the United States but also—and later—to sponsor worldwide leadership in communications, transportation, and military technologies. While this type of debt might also be understood to be paid by the health and lives of military persons and civilians alike (both those killed by weapons and those affected by testing, as in the case of thousands of military persons affiliated with atomic testing in the South Pacific), it lays claim to the morality of righteous causes. The case for deficit spending for defense in the United States after World War II, then, is doubly warranted: it is an investment in safe *and* economic futures. Similarly, deficit spending during economic crises, the aid packages quickly assembled and distributed in response to the subprime mortgage crash in 2008 and to COVID-19 in 2020, for example, are narrated as necessary and moral investments in safe and economic futures. Even with significant political critique, both are packaged as vital investments in national economic recovery.

Notably, warrants for student loan debt are likewise invested in safe and economic futures; they also promise more equitable futures as they rhetorically pair access to education with the ability to pay for it. Backed by the federal government, they signify as a vetted, legitimate debt, especially when juxtaposed with the reputation of other types of consumer debt: auto, credit card, payday loans, and so forth. Despite the parallels with other nationally sanctioned debts (for defense and crisis), however, the warrants and promises of student loans suggest them as distinct from other types of debt in the United States. As Beth Akers and Matthew M. Chingos propose in *Game of Loans: The Rhetoric and Reality of Student Debt*, in general loans can be defined as "a transaction between an individual and her future self," which is reasonable when "your future self will be much wealthier than your present self" or when a purchase will "benefit your future self" but destructive when used to "finance purchases that we can't really afford" (6). But they disaggregate student loans from this general definition, explaining that rather than indicate a postponed expense, student loans are "a means for transferring wealth from a future period of relative prosperity to the present" (6). What is more, they continue, debt associated with financing education not only makes it possible for "consumers to smooth their consumption over time, . . . but the debt itself is what generates the opportunity for the heightened future prosperity" (6). Whereas other types of unsecured debt—debt that does not have the backing of equity that might be repossessed in the case of default—primarily fund consumption, Akers and Chingos explain that student loans combine consumption in the present (as students use loan money for the *experience* of college) with investment in the future (insofar as college degrees underwrite professional opportunities with higher pay).

Excavated from an equation of consumer debt with extravagance, student loans signify, instead, as a pathway toward equitable futures, participating, in the words of the oft-cited education reformer Horace Mann, in a narrative of US education as "the great equalizer of the conditions of men—the balance wheel of the social machinery" (qtd. in Mullen 4). The sociologist Ann L. Mullen recounts the emergence of this reputation, citing the "remarkable campaign" of the latter half of the twentieth century to "increase the accessibility of higher education in the United States, premised on the value of offering young adults an equal opportunity for success on the basis of hard work and merit" (3). This rhetorical campaign was matched by public (federal and state) investments, resulting in the doubling of postsecondary institutions in the United States between 1950 and 2000 (from 1,851 to 4,084 institutions; Mullen 3). As Mullen explains, the introduction, expansion, and improvement of grant and loan programs during this period resulted in incredible increases in postsecondary enrollment (from 2.3 million to 15.3 million students), which not only increased how *many* students enrolled but *which* students enrolled.[2] The increased access and changed demographics that Mullen cites confirm the broad appeal of the case for college, such that "going to college has evolved from a rare privilege typically accorded only to the children (especially the white male children) of the middle and upper classes to a common part of the life course for a large segment of the U.S. population" (Mullen 4).

Although Mullen ultimately contextualizes these significant gains in access with respect to the *types* of institutions available to and attended by different groups and the significant effect of these differences on student outcomes and incomes (a point to which I return later in this chapter), the expansion undeniably shapes the US public imagination of postsecondary education as fundamental to sponsor or enhance employment opportunity and mobility as well as financial stability. Premised on competing narratives—as preprofessional or vocational training, on the one hand, and a liberal arts holistic education, on the other—the benefits of a college degree make multiple rhetorical appeals. College can code as a path toward steady employment, protection against underemployment or unsafe working conditions, and preparation to compete in a global economy. It can also, as Mullen explains, uphold generational legacies and confirm access to upper-class networks and privileges. Moreover, as Zaloom argues, "Pursuing a college education fulfills crucial cultural mandates that being *middle* class requires," demonstrating the moral uprightness of parents committed to their children's futures (7, emphasis added).

This variety of appeals to the value of a college education is rhetorically distributed and circulates through numerous media and institutions. Financial costs notwithstanding, the benefits of a college education are asserted as worthwhile or moral choices, as an investment in the future. This is manifest in the labeling of pre-K–12 courses, curriculum, and entire schools, for example, as "college prep" or when schools cite their rates of college acceptance. Human-interest stories and popular media accounts that follow the unlikely admission of students from poor, marginalized, or disenfranchised neighborhoods equate getting into college with success. Such naming and citation invoke the value of college for students (and their families), affirming its importance often without mentioning its costs. This value is also corroborated by marketing campaigns for colleges and universities themselves—distributed in a variety of media and reliant on tropes of working-class individuals using college degrees to secure stable employment. Perhaps most importantly, it is confirmed by job advertisements and applications that list specific college degrees as a minimum qualification for consideration to interview.

Significantly, as college degrees have replaced high school diplomas as a minimum qualification for entry-level work in a range of fields, and advanced degrees are all but required in many professional fields and have thus come to shape school choice, curriculum, and extracurricular activities for children and have prompted adults to return to school (full- or part-time, in person or online, in traditional and for-profit universities), the material need for student loans has skyrocketed. That is, whereas public (financial) support between 1950 and 2000 shifted enrollment of eighteen- to twenty-four-year-olds from one in seven (in 1950) to one in three (by 2000), in the last decade of the twentieth century, the federal government and banks "came to agree that debt was the way students should fund college education" and restructured financing to include private lenders (Zaloom 13). In short, rhetorical support for the *need* for higher education was matched by the availability of funding to meet that need.

Despite student loans' widespread reputation for sponsoring what Zaloom calls "open futures," Sara Goldrick-Rab explains how the twenty-first century has made student loans both essential and insidious for college attendees: "Just as Americans decided that college was essential, states began spending less on public higher education and the price of college rose. At the same time, the financial aid system, long intended to make college affordable, failed to keep up with growing student and family need. Student loans became the stopgap. And to make matters worse, for nearly 80 percent of the public, family income declined" (1). In the context of significant reductions of federal and state contributions to public colleges and universities (Fuller), student loans become vital for *most* students to pay or supplement tuition, fees, and other costs associated with college attendance. Indeed, as cited by Debt.org, *average* student debt (in 2017) for undergraduate degrees alone was $37,172 ("Students"). This average is even more for graduate students, who are limited by the time commitments of programs and funding opportunities (or total lack thereof, in the case of medical students, for example) and require substantial backing to pay not only for tuition and fees but the costs of living: rent, utilities, insurance, food, child care, and so on.

Notably, the marked value or necessity of college education—and the student loans needed to underwrite it—cannot be disarticulated from postsecondary institutions themselves, which are critiqued as participating in the ever-increasing costs of attendance by scaling tuition and fees to match the widespread availability of student loans, appropriately termed a "high tuition, high aid" model. As Matthew B. Fuller explains in his "History of Financial Aid to Students," this critique can be traced to Ronald Reagan's secretary of education, William J. Bennett, who vociferously decried increased spending and "argued that colleges and universities were—and had been for some time—increasing tuition simply because federal student aid was readily available" (55). As Fuller explains, Bennett "fueled a growing societal distrust of higher education costs," known as "the Bennett Hypothesis" (55–56). Whereas Fuller rejects this hypothesis, it nonetheless finds purchase in discussions of culpability for student loan debt, blaming institutions themselves for exponentially increased costs of college attendance.

Importantly, the lack of evidence to confirm the Bennett Hypothesis does not wholly exclude postsecondary institutions as participants in the rhetorical emergence of the *need* for student loans to finance college education. As the sociologists Armin Beverungen, Casper Hoedemaekers, and Jeroen Veldman point out, the image of college education as a public good in a neoliberal economic context reduces accountability (of the institutions) to a matter of financial performance and makes the university "a key actor in the construction of neoliberal consent" (64). Building on Jeffrey Williams's articulation of a "pedagogy of debt," Beverungen, Hoedemaekers, and Veldman argue that given the financialization of the universities, student debt should not be understood merely as "financing" but as "a mode of pedagogy." They continue: "Student debt in the USA and in the UK has come to serve as a tool for 'market conscription.' Debt teaches several lessons to the student: that 'higher education is a consumer service,' that studying is a question of 'career choice' and that the worth of a person is measured 'according to one's financial position.' These lessons promote a worldview where 'the primary ordering principle of the world is the capitalist market' and wherein 'the state's role is to augment commerce'" (64). As Williams pointed out in 2006, while many people have critiqued the "corporatization" of the university for the creep of capitalism into research, labor, and administration, few studies acknowledged the "privatization of student debt" as another key factor (157). Extending this argument in 2012, Beverungen, Hoedemaekers, and Veldman propose that the university itself is "the incubator" of more widespread financialization and neoliberalism writ large, insofar as it offers a "narrowly defined ... gateway to a better job and higher earnings," whereby student loans indicate "'a personal investment in one's market potential rather than a public investment in one's social potential,' where consequently 'each individual is a store of human capital, and higher education provides value added'" (64). In other words, the financialization of the university welcomes students into the logos of neoliberalism, interpellating them as economic actors always already beholden to finance.

The effects of this incubation are manifest in the work of the economist Sandy Baum, who, dissatisfied with the rhetorical construction of student-debt-as-crisis and dismissing media representations of the problems with student loans as political pandering, describes the rationale for student loans as follows: "People have limited resources before they get an education, but that education is an investment that will boost their incomes over a lifetime. They can use part of the earnings premium to repay the debt. That's the same concept as borrowing to start a business" (7). Whereas Beverungen, Hoedemaekers, and Veldman via Williams critique the "pedagogy of debt" that persuades students (and their families) of the inevitability of financialization of education in a neoliberal economy, Baum insists that its benefits outweigh the costs. As evidenced by Zaloom's interviews with middle-class families seeking to finance college, Baum's argument emerges as a compelling rhetorical commonplace: "Borrowing for college is a sensible idea" (7).

Defining the Terms of Student Loan Debt

At issue in the implicit disagreement between the authors cited in the previous section is not only the idea that student debt is sensible or smart—which frames it as a question of both quality and policy—but, I would argue, the definition of debt itself. Using the terminology of stasis, we can see how identifying the point at which disagreement is articulated helps shift attention away from the debt as a predefined and foregone conclusion to a rhetorical question of belief and enthymematic history and reasoning. Clearly diverging in characterizations of the qualities of debt (rational and sustainable versus ideological and untenable) and thus articulations of appropriate policies pursuant to these qualities (encouraging or rejecting debt as a worthwhile risk), the scholarship cited previously offers fundamentally different definitions of debt itself. Whereas Baum and other critics of the media framing of student-debt-as-crisis define debt as an individual, rational (and moral) decision made by individuals weighing the costs and benefits of debt-for-education, Williams, followed by Beverungen, Hoedemaekers, and Veldman, defines debt as a system of finance that, however problematically, teaches students (and their families) how to become successful debtors or, as I discuss later in this chapter, debtors capable of recouping their investments through the cultural capital afforded by a college degree.

Importantly, whether debt *counts as* or can be justifiably framed as a crisis in these diverging conceptualizations hinges on whether—and to whom and how—debt attaches. Scholars including Baum and Akers and Chingos reject the idea that debt is worthy of the characterization of crisis, suggesting that the chasm between the "rhetoric" and "reality" of debt is significant by deferring to statistical representations that show that student debt is working "for most" (Baum) and that there "is no evidence of a widespread, systemic student loan crisis, in which the typical borrower is buried in debt for a college education that did not pay off" (Akers and Chingos 4). And perhaps using their metrics in relation to crisis as an exigence equally distributed in normative ways, others would agree with their rejection of that framing. But predicating the existence of a crisis on "most" or the "typical borrower" categorically discounts differential relations to debt, relying on averages to dismiss outliers. Crisis rhetoric here is considered hyperbolic when "most" is a sufficient condition to evaluate the success of student loans. Accounting for the historical emergence of student loan debt in the United States, however, as I demonstrate shortly, reminds us that norms are not merely statistical or numerical but racialized and gendered, offering terms of inclusion and exclusion for who counts and how they are counted. The "typical borrower" is one who is narrated as an individual making sensible and rational choices about the risks and rewards of debt but whose relationship to finance and debt for education, created in a long history of exclusion and abjection, has been ignored.

Juxtaposing denials of student debt crisis rhetoric, many scholarly, financial, and popular media texts announce the crisis of student loan debt using much-different metrics to identify it as such. The dramatic shift in ratio between student debt and other consumer debt (mortgage, credit card, auto), the overall total of student debt in relation to gross domestic product (GDP), the percentage of students who *require* student debt to attend college versus those who qualify for financial aid or have resources adequate to pay for college, and the individual and shared stories of the lived burden of debt articulated by individuals and families are some of the most popular ways to evidence claims of crisis. This evidence does not reject the idea of a typical borrower so much as recast the terms of evaluation. Crisis continues to be warranted through numerical calculation, but rather than in relation to number of students served, it indicates the crisis of debt in relation to larger economic measures. And while these measures *can* admit outliers—identifying specific stories of individuals being overwhelmed by debt, for example—they continue to frame crisis in terms of acceptable norms. Student debt crisis *exists* when it disrupts acceptable cost-benefit ratios. Debt ascends to crisis when it threatens financial futures on a broad scale. And crisis remains a normative evaluation of debt.

Using distinct and different measures of crisis, then, each of these approaches substantiates *how* or *whether* debt emerges as a crisis on the basis of the accounting work used to justify the claim. Moreover, despite using different methods to account for or evidence crisis, each of these approaches to the rhetoric *of* student loan debt presupposes individuals making rational decisions *about* debt, and thus neither can account for the emergence of rhetoric *in* debt, which allocates risk differentially, sponsoring debtors who emerge as moral and justified and others who are irresponsible or (financially) illiterate. In the following sections, then, I build on contemporary studies of debt that are attuned to its persuasive and subjectifying functions (as discussed in the introduction and chapter 1) and show how pivoting to a rhetoric *in* debt at a national level of scale offers a more nuanced perspective from which to contend with debts and debtors and with which to critique and intervene in its patterns of (mis)use and violence.

Identifying New Metrics

With even a limited sense of the diachronic emergence of discourses of the *need* for student debt on a national scale, it begins to become clear *how* student debtors emerge as individuals making calculated choices about the costs and benefits of a college education. That is, despite being fundamentally entangled with histories of (in)access and exclusion and questions of federal and state education policies and shifts in political tides as well as neoliberal economic practices more broadly, the student-as-debtor is nevertheless produced by and tasked with making individual choices about how they will finance education that is deemed necessary to create (or maintain) economic and employment opportunities. In other words, this national discourse of the *need* for college education (and corresponding student debt) reduces students to individual, rational, economic actors, flattening any differences between access to and experiences and effects of debt to issues of calculation and probability. However, as discourses of student debt need and crisis circulate at a national level of scale—in both academic studies of debt and news and popular media accounts—they stick differently to different bodies, marking them as more and less risky, more and less prone to poor decision-making, more and less capable of accruing unmanageable debt. Drawing on the methodology I theorize in chapter 1, it becomes clear how the reduction of need to an issue of individual financial literacy and rational cost-benefit analysis misrecognizes how debt circulates and sticks based on patterns of use, which not only assess but create worthy debtors and reinscribe normative evaluations of credit and risk that are class-based, racialized, and gendered. By turning to interdisciplinary scholarship that focuses on differential access, then, it becomes possible to trace the emergence of this rhetoric *in* debt, surfacing how, and with what effects, individuals emerge as worthy—or not—of investment.

Caitlin Zaloom's work in *Indebted: How Families Make College Work at Any Cost* begins to acknowledge the differential effects of debt. Explicitly focused on the middle class, Zaloom uses interviews with individual families to better account for how the need for educational financing is lived out in a variety of ways. Her work extends a tradition of research that exposes how education reproduces class differences. As Dalton Conley argues, citing the germinal study *Equality of Educational Opportunity* from 1966, education does "an excellent job of reproducing the same class differences that children brought to it in the first place" (56). Confirming this conclusion more than thirty years later,

Zaloom's and a number of other recent studies reveal that the promise of an open future offered by college matriculation is not straightforward, simple, or equally available.

This promise can be probed, for example, via attention to the probability of loans to exacerbate economic and other vulnerabilities. As concluded by Rachel E. Dwyer, Laura McCloud, and Randy Hodson in their study "Debt and Graduation from American Universities," increased access to college, combined with reliance on "significant loans," results in "added levels and types of vulnerability, . . . particularly students from less advantaged backgrounds" (1134). This is corroborated by Christopher Newfield in "Student Debt and the Social Functions of Consolidation College," in which he argues that the benefits of education are polarizing (especially along race and class lines). That is, despite rhetorically signifying as necessary for individual economic mobility and stability and thus ostensibly true *in general*, student debt "lowers the net value of college for its graduates" in three distinct ways (199).

First, Newfield cites the damning correlation between household income and student debt, finding that since 2003, income has not kept pace with student debt, a factor that disproportionately affects the middle and lower classes, making debt all but unavoidable for people without generational wealth or a very high income-to-expense ratio (199). In this context, the second factor he identifies that reduces the value of college is even more damning: "the stagnation in college completion for the bottom half of the U.S. population by income" (199). Whereas college has almost unilaterally become more important, more expensive, and more reliant on student loans, graduation—and thus the *benefits* of a college degree and associated debt—are not equally distributed or lived across socioeconomic classes. Expanded access to college, as evidenced by statistics of increased enrollments across classes in the second half of the twentieth century, then, is not a sufficient indicator of its value because it is graduation rather than matriculation that (statistically) offers economic and employment opportunities and their attendant financial stabilities. As Dwyer, McCloud, and Hodson confirm, student loan debt can either support *or* undermine college education because "graduation is a first crucial step in the attainment of a middle-class lifestyle" but is not itself guaranteed (1134). In a study of the effects of debt across public and private institutions, which includes students from a variety of socioeconomic backgrounds, the authors concluded that "those who were expected to benefit most from expanded college access are also most vulnerable to the risks of carrying too much debt" (1149).

As noted earlier, a crisis rhetoric of student loans in general does little to account for how they work (or not) for different kinds of subjects. The student who must withdraw from college to take a full-time job or to take care of their own mental health and who does not graduate, for example, is written off as unable to pay debt while their debt remains on the books. So too is the student who leaves college because they do not feel at home, because their language(s) or literacies are not recognized, or because—even with loans—they cannot afford to remain in school. Given the patterns by which debt *attaches* to and narrates bodies, however, the inability to graduate and capitalize on extended credit is narrated as a personal failure. In other words, in an accounting system organized by inputs and outputs (credits and debts), failure to *make good* on a debt (not only by paying it back but by building on its promise of an open future) secures or denies the credibility—and credit-worthiness—of students rather than the context in which they take out (or take on) a student loan. Whereas a ledger might account for tuition, board, and books, aligning those costs with available credit, it does not consider cultural or emotional costs of a college education and thus reasons beyond economic ones that a student might default on a loan.

Perhaps surprisingly, as reported by Josh Wright in the *Boston Globe*, statistically the *amount* of student loans a student takes out has an inverse relation to their likelihood to default. In his words, "Over half of student loan borrowers (around 25 million people) owe less than $20,000, but they have higher default rates than the borrowers who owe more. The student borrowers with over $100,000 in federal student debt (about 7 percent of borrowers) are, in fact, the least likely to default on their loans." Wright attributes this trend, in part, to disparate information literacies and accessibilities, citing complex funding structures and default policies that confuse borrowers. In other words, borrowers with more student loan debt often have more normative financial literacies; they are not more likely to pay off their loans *only* because of simple economic advantage but because they can better anticipate and navigate the requirements of finance. Dwyer, McCloud, and Hodson underscore this logic in their own conclusions, suggesting that in a context of "declining state subsidies and increasing private debt," educating students about debt is crucial to carrying out the promise of increased access to education: "If the burden of increasing college enrollments must fall to individual students, then we may need far more financial education and support as students with unequal resources and networks of social support make decisions and navigate a complex financial aid system"

(1151). For Wright, as for Dwyer, McCloud, and Hodson, loan default can be better mediated by better education about financial processes. As I discuss in more detail in the sections that follow, however, casting default in terms of individual financial literacy elides a more complex accounting for differential debt, redacting the emergence of (normative) literacies as entangled with the emergence of debt and eliding the participation of literacies in making "high risk" borrowers.

Pathologizing Financial Literacy, Promoting Dominant Pedagogy

The effect of positing individual financial literacy as the solution to problems (crises) associated with student loan debt can be illustrated by way of Sandy Baum's *Student Debt: Rhetoric and Realities of Higher Education*. Ostensibly corroborating the value of teaching financial literacy to students to help them avoid drastic economic consequences of illiteracy, Baum suggests that "instead of sweeping or simplistic policy proposals, we should be focusing on the individuals and groups of individuals who are being harmed by our current loan system" (12). Without using the language of financial literacy explicitly, Baum links systemic outcomes to individual choices and faulty cost-benefit analysis and later suggests that defaulting on loans can be attributed to a matter of "attitude and priorities" (37). Further, and without commenting on how different needs for debt follow and emerge from historical oppression and inequities, Baum moralizes debt to confirm stereotypes of borrowers: those who are willing to sacrifice to pay off debt versus those who are not. Only superficially sensitive to different value sets that motivate financial decisions—she admits that "it is not easy to define 'necessities' and no one can prescribe priorities for others"—Baum illustrates differences between types of borrowers by contrasting (hypothetical) people who "would rather live in their parents' basement and have the opportunity to travel" with those who "would choose a fancy apartment" or "being able to eat out or buy nice clothing" (37). Baum's choices of imagery here suggest that the ability to pay off student loan debt is not about necessities but travel and unnecessarily extravagant housing, food, and clothing. Moreover, her reference to basements to which students can retrench indicates underlying assumptions about intergenerational or familial wealth.

Elsewhere Baum acknowledges distinct patterns of risk for specific groups of students who require student loan debt but nevertheless frames such risk in terms of the choices made by such students:

> We know that high-risk students who enroll in for-profit institutions are much more likely to end up with unmanageable debt than are academically prepared students who enroll in public four-year colleges. We know that students who borrow for programs they are very unlikely to complete are most likely to default on their debts. We know that too many graduate students are borrowing very large sums to pursue occupations that will not generate the earnings required to pay their loans, while those who borrow even more for professional school are likely to repay. We know that people who have experienced serious medical problems or who have trained for occupations later decimated by technology or by outsourcing are likely to struggle despite having made apparently good decisions about financing postsecondary education. (12)

Interpreting what "we know," it becomes clear once again that for Baum, "unmanageable" student loan debt is the by-product of poor decision-making. Academically underprepared students should know better than to enroll in for-profit institutions. Students who may not finish their programs should not borrow money for college in the first place. Aspiring graduate students should not use debt to fund programs with limited exchange value. People with serious medical problems should better anticipate their inability to repay. And any students who use postsecondary education to fund jobs that might be replaced or outsourced should reconsider their plans. For Baum, these are issues of financial literacy and forecasting. With support and education to make better decisions, she argues, students can avoid these risks. This argument is not hers alone, however, but synecdochic of economic orthodoxy and neoliberal logic, in which individual and rational economic actors are held responsible for their choices.

Notably, an attribution and analysis of individual responsibility illustrates what the education scholar Chris Arthur (following Henry Giroux) calls the "public pedagogy" of financial literacy education (FLE; "Financial Literacy"), through which popular discourses "influence a society's dominant cultural mores and commonsense understandings" ("Debt" 176–77). As discussed in the introduction to this book, debt does not merely exist but rhetorically functions as the conclusion of enthymematic reasoning—it is taught and learned through commonplaces, norms, and fragments of discourse that allow it to go unquestioned. In addition to unstated premises of debt, however, discourses of FLE public pedagogy of "debt, spending, saving, risk and investment influence how individuals view the world, themselves, their relations, and others" and emphasizes the need to "improve and expand the teaching of financial literacy so the insecure and indebted can improve their lives" (Arthur, "Debt" 177). Citing explicit, funded, FLE programs that span rich and poor countries alike, Arthur shows how FLE becomes a commonsense response to debt, teaching individuals *in* debt how to navigate financial industries and obligations in order to get *out* of it.

Considering Baum's proposal to teach individuals how to make better decisions about student debt—whether or when it is worth it—as an instance of FLE, we can see how this form of public pedagogy not only addresses but more fundamentally produces "high risk" borrowers. That is, financial choices that do not pay off contribute to, rather than merely reflect, assessments of literacy. Such public pedagogy thus might be understood in terms of what the rhetorician Lynn Worsham refers to as "dominant pedagogy," "a structure that produces individuals and groups who are recognized as such because they have internalized the legitimate point of view" (221). This point of view is not disinterested. Its dominance and authority are maintained through violence, "through its power to impose the legitimate mode of conception and perception, through its power to conceal and mystify relations of domination and exploitation" (221). What is more, she continues, "pedagogy is an apparatus for creating, maintaining, and perpetuating the legitimacy of the interests of the dominant group across many different kinds of discourse that cultivate 'the educated individual' as an ideal type of pedagogical subject who possesses the propensity to consume the legitimate products of dominant culture and is predisposed to be used and consumed according to its interests" (221).

Working from Worsham's definition of "dominant pedagogy," we can identify how student loan debt can be both necessary and differentiating. Tied to the legitimacy of finance and indicative of financial literacy, it rhetorically and affectively hails students and families through a narrative of equal access, directing them toward a "legitimate product of dominant culture": college education. But this hailing work simultaneously creates borrowers on the basis of dominant interpretations of risk and reward, not only saddling them with material debts but with the consequences of "individual" decision-making that, as Baum's argument demonstrates, follow specific patterns of risk and risk assessment. Like other pedagogies enlisted in the work of dominant pedagogy, FLE purports to be neutral and provide equal access and in so doing masks its own truth: literacy emerges in normative relations, relations of power. It is enforced affectively, sticking pride or shame to individuals and groups to encourage (or discourage) financial behaviors. Accordingly, demonstrating financial literacy cannot be equated with avoiding debt. As Andrew Ross reminds us, "The goal is to keep us on the hook until we die" (216). "Financial literacy" is, instead, the name given to the right kinds of debtors and the right kinds of debts.

Popular and academic texts premised on resolving the problems associated with significant student loan debt through financial literacy initiatives or education, designed to teach individuals how to make wise decisions, not only reinvest debt and literacy in individuality but misrecognize the role of financial literacies themselves in *producing* differentially indebted subjects as well as the affective role of pedagogy in disciplining economic subjects. In other words, the public pedagogy of financial literacy both relies on and disavows its own "pedagogy of debt" (J. Williams). Importantly, while targeting individuals or, as Arthur argues, "offloaded" onto individuals ("Debt" 176), the responsibility to manage imbrication in finance capitalism—including student loans—is not distributed to individuals in equivalent ways. Rather, invoking Sara Ahmed (as discussed in chapter 1), we might say it *sticks* to them, managing relations, feelings, and futures through the threats and promises of economic opportunities and employment possibilities. A "pedagogy of debt" suggests that inequity can be ameliorated and (economic) anxieties addressed through individual action; individuals who pursue literacy education can learn how to use debt effectively and thus access education benefits equitably.

Accounting for Race and Student Loan Debt

Variability in financial literacies (as discussed by Wright), however, cannot be accounted for on an individual level of scale but are intimately entangled with Newfield's third factor of debt devaluing college: race. While racial disparities in rates of graduation have lessened, he argues, "they are still significant"; meanwhile, "the increase in overall graduation rates hides disparities in the type of institution attended" (199–200). Implicitly contextualizing Baum's assertion that high-risk students are more likely to default on loans for for-profit institutions, Newfield explains that minoritized students in particular often choose more "affordable" colleges without sufficient context to understand the risks of such choices: "Debt aversion may be pushing students of color towards institutions with fewer resources and lower graduation rates, which then passes the inequality of the higher education system on to the current generation of students" (200). Moreover, as Dalton Conley points out in *Being Black, Living in the Red*, there is a strong correlation between college selectivity and overall assets as well as college selectivity and neighborhood income, both of which accumulate asymmetrically along racial lines. Indeed, the seemingly individual decision to attend a more affordable college suggests a *lack* of financial literacy by students of color and their families, who evaluate costs and benefits in strictly fiscal terms, without considering the myriad factors that impact the value of a college degree. But the idea that making correlations between higher costs of more prestigious institutions and the added value they offer would presumably direct more students toward them overwrites significant histories of racialized wealth and literacies that underwrite individual "choices" about college attendance.

In a book-length study of students who went to Yale versus Southern Connecticut State University (institutions that are geographically separated by only two miles but are quite distinct with regard to reputation, costs, and the socioeconomic and racial makeup of the student population), Mullen further complicates this individuating of decision-making: "most of the Yale students," her interviews revealed, "had in fact never actually *decided* to go to college" (72, emphasis added). Indeed, in place of deciding to attend college, "going to college was simply the next step for the Yale students, one deeply ingrained in their habitus" (73). Mullen explains that when Yale students were asked why they attended college, their answers "did not rest directly on the extrinsic goal of getting a good job or preparing for a specific career; rather, college was simply what one did, suggesting a broader purpose framed around building a particular kind of self rather than preparing for a particular profession" (73). Mullen goes on to explain that while the students attending Southern Connecticut explicitly articulated rationales for attending college in terms of being "engaged in a quest to get ahead," the Yale students "did not attach a goal of social mobility to their education" but instead imagined futures and future jobs "not so different from those held by their parents" (73).

Primarily focused on class, Mullen's study nonetheless reveals the dominant pedagogy's misrecognition at work when individual decision-making—and the attendant cost-benefit analysis of student debt—is assumed to govern college selection unilaterally. Students with more means, with family wealth, or with a family history of college attendance are not making better or more rational choices or performing more financially literate behaviors but, ironically, sheltered from the need to make choices at all. A reputation of responsibility and wise decision-making nonetheless *sticks* to them. By contrast, students with less means and in more need of debt, who do not have a family history of college attendance, forecast the risks and rewards of college choice in service of specific social and professional aspirations. Notwithstanding this complex decision-making, the use of debt by these students can nonetheless stick to them as potentially risky behavior, only determined moral and worthwhile if it pays off in the future, in forms that might include a direct pathway to stable employment, subsequent promotions, and built-in security. Accounting for the patterns and differential stickiness of debt reveals how the financial literacies required or assumed of students do not express individual rationality (or morality) but sociocultural history and habitus (Mullen). These are not characteristics of students—or even their cultures—but these characteristics nevertheless *stick* to them, accumulating adhesive strength within an economy of racialized and classed values. As Mullen draws on Bourdieu to argue, the "concept of habitus suggests that . . . class differences in educational choice may be partly explained in terms of the perception of one's chances for success," and "self-exclusion may occur through a perception that 'that's not for the likes of us' and a consequent adjustment of expectations to chances" (85). Such explanations do not reflect individual financial literacy divorced from context, however, but emerge and make sense to students and their families with the force and weight of histories of access, which discipline individuals to frame expectations in terms of probabilities.

Further troubling any easy equation of race with financial literacy, as discussed in the introduction to this book, Darrick Hamilton and William A. Darity Jr. expose and reject the idea that financial literacy—imagined as a capacity of an individual—can be used to explain differences in wealth holdings between white persons and persons of color, arguing that this language "does not offer sufficient attention to the intergenerational and iterative role of wealth creation" (60). Without reducing literacy to a singular, positive capacity, however, we *can* consider how intergenerational relationships and relations to (racialized) financial policies, programs, and practices sponsor and constrain *how* people understand and engage with financial institutions and opportunities, including student loans. Indeed, without denying the cultural, colonial legacy and weight of literacy as a normative evaluative heuristic, we can consider how different relations to normative financial literacies extend to student loan application, management, and repayment possibilities, as well as to the costs themselves of different institutions, which require specific economic histories and (intergenerational) relations to seem *worthwhile*. While these are not *only* tied to race, they nonetheless interface with and are bound to racialized histories. Families that have historically been served by the market and financial and educational institutions—middle- to upper-class white families, for example—may have more opportunities to develop normative literacies, which can be passed down generationally, for navigating their financial bureaucracy or, as Mullen suggests, less need to do so (relying on tacit, habituated expectations). They are interpreted as performing (individual) literate behavior in a racialized economy of meaning: financial literacy becomes synonymous with whiteness. Families that have historically been denied access to markets and financial institutions, including families of color, on the other hand, developed historical literacies for alternative markets and economic activities, potentially warned by successive generations of the dangers of trusting mainstream markets or finance. Such literacies, which underwrite financial survival and success, are marked, in the racialized economy, as illiteracy.

At a national level of scale in discourses of student loan debt and in the accounting metrics that produce statistics about debt, however, financial literacy does not signify as a name for racialized, intergenerational, and highly oppressive relations. Instead, it is used to mark individuals who possess (or lack) the capacity to make well-informed financial choices and moralize their behavior accordingly. Students who seem to use debt *well*, who seem to be able to calculate and forecast accurately the futures that debt makes possible, are understood as responsible and worthy individuals. Indeed, they are not understood to be debtors in a pejorative sense but to be investors. This is despite, as Mullen's study makes clear, the asymmetric distribution of decision-making itself, which is most necessary for students with less or limited means who use a college education for class mobility and increased economic opportunity (as opposed to socioeconomic confirmation).

Contextualizing relationships to normative economic or financial literacies, Melvin L. Oliver and Thomas M. Shapiro invoke Marcia Millman's work to identify "cultural capital" as the currency most likely to be passed on by middle-class families, suggesting that in the twentieth century, "the primary legacy of middle-class parents to children has been 'cultural' capital, that is, the upbringing, education, and contacts that allowed children to get a good start in life and to become financially successful and independent" (64).³ Rather than suggest that this capital belongs to any specific (racialized or classed) group, Millman's work emphasizes how relationships to finance are shaped within cultures and communities and across generations. This is corroborated by Hazel Christie and Moira Munro in their study of British university students' "perceptions of the costs and benefits of the student loan." In a financial educational landscape similar to the United States—where decreasing public funding has been replaced by increasing reliance on student loans—Christie and Munro argue that "class location is not simply given as an explanation for the decisions made by individual students"; instead, it is cultural capital that provides "uneven access to the assets and resources that bestow already dominant middle-class families with more knowledge about (the right kind of) higher education" (625).

As demonstrated by Christie and Munro's study of university students, the effect of this (inter)generational knowledge means that "the risks and costs of attending university are experienced differently depending on parental resources, and that the strategies evolved for dealing with these risks are also differentiated" (625). Mullen corroborates as much in the context of her own study of Yale students versus Southern Connecticut State students, explaining how students in the latter group made choices with reduced resources and context clues for doing so, drawing on limited (and sometimes inadequate) information culled from a paucity of sources (e.g., a friend or family member or college fair; 113). Mullen thus problematizes conceptualizing this process as individual, proposing that prior to any choice made by a student, "the range of options had been either kept open or narrowed down by the resources related to that student's social background" and that the "students' choices differed just as much as the contexts in which they made those choices" (117). Although neither Mullen nor Christie and Munro explicitly study race, drawing their work together with Millman (vis-à-vis Oliver and Shapiro) frames Newfield's claim about the devaluation of a college degree in relation to debt for people of color: the concept of cultural capital as intergenerational directs attention to why students of color might choose more "affordable" colleges despite lower graduation rates (ironically, most likely in an effort to *demonstrate* financial literacy). It is not merely an individual choice that weighs costs and benefits but a choice circumscribed in relation to differential histories of access and exclusion to both education and finance.

Centering racialized disparity, and in addition to normative cultural capital and financial literacies being passed on intergenerationally, Oliver and Shapiro also address the affordances and constraints of wealth itself for creating what Zaloom calls "open futures": material and liquid assets. As Oliver and Shapiro argue (and as discussed in the introduction), racialized wealth disparity is the effect of radically inequitable access to financial opportunities: "skewed access to mortgage and housing markets and the racial valuing of neighborhoods on the basis of segregated markets results in enormous racial disparity" (9). Importantly, this access is baked into economic policies and commonplaces, and its effects are left largely unquestioned. As Monica Prasad notes in *The Land of Too Much: American Abundance and the Paradox of Poverty*, for example, "The American tax code is riddled with tax preferences. Tax preferences were enshrined in the American tax state at its very origins, with the income tax act of 1913 including a deduction for home-mortgage interest" (154–55). This ongoing tax preference prioritizes home buying without acknowledging the many policies and practices designed to exclude people of color from participating in it. Housing discrimination is not only well documented historically but continues to surge, as evidenced, for example, in the explicit predatory lending programs and explicit racial redlining that contributed to the subprime mortgage crisis of 2008 (see Rothstein; Trounstine). This discrimination affects not only neighborhood home values and related wealth (created or denied by such) but resources available within school districts and consequent educational inequities. Both legal (tax code) and extralegal (tacit segregation) financial practices contribute to intergenerational wealth possibilities and limits that are distributed along racial lines. And this wealth necessarily sponsors and constrains who is hailed by a college education (and to which colleges) as well as for whom debt is needed.

In other words, the significant difference in wealth held by families of color versus white families in the United States not only shapes *how* students and their families interpret student debt but shapes the necessity for and value of student debt. Corroborating the insights of Shapiro and Oliver and Hamilton and Darity about the impact of racialized wealth holdings, Conley offers the following example to illustrate some of the differences:

> Over and above traditional measures of socioeconomic status such as income and occupation, parental asset levels may affect several dynamics that have importance in explaining who succeeds educationally and who does not. Wealth (net worth) may reflect long-term family legacies that have been discounted by the usual analyses of income or occupational data. For example, parents who are professionals, who come from a long

line of professionals, and who have inherited substantial wealth might be better able to solidify their children's educational outcomes than another set of parents who are professionals and who have an equivalent income but who are burdened by debt from student loans and thus cannot play as large a role in aiding their children's education. In other words, two families with the same household income might have vastly different resources at their disposal to provide advantages to their children. These advantages can be as tangible as extracurricular and private education, financial support during college, or in-kind aid such as providing educational materials. (57–58)

If, as proposed by Zaloom, college education sponsors ascendance to or security in the middle class, these racialized differences in wealth accumulation and holdings not only pave the wave for different experiences of debt across racial lines but racialize the significance of wealth and debt, confirming rhetoric about student loans as always already in debt (to histories, to literacies, to relations). Ostensibly providing "equal access" to college education, student loans—and their effects—are, again, disproportionately required for students of color to gain access.

To be sure, as Hamilton and Darity point out, differences in debt accumulation in the United States between races is *not* inversely related to differences in wealth accumulation. Despite dominant, racist cultural narratives that position people of color as living off the state, Hamilton and Darity propose that "after controlling for basic socioeconomic and demographic characteristics," there is "no significant difference between Black and White unsecured debt holdings, while both Asian and Latino families had significantly less unsecured debt than their White family counterparts" (62). Using Survey of Income and Program Participation (SIPP) data, however, they do find "significant differences by race" for the "other" category of debt, which includes student loan debt: "Among the relatively well-off students who are able to attend college, Black students are 25 percent more likely to accumulate student debt and are, on average, borrowing over 10 percent more than their White student counterparts. . . . To compound the liability of debt, Black students are one-third less likely to complete their degrees, often because of the greater financial burden that precipitated student loan borrowing in the first place; 29 percent of Black students and 35 percent of Latino students who leave college after their first year do so for financial reasons" (62). Of course, with or without a degree, persons of color face employment and real estate discrimination that contributes to difficulty paying off student loan debt. That is, with fewer employment prospects, proportionally lower pay, and predatory real estate lending terms, the weight of student loan debt for people of color is compounded. Moreover, as Hamilton and Darity point out, "given their greater vulnerability to income volatility and little to no liquid assets, Black and Latino families have a greater need for unconventional predatory lending products such as payday loans as a last resort to deal with any number of financial exigencies or budgetary shortfalls" (63).

As previously discussed, this dearth of assets and corollary need for student loans cannot be reduced to an issue of individual choice, responsibility, or literacy but is best explained, again, by opportunities and barriers to intergenerational wealth accumulation. Citing the 2015 Pew Charitable Trust report on American debt, Hamilton and Darity argue, "The racial wealth gap has more to do with a lack of assets for Black and Latino families than racial variation in debt or an abundance of debt on the part of Blacks and Latinos. Instead . . . inheritance and other intergenerational wealth transfers benefit Whites to a much larger extent" (64). What is more, while the *lack* of wealth disproportionately undermines the economic well-being of persons and families of color, structurally demanding more reliance on student loan debt to provide "equal access" to education, the *presence* of wealth does not insulate students of color against the inequities of access to or benefits of education. Fenaba R. Addo, Jason N. Houle, and Daniel Simon argue in "Young, Black, and (Still) in the Red: Parental Wealth, Race, and Student Loan Debt" that "it is not evident that wealth provides the same protective effects across races" (66). In discussion of their qualitative, longitudinal study of students, in which they prioritize family and individual characteristics in the context of racial identification, Addo, Houle, and Simon attribute the unbalanced protections of wealth to its forms: "We propose that one reason that wealth may not protect black young adults from debt is because their parents may be more likely to possess forms of wealth that are less fungible (transmittable) across generations" (74). They also connect the inequities in the benefits of wealth to "postsecondary experiences, young adult social and economic outcomes, and . . . discrimination" (66). Indeed, whereas wealth has a positive correlation with upward mobility for white young adults, the research conducted by Addo, Houle, and Simon indicates *downward* mobility for Black young adults from wealthy families, citing the difficulty of retaining wealth in always-racialized economic contexts of education and employment (74).

Synthesizing this scholarship, it is evident that while patterns of wealth holdings *begin* to offer a picture of racialized differences in student loan debt, such patterns must be contextualized with regard to how they emerge and function, sticking responsibility and risk differentially across racial lines. Student loan crisis, like debt itself, does not merely exist as an imbalance in a ledger but emerges in the context of asymmetrical histories and racialized economies of meaning. Drawing in diachronic analysis of financial literacy and wealth accumulation shifts accounting metrics away from individual decision-making and toward the emergence of debtors *in relation* to complex histories, practices, and policies of debt articulation. Accounting for rhetoric *in* debt requires looking across scales to track the complex emergence, stickiness, and salience of its materializations.

Accounting for Gender and Student Loan Debt

As we continue to track how and for whom student loan debt matters, gender also surfaces as significant to its differential requirement, access, and benefits. Or, put otherwise, student loans are disproportionately required for women to gain access to professional employment opportunities and financially "open futures."[4] Without the same history of racialized access to education and finance but certainly compounded by the complex relations between gender and race, the historical inequity in women's access to higher education likewise circumscribes the differential effects of student loan debt. As Dwyer, Hodson, and McCloud argue in "Gender, Debt, and Dropping Out of College," this is due, in part, to the fact that "occupational segregation and the gender pay gap for women are especially large among jobs that do *not* require a college degree, and so women experience a greater relative college premium than men" (31, emphasis added). Put another way, there are more opportunities for men to find labor or employment without a college degree that offer comparable financial security to those available *with* a college degree, while employment opportunities for women are much more polarized: without a college degree, women are limited to much-lower-paying jobs. Thus, in the words of the authors, "Women may feel more pressured to take on debt to finance college than men because women have fewer options for decent pay in jobs that do not require a college degree" (31).

The gendered history of access to higher education interfaces with the availability of credit and debt in complicated ways. Whereas a long history of explicit, policy-based exclusions kept women out of universities themselves, specific institutions, and entire fields since the establishment of the first institutions of higher learning in the United States, more recently, women in the United States are now more likely to attend *and graduate from* college than are men (Dwyer, Hodson, and McCloud). Moreover, while debt opportunities were until quite recently all but unavailable to women—whose credit was established and attached to normative heteropatriarchal relations to their fathers and husbands—that is no longer true (Dwyer, Hodson, and McCloud 32). These shifts in education and credit/debt opportunities that pave the way for women to access student loans necessary to pay for college education, however, continue to be entangled and emerge within gendered norms, which make a college degree more important for women in "forming an adult female occupational identity" while reinforcing "gender essentialist beliefs that women are well suited to careers in care work and human development" (32). In other words, the significance of a college degree is narrated in gendered terms.

Beliefs about the role of college education for women, of course, emerge from histories including those described by Jessica Enoch in her study *Domestic Occupations*, in which women were only admitted to scientific fields of study when such study became attached to household responsibilities. Combined with teaching, domestic sciences (or home economics) became an acceptable use of college (and instruction in the sciences) for women in the late nineteenth and early twentieth centuries in the United States. Although education opportunities today are no longer *explicitly* segregated by gender (and, indeed, the passage of the Title IX education act makes this illegal), these histories of gendered exclusion echo in the educational choices of men and women enrolled in college today. This is especially stratified, as Mullen argues, in nonelite institutions—those attended by students using college for professional futures and class mobility. In her study of Southern Connecticut State, for example, Mullen found that "because majors were so tied to future occupations for the Southern students, gendered patterns of choice reflected gender-typed notions of appropriate work for men and women" (167). In elite institutions, on the other hand, where the rationale for education is less directly tied to specific careers, gendered patterns by major are less significant. Mullen's study suggests (1) that the student loan debt required to finance education implicitly underwrites gendered inequity there, which both demands its use for women to access higher-paying professions and also directs them to those that are highly care-intensive, and (2) that gendered inequity is compounded by socioeconomic status.

The debt-sponsored gendering of higher education tacitly contributes to what Miranda Joseph identifies as gendered pathologies of finance, in which women are assumed both to lack financial acumen and thus the ability to respond to financial exigencies and to tend toward overconsumption and thus consumer debt. A neoliberal economy governed by "the pedagogy and ideology of responsible entrepreneurial action," she explains, is "shored by pathologized, feminized hyperactivity on one hand and the equally pathologized, feminized specter of paralysis on the other" (114). While these stereotypes do not accord with studies of *actual* spending patterns or behavior of women, they do follow normative gendered characterizations of overly emotional women who worry more, who spend more, and who depend on the rationality and decision-making of men in order to make wise financial decisions. Joseph, for her part, does not seek definitive, positivist descriptions to account for different gendered relations to spending or debt, however, but takes a "Butlerian approach to the endlessly reconfirmed 'fact' of gender difference—women worry more than men"—and "rather than debunking the finding itself ... understand[s] its pervasiveness to suggest that being a woman is predicated upon being a worrier" (112).

Following Joseph (herself following Butler) likewise reframes the gendered "facts" associated with student loan debt, disarticulating the gendered patterns from directional interpretations of individual decisions about the costs and benefits of a college education. That is, whereas Dwyer, Hodson, and McCloud usefully account for the statistical differences between the amounts of and uses for student loan debt between men and women, Joseph directs attention to how such differences underwrite the emergence and performance of gender itself. This is not merely a shift in directional causality but an insistence on the coemergence and commingling of gendered rhetoric and student debt; women become so as they perform finance—including debt—in particular ways. In the contemporary US, this includes using student loans to secure education that sponsors specific professional opportunities that would otherwise be unavailable. It also means gravitating toward care-intensive jobs. Moreover, it means a greater likelihood of graduation and debt repayment despite being paid less for similar jobs (Dwyer, Hodson, and McCloud).

Considering the gendered performance of financial literacy and debt, Joseph is careful to note how financial expectations, including the availability and use of debt, cannot be divorced from racialized histories, opportunities, expectations, and values. Citing the infamous Moynihan Report of the 1960s, which attributed racialized poverty to the "matriarchal structures" of Black families and blamed the education and power of Black women for the seeming failures of Black men, Joseph evidences how financial literacies stick differently to gender across racial differences. At the same time that white women were considered dispositionally incompetent to navigate the complexities of financial decision-making or personal finance, for example, Black women were critiqued for hypercompetency, narrated as undermining the economic flourishing of Black families by emasculating men. More than a simple double bind (damned if you do, damned if you don't), financial literacy and performance are disciplined by impossible gendered and racialized expectations. As Enoch explains in her study of historical rhetorics of women's work, gender and race are not separate evaluative criteria so much as the complications of dominant discourses—predicated on the white middle class—encountering "differently raced, cultured, and classed women" (7).

Intersecting Subjectivities, Invitation to Accounting

Intersections of race, culture, class, and gender to circumscribe the emergence and effects of debt for particular bodies are, of course, insufficient to account for all of the complexities of subjectivity and student loan debt. Normative physical and cognitive ability and mental health, for example, are intricately interwoven into dominant discourses of college education, presuming—in ways tacit and explicit—who is worthy of a college education and thus who must be accounted for in the funding streams and delivery modes of higher education. While scholars in rhetoric consider the effects of inequitable access to and pathologizing disability of education (see, for example, Price; Dolmage, *Academic Ableism*), rhetoricians would do well to consider how student loans recognize—and not—the needs, both financial and educational, of borrowers of all abilities and how this politics of recognition intersects with other histories of access and exclusion. As Jay Dolmage argues in *Disabled upon Arrival*, "rhetoric needs disability studies as a reminder to pay critical and careful attention to the body" (2).

Grounded in disability studies, rhetoric could, for example, investigate the legal basis for recognizing (and not) embodied differences of student loan borrowers. Section 504 of the Rehabilitation Act of 1973, of course, "prohibits discrimination on the basis of disability in programs and activities that receive federal funding," while additional statutes of the Americans with Disabilities

Act prohibit discrimination of public places (US Department of Labor). But to qualify for protection or accommodation under these laws, students must have sustained, substantive, and documented disabilities. While *access* to student loans—especially federal student loans—should be guaranteed for those who qualify under these laws, then, it also depends on legal recognition that does not fully account for a full range of nonnormative embodiments and experiences. Students and their families (both implicated in borrowing) who do not meet or cannot evidence that they "have a physical or mental impairment that substantially limits one or more major life activities," "have a record of such an impairment," or "are regarded as having such an impairment" (Legal Information Institute) are not afforded the legal protections *or* assistance that those who can document a recognized disability are. The consequences for this politics of recognition are significant, including, for example, ability—or not—to qualify for the loan discharge recently offered to 323,000 borrowers "who have a total and permanent disability (TDP)," as indicated by their records in the Social Security Administration (US Department of Education).

This categorical discharge of loans is an important step to providing relief to student loan borrowers in part because it recognizes them in relation to contextualizing factors. Moreover, unlike examples of those needing social credit who must perform repeated *worthiness* for social services as social credit (like those relayed in the introduction), the automation of this discharge purposefully rejects process-based denials: those who qualify via matching Social Security Administration data cannot be denied based on a failure of correspondence (US Department of Education). But categorical strictures for *qualifying* for TPD nonetheless rely on legal and medical recognition of specific conditions that must be met with bureaucratic and medical literacies. This and other categories of disability thus (re)produce polarizing terms of inclusion and exclusion whereby some debtors are worthy of (loan) forgiveness and others simply do not qualify; in so doing, they also (re)produce embodied difference as a matter of individual ability or capacity rather than the effect of histories, discourses, and normative relations.

Not only akin to but interfacing with the classed, gendered, and racialized work of debt, attention to diverse embodiments and their complicated relationship to legal and medical systems would highlight how impossible expectations for financial literacy are narrated in terms of simple, calculable finances and (normative) financial literacy that emerges as an effect of specific histories and technologies. Impossible expectations for specific subjects or bodies to perform financial literacy is especially significant given the recent studies into the effects of student loan debt on employment opportunities, long-term finances, physical and emotional health, and overall well-being. That is, while "student loans are often said to be 'good debt,' providing individuals with the opportunity to invest in themselves as human capital" (Nissen et al. 245), interdisciplinary scholarship considers how it can dissuade students from graduate school (Millet), limit occupational choices (Rothstein and Rouse), stall home ownership (Berger and Houle), and undermine well-being (Nissen et al.). In the context of the discrepancies in need for student debt across race and gender, these effects disproportionately land on people of color and women, the by-products of a system of access that is distributed through loans. As explained by the sociologists Brandon A. Jackson and John R. Reynolds in their 2013 study "The Price of Opportunity: Race, Student Loan Debt, and College Achievement," for example, "Considering black students' greater reliance on loans and risk of defaulting, attention must be paid to the consequences student loan debt has for wealth accumulation, the passing of economic advantages across generations, and other ways beginning adulthood in debt may affect future life chances" (356). Moreover, Addo, Houle, and Simon argue, "Recent research shows that student loan debt is associated with delayed childbearing... and marriage,... and as such rising debt may contribute to growing racial differences in successful transitions to adulthood" (74). In short, "Given that blacks experience lower labor market returns to college than whites... while also facing higher debt burdens and dropout risk, black young adults take a great deal more risk of enrolling in college, and reap fewer rewards to that risk" (Addo et al. 74). Despite signifying as a universal means to economic security and open futures, then, student loan debt exacerbates inequality, sticking to histories and vulnerabilities, punctuating inclusion and exclusion, and taking rhetorical cover as individual, financial, mathematical choices.

As discussed throughout this book, inclusion and exclusion are not periphery but *central* to the function of (credit and) debt. Whereas student loans signify as distributing educational opportunities and their related cultural capital by allowing a greater range of students to pay for college, they depend on normative cultural hermeneutics that understand the cost-benefit ratio of student loans as self-evident. But calculations of cost and benefit, future value and liability, cannot be divorced from their diffuse cultural and familial contexts, in which credit and debt have long histories of differential access and abuse, of "shaping social inclusion and exclusion, ... life chances, and ... oppressive social relations" (Dwyer, "Credit" 239).

Despite high costs and statistically inequitable benefits as well as increasing public attention to the student loan crisis, then, in public discourses, college education and its dependence on finance (debt) retain their reputation as worthwhile, even moral. They are, returning to Zaloom, understood as a worthy investment—worth the risk—when they secure an "open future" for the next generation (8). As she points out, the morality of this investment is ideological and class-based, invoking what it means to be a "good parent," but also organized by the moral vision of finance. In her words, "As middle-class families use investment and debt to fund college education, they encounter the financial system's particular moral vision" (5). Ironically, debt, when it takes the form of investment in the next generation's ability to be financially autonomous, is marked as morally upright. Despite entangling parents and children alike in shared financial futures and outcomes, student loan debt codes as the voluntary choice of parents persuaded that financial autonomy is worthy and *possible* for their children. This moral logic recombines commonplaces from other narratives of and relationships to debt and autonomy in which they are antithetical, inviting student loan debtors into a paradoxical moral economy where debt relations are necessary for autonomy.

Such logic underwrites Baum's assertion about what she refers to as "the reality" (as opposed to "the rhetoric") of student debt: "Borrowing for college is opening doors for many students. It is helping far more people than it is hurting" (5). But this cost-benefit analysis is based on calculations that *do not account for* disproportionate effects, instead prioritizing quantity of students helped versus hurt to determine value. The inability to account for disproportionate effects, as Joseph argues, however, is not merely a matter of (mis)representation. Following Foucault, she proposes that statistics are not "an inadequate representation but rather . . . *the* preeminent technology of governmentality, enabling the production and management of populations—the exercise of power through the selective and directive encouragement of life captured in the term *biopolitics*—as well as disciplinary strategies directed toward the formation and management of individuals" (xix). Rather than discount or dismiss statistics, then, Joseph argues for their necessity to "identify disturbing social patterns." "We must also," she continues, "recognize the limits of such statistical pattern recognition as a descriptive step on the path toward another level of analysis that would allow us to see/grasp/articulate/understand/conceptualize the dynamics generating those observed patterns" (xx).

We can see such statistical identification at work—and working toward redressing inequity—in Thomas M. Shapiro's 2017 follow-up to *Black Wealth / White Wealth*, which draws together statistical data with longitudinal interviews (from over a decade of check-ins with the same families) to suggest that one crucial way to help intercede in the "toxic inequality" of the racial wealth gap is to "champion affordable and equitable access to higher education" by not only holding tuition increases to the rate of inflation and increasing investment in public education (209) but "expanding early debt assistance programs" and providing more opportunities for debt forgiveness for low-income students (210). These proposals, Shapiro shows, would not merely "help more people" in general but redress specific, historical, structural inequities: For low-income students, the effects of debt forgiveness "would be far greater among households in the twenty-fifth percentile of wealth, where it would reduce the black-white disparity by nearly 37 percent. Among such low-wealth households, eliminating debt for just those making $25,000 or less reduces the black-white wealth gap by over 50 percent" (210).

Recent policy proposals for intervening in the student loan "crisis," however, do not address the differential *need* for or *emergence* of student loans on the basis of historical and continued racialized and gendered inequities but confirm, instead, student loan debt as an individual problem that has accumulated to the point that it threatens the stability of economic futures. It is a crisis, then, not *as* it undermines the economic livelihood *of* those individuals but because the number of individuals has reached a point where the overall student debt holdings in the United States undermine economic growth. In the context of a progressive political shift toward rhetorically surfacing student loan debt *as* a crisis, then, its differential effects can only be addressed, only be redressed, when we begin to account for rhetoric *in* debt.

3

"Dividuals," Community Development, and Accounting for Municipal Bond Debt

As explored in chapter 2, in the twenty-first century in the United States, student debt rhetorically signifies *both* as a mediator of equal access to postsecondary education, leveling historical asymmetries by offering every student the chance to fund a college degree, *and* as a mathematical and moral obligation of individuals who forecast the costs and benefits of borrowing money in the present for an education that *should* pay off in the future. In this economy of meaning, students whose debts are manageable demonstrate wise decision-making and financial literacy. They are worthy creditors who understand how to leverage debt for "open futures" (Zaloom). By contrast, those who are overwhelmed by debt evidence a lack of judiciousness, perhaps having taken on more debt than is prudent, chosen an institution with low levels of graduation or job placement, selected a major that is unlikely to lead to steady employment, or spent money on a lavish lifestyle rather than prioritizing repayment. It is as the debt proves to be unmanageable that they become creditors incapable of responsible risk assessment and, consequently, become risky themselves. Drawing on a methodology of accounting for rhetoric *in* debt as theorized in chapter 1, however, reveals how financial literacy and decision-making are not merely the attributes *of* individuals but *stick* to specific bodies and groups on the basis of histories of policies and practices of radical differentiation. More specifically, by analyzing the emergence of student debt, I identified how it rhetorically flattens complex histories and misrecognizes systemic inequities under a normative rubric of individual, mathematical, and, ultimately, financial responsibility and literacy.

With a specific history in the United States—indeed, as Miranda Joseph argues, "any particular indebtedness must be the product of history" (x)—the case of student debt explored in chapter 2 nonetheless serves as symptomatic of the ways debt rhetorically circulates and emerges in racialized and gendered patterns, assigning meaning and morality differentially. Akin to student debt, other types of consumer debt (mortgage, credit card, auto, pay day, etc.) likewise stick to and assess risk on the basis of complex relations that cannot be disarticulated from larger economic and cultural histories and relations fundamentally shaped by oppression, violence, and vulnerabilities.

In this chapter, invoking the methodology of accounting for rhetoric *in* debt and building on the analysis in chapter 2, I consider how the *stickiness* of debt and its differentiating, differential effects are not produced only discursively or ideologically. Or, rather, I consider how discourse and ideology—and rhetoric itself—are always already material, emerging with, operating through, and entangled with networks and technologies and infrastructures that participate in the conditions of possibility for economic activity, including debt. In practice, this means that any close analytical work of texts, including, for example, the "Terms of Use" that admit would-be investors to specific financial arrangements (which I analyze in this chapter), must be contextualized within the material systems in which they participate and which constitute debtors.

Debt and Subjectivity

As interdisciplinary critical debt scholarship makes clear, and as illustrated by the case study of student loan debt in chapter 2, debt does not merely describe economic activities but "produces, distributes, captures, and shapes subjectivity" because, as Maurizio Lazzarato argues, "what one defines as 'economy' would be quite simply impossible without the production and control of subjectivity and its forms of life" (*Making* 32, 33). Whereas so-called individual debts—like consumer debt—work at the level of ideological and moral interpellation and discipline, producing debtors affectively conditioned to understand and participate in market activities in normative ways in order to perform financial literacy, employability, and creditworthiness, Lazzarato draws on Marx to offer more detail about "the way in which debt/money has a 'hold' on subjectivity" because "morality, the promise, and one's word are mostly *insufficient* to guarantee debt repayment" (*Making* 145, 146, emphasis added). He continues,

> To have a real "hold" on subjectivity, there must also be legal and police "machines" (Marx) as well as mnemotechnical "machines" in effect which work on and manufacture the subject (Nietzsche). Based on Deleuze and Guattari's work, it is possible to articulate the joint action of "morality"

and speech on one hand, with machines on the other. Debt/money involves subjectivity in two different but complementary ways. "Social subjection" operates molar control on the subject through the mobilization of his conscience, memory, and representations, whereas "machinic subjugation" has a molecular, infrapersonal, and pre-individual hold on subjectivity that does not pass through reflexive consciousness and its representations, nor through the "self." (146)

To illustrate the relationship between social and machinic subjection vis-à-vis debt, Lazzarato invokes the language of Gilles Deleuze and Félix Guattari and offers the example of an automatic teller machine (ATM), which "asks you to respond to the demands of the machine, . . . requires you to 'enter your code,' 'choose your amount,' or 'take your bills'" but does "'not require acts of intellectual virtuosity'" (147). He concludes, then, that "there is no subject who *acts* here, but a 'dividual' that *functions* in an 'enslaved' way to the sociotechnical apparatus of the banking network. The ATM activates the 'dividual' not the 'individual'" (147–48). Returning to the concept of debt, Lazzarato explains that "debt/money asks neither trust nor consent from the dividual. It asks only that he function correctly according to received instructions. And the same is true for all machines that we encounter every day. Following the prescribed orders determines access to information, to money, to plane and train tickets bought on the internet, parking ramps, computers, bank accounts, etc." (149).

Lazzarato's work here necessarily shifts attention from how individuals are persuaded by the moral implications of debt to how they are imbricated in material systems of debts, which work on both "dividuals" and individuals. A different account of student debt, then, might more explicitly focus on the machinic subjection as fundamental to its scalar work. As Caitlin Zaloom argues, student and family relationships to debt fundamentally emerge from and are shaped by the technical applications required to apply for student aid and student loans. The Free Application for Federal Student Aid (FAFSA), available online and required of all students needing financial support, for example, rests on answers and documentation about family income, assets, and potential contributions, which are interpreted algorithmically to estimate federal aid, loans, and expected family contributions. The machinic function of FAFSA invites individuals and families to provide personal and financial information as quickly and accurately as possible, a necessary step in the application for the student loans that is all but automatic. Using Lazzarato's terminology, we can see how it is not just individuals who are hailed to answer probing questions but "dividuals" who react, often by rote: "What you are asked to do is react appropriately, react quickly and without making errors, otherwise you run the risk of being momentarily excluded from the system" (*Making* 147). And indeed, individuals are prompted to fill out FAFSA forms no matter their perceived need for them; they enter personal information without questioning the value or meaning of the action, induced by machinic subjection to participate as potential debtors.

A more traditional rhetorical or ideological analysis of FAFSA—which might attend to its framings and phrasings, how it interpellates debtors through what it presents and what it elides—might miss this critical component of its function. That is, whereas FAFSA hails and corroborates subjects ideologically, requiring individual and familial financial information that, Zaloom explains, relies on the "household budget" as a normative gendered and middle-class value (74–75), and its questions and prompts are *not* always easy for students to answer, suggesting that it invites decision-making and questions (77), its function as *the* gatekeeper to college admission and financial support means that it is also operates machinically. So even when students and families struggle to find and provide the information to fill out the form correctly, they do not decide whether they will fill it out but do so automatically, tacitly accepting its necessity as the cost of doing business.[1]

Although student loans offer a compelling example of the entangled work of social and machinic subjection to the emergence of rhetoric in debt, in this chapter, I turn to an adjacent case of municipal bonds to demonstrate the affordances of this shift. Municipal bonds—the debt issued by states, counties, and municipalities to fund capital expenditures (Investopedia)—not only are primary to the economic architecture and infrastructure of the United States but fundamentally participate in conditions of possibility for subjectivity and livability, differentially allocating credit, value, and risk to spaces, projects, and peoples deemed worthy (or not). Like student debt, municipal debt relies on the entanglements of social and machinic subjection. It also signifies, as I discuss in more detail shortly, as a mathematical calculation based on rational analysis of (present) costs in relation to (future) benefits undertaken by financial literates seeking a "safe bet." Like student debt, too, the rhetoric *of* municipal bonds gives cover to its sticky, differential work and holds on subjectivity. Whereas student debt sticks to individuals who seem to make decisions *about debt*, however, municipal bonds signify as a bureaucratic and infrastructural process and financial product. When such bonds fund successful projects (i.e., projects for which creditors recoup their investments), they evidence savvy investment, sticking to individuals as wise investors, wary of risk and thus invested in a financial product that is highly likely to offer significant return. Unsuccessful projects, by contrast, compound lived precarities within municipalities, sticking risk to any who would benefit from municipal projects through public housing, transportation, education, and so forth. These thwarted benefits—including austerity measures and the privatization of public and social services—are the accepted, acceptable risks of municipal bonds. While bond owners and their proxies (human and algorithmic) are charged with making decisions about risk or following machinic prompts through which they formally accept specific risks, the effects of those bonds differentially emerge and stick to those who are already economically disenfranchised: people with housing, food, and employment insecurity; people without adequate health care; undocumented persons; people of color; and Indigenous peoples; among others.

In this chapter, then, I draw on a methodology of accounting for rhetoric in debt to track how municipal debts emerge, circulate, and stick across spatial scales through both social and machinic subjection. Whereas in chapter 2, I emphasized the former, calling attention to how temporal scales (or histories of social and political exclusion and violence based on racism and sexism) produce and delimit possibilities for how debt sticks to subjects via "financial literacy" and a "pedagogy of debt," in this chapter, I shift attention to the latter, considering how the material, machinic relations (themselves invested in histories and practices of differential oppression) allocate and stick the risk of municipal debt in radically inequitable ways. I begin this work with a (brief) review of the history of municipal debt in the United States, arguing for its importance to understanding contemporary political economy in relation to practices of colonization and (geographical) racialization. Thereafter, I turn to media and technologies through which municipal bonds—drawing on Sara Ahmed's language—both surface and recede. In other words, to account for rhetoric *in* debt, I identify not only what matters contribute to municipal debt but *how* they matter and for *whom*. Whereas student debt flattens racialized and gendered intergenerational relations under the sign of individual students who *need* a college education and the means to finance it, I argue that municipal debt mystifies complicated and inequitable community relations by way of development rhetorics that tout public projects and services without addressing the asymmetrical risks of such debt.

Emerging Nation, Emerging Debt

As reviewed, in brief, in chapter 2, debt occupies crucial ground in what Joshua S. Hanan refers to as the "economic imaginary" (of the United States). With roots in colonial practices of trade and the legacy of European economic theories and accounting, debt was also centered, according to William Rodney Herring, in the political debate of those who came to be known as the nation's founders, who considered its possibilities and constraints. Recounting economic arguments made by James Madison and Alexander Hamilton, Herring reveals their different assumptions and consequences: while debts as obligations (from the perspective of Madison) must be repaid, debts framed as opportunities (according to Hamilton) could create perpetual capital only insofar as they were *not* repaid (by extending their service, or what we might now call interest payments; "Rhetoric" 59–60). Set in motion in explicit arguments about the appropriate *national* response to Revolutionary War debts, this bifurcated reputation of debt haunts development rhetorics at municipal levels of scale, inviting investors to imagine municipal debt as an opportunity for payoff.

It was not until a half a century later, when urban centers were rapidly growing in population and density and "internal improvements" became paramount to their success, that municipal bonds began to emerge as a debt opportunity (Sbragia). In context of the *need* for significant monies to fund municipal improvements, individual investors were wary of the possibility of a return on investment, and corporations were not yet "familiar to American investors and therefore needed the 'legitimacy' granted by government in order to attract capital" (Sbragia 33).[2] But transportation in particular became enormously important as more of the US populace moved to cities and thus required food and other goods to be brought *to* them. Moreover, according to Alberta Sbragia, successful improvements to transportation bred rivalries as cities competed for access to supply lines for imports and exports (both foreign and domestic). These rivalries not only shaped which and how cities grew but invited municipalities to pattern their own public projects on the successes of other cities. The overwhelming success of the government-backed bond funding of the Erie Canal by the state of New York, for example, served as a crucial progenitor in shaping how the nation acquired capital adequate to its public and infrastructural needs because it so significantly changed transportation options and routes. Other states quickly followed suit to build canals funded by public bonds in hopes that they could replicate the success of the Erie Canal, which recouped costs and repaid bonds quickly through the tolls it charged for use (Sbragia 29). As Sbragia argues, "The success of New York State in attracting investment capital to finance the Erie Canal encouraged other state governments both to view debt as a suitable financing mechanism and to view themselves as the most appropriate borrower" (33).

Perhaps more important to the development of municipal debt was the shift from bond investment in canals to railroads, which, because they did not require water access, became a viable option for many more towns and cities hoping for the benefits afforded by ease of transportation. Individual states used bonds to finance railroads themselves, but cities also participated; rather than "build their own railways," however, local governments acted as "catalysts," using bonds to give "financial help to private companies that were promising to build a railroad" (Sbragia 45). In the second half of the nineteenth century, cities also increased their investments to include a broader range of public projects, primarily transportation but also including manufacturing (55).

This shift by cities to rely on and help financial companies to support urban development signified, according to Sbragia, a "conventional view" wherein "capital calls the tune," such that "private interests use or constrain public authority" and local officials "are forced to be extremely responsive to business, whose local decisions are critical for the fiscal health—and thus credit rating—of any locality" (11). Without denying the impact of capital or private interests, however, Sbragia offers a competing interpretation: "that the system of public capital finance is driven by government rather than by the capital market. In the area of capital investment, higher levels of government—rather than the capital market—determine the relationship that local governments will have with that market" (13). More specifically, Sbragia argues that governmental regulations created the limits within which municipal-bond-market practices emerged and continue to emerge, such that "American local governments have used the market as a vehicle, or instrument, to circumvent legal restrictions on their borrowing" (13). Sbragia shows that governmental restrictions, ostensibly intended to minimize bond issuance and borrowing, inspire "new financial instruments specifically designed to evade" them and encourage municipalities to leverage "the creativity of the financial market for their own purposes" (13). Rather than only private interests or local governments exercising unilateral control, then, they respond to and encourage each other: restrictions produce creative responses that in turn invite restrictions and inspire yet more creative financial products. As I discuss in more detail later in this chapter, the consequences of these laws and financial products do not merely shape those institutions but organize the lives and livability of municipal constituents in differential ways.

As explained by the political science scholar Steven P. Erie contextualizing the urban growth of Los Angeles (between 1880 and 1932), local governments and businesses most often work together to sponsor development, but it is nevertheless shaped more acutely by one or the other on the basis of history and policies. Nevertheless, for Erie, the difference between entrepreneurial- and state-led growth is always relative, reflecting "influence and autonomy of private sector-versus-public sector actions in shaping urban growth and to the relative importance of private-versus-public development strategies" (521). Analyzing the shift in importance of private and public investment in Los Angeles, Erie identifies five dimensions that reveal its specific dynamics—market-state relations, intergovernmental relations, citizen-state relations, territorial relations, and local-state apparatus—ultimately arguing that "urban growth cannot be understood historically apart from the municipal bond market" and "municipal labor policy" (522). As his list suggests, the municipal bond market shapes not only the relationship of the city to investors but, more fundamentally, its spaces, places, peoples, and possibilities. As I argue in the next section, any accounting of these relations also requires attention to histories of radical exclusion on which they also rely.

Same Bonds, Different(ial) Effects

Relating the history and ascendance of municipal bonds to the national—and spatial—character and growth of the United States and specific regions, states, and cities, as well as the significance of municipal bonds to US policy, Sbragia and Erie only briefly acknowledge their inequitable effects. Sbragia, for example, contrasts the use of bonds in Europe—which used bonds to provide for the poor—with their use in large cities in the United States, which "spent fortunes on giant engineering projects for the convenience of the prosperous, but bathhouses for the uplift of the poor were an afterthought" (66). She also parenthetically admits that in the last decades of the 1800s, services in cities in the US South "largely excluded black neighborhoods," which "did not receive water and sewer lines, had unpaved streets, and were generally far from fire stations" (67). Erie, for his part, notes that "a draconian labor policy was an essential component of a state-centered growth strategy" (523), and reliance on low-turnout special elections sponsored the success and ubiquity of municipal bonds in Los Angeles. Neither scholar, however, historicizes the emergence of bonds within the racial, gendered, and colonial histories that are central to US territorial expansion or geography.

These accounts corroborate the history of the United States as a history of debt, centering municipal debt as key to understanding how both municipalities and the municipal bond market emerged and took shape in the ways they did and continue to do so. They nonetheless sideline core conditions of possibility for US territorial and urban growth—colonial settlement and chattel slavery and their afterlives—and continued segregation and asymmetrical allocation of resources, revealing the (historical) rhetoric *of* this type of "public" debt as based on either a profound misrecognition or denial of the diversity of that public. Indeed, the influx of people and goods to urban centers in the North and western territories, towns, and cities and the consequent need for development cannot be disarticulated from policies of Manifest Destiny and slavery or the violent practices of colonization and Jim Crow. Explaining territorial expansion in *American Indians and the Rhetoric of Removal and Allotment*, however, Jason Edward Black characterizes it as "a principal colonizing ideology of the early US government," which "dictated that there was a need for physical places and cultural spaces for the nation to thrive" (9). He continues, "Within the complex of nineteenth-century US governmental ideologies, such territorial 'place' was necessary to 'the nation's rapidly-industrializing economy.' Additionally, the 'space' that was attached to the physical land was vital to build a nation 'based on the assumption of racial and cultural superiority as well as an insatiable desire for land, expansion and empire'" (9).

While land acquisition and use were organized by colonizing ideology, claiming Indigenous land and displacing and murdering Indigenous peoples, economic development—of both the United States itself and its local municipalities—depended on forced labor of first enslaved and then radically disenfranchised peoples. As succinctly articulated in the introduction to Nikole Hannah-Jones's "1619 Project," "In August of 1619, a ship appeared on th[e] horizon, near Point Comfort, a coastal port in the English colony of Virginia. It carried more than 20 enslaved Africans, who were sold to the colonists. *No aspect* of the country that would be formed here has been untouched by the years of slavery that followed" (emphasis added). These organizing forces not only shaped but more fundamentally sponsored and continue to sponsor the landscapes of municipal development in the United States, where Indigenous lands remain occupied and communities of color are tolerated only until such spaces are marked for "development."

Occupied land and forced labor that allowed US municipalities to exist morphed into policies and practices of segregation within cities, whether explicit or tacit. For example, voting-rights laws enacted after the Civil War violently prevented Black residents from voting, not only for government representation but for bond measures as well. Racial covenants that spanned the country prohibited nonwhite persons from living in white neighborhoods, attending white schools, or accessing white community spaces (see Rothstein). Such laws were, furthermore, as Miriam F. Williams argues, "veiled" in "detached, complex, and jargon-filled language that we now call 'legalese,'" which effectively evaded explicit "mentions of race and racial discrimination" (2). The technical literacies required to navigate this jargon by those who were most likely to be affected were all but prohibitive; they not only shaped (and shape) which projects were proposed and funded but, consequently, which neighborhoods were maintained and which had (or were denied) access to public works and resources.

While the full history of the emergence of contemporary municipal debt is beyond the scope of this book, the early uses of municipal debt to fund US infrastructure and development must be understood in the context of the differential risk and value already at work in shaping US politics and financial practices. The value accorded to the lives and living conditions of people of color, including Indigenous peoples and immigrants as well as the enslaved and their progeny, were limited to exchange value, important for labor but not worth the investment of such amenities as water and sewer, electricity, public services (including fire or police departments), educational institutions (schools and libraries, for example), or recreation (parks, trails). As Richard Rothstein argues in *The Color of Law: A Forgotten History of How Our Government Segregated America*, "We have created a caste system in this country, with African Americans kept exploited and *geographically separate* by racially explicit government policies. Although most of these policies are now off the books, they have never been remedied and their effects endure" (xvii, emphasis added). Focused specifically on Black-white segregation, Rothstein's work can be extrapolated to other groups that likewise have been legally and forcibly prevented from receiving the benefits of municipal investment. Municipal bonds—debts articulated as worth public investment—thus intensify rather than contest lived inequities, directing resources and development to projects and spaces deemed *worth the risk*. In other words, extending Sbragia's argument that federal and state restrictions became the boundary conditions for municipal debt to take shape in particular ways, we must consider how colonial and racialized sociocultural and legal practices likewise contribute to such conditions, assessing value and risk appropriate for and worthy of public investment.

Emergence of the Contemporary Bond Market

Alongside the importance of the history of municipal bond debt to understanding its differential work, the history of the *market* for municipal bonds is likewise critical. That is, as I review in this section, the current popularity and reputation of municipal bonds in the United States follow a history of expansion and contraction in relation to a variety of economic trends and legislative measures. Whereas mid-nineteenth-century investment in transportation, education, and urban development significantly increased municipal debt (as described earlier), shortly thereafter, in 1873, railroad default (when construction outpaced demand) resulted in its stark decline. The 1913 creation of a permanent federal income tax that specifically excluded municipal bond income as taxable reinvigorated the bond market, which continued to thrive even through the Great Depression. And while World War II saw another marked decline in bond issuance (with attention directed to the military-industrial complex rather than the US infrastructure and development), by the mid-1960s, bond debt once again thrived (triple its World War II amounts; Sbragia). Perhaps most influential for the current form of bond debt, however, was the introduction in 1973 of municipal bond insurance, designed to protect investors from fraud, and the creation two years later of the Municipal Securities Rulemaking Board (MSRB), which first regulated municipal bond dealers and later advisers and now also manages the Electronic Municipal Market Access (EMMA), where official statements, disclosures, and market data for municipal bonds are made public (Brodskey). Overseen by the Securities and Exchange Commission (SEC), the MSRB and EMMA not only explicitly promote transparency and education for investors but rhetorically secure municipal bonds through their association with close federal oversight. The reputation of the municipal bond market as safe and regulated was also confirmed by the appointment of Arthur Levitt as the chairman of the SEC in 1993 (Butler et al.). Previously organized by unspoken "pay-to-play" policies, the reputation of the SEC dramatically shifted when it "brought nineteen municipal securities enforcement cases in the three years immediately following Levitt's appointment" (Butler et al. 2878). These cases, as explained by Alexander W. Butler, Larry Fauver, and Sandra Mortal in their study of the link between political corruption and municipal finance, incentivized the municipal bond industry to "cease making pay-to-play political contributions," and in 1994, "the SEC established a rule that investment houses making political contributions could not sell bonds from that city/state for two years" (2878).

Increasing popularity and changing regulations have contributed significantly to the current form and uses of the municipal bond market in the United States. As reviewed by W. Bartley Hildreth and C. Kurt Zorn in their 2005 retrospective of the previous twenty-five years of municipal market changes, not only did market activity show dramatic increases (from $400 billion to $2 trillion), but changes to tax law and the economy itself invited increasingly "creative" uses of bond measures and markets (127–28).[3] The introduction of an electronic marketplace to distribute information and access to the municipal bond market, coupled with corresponding financial products created in response to changing tax codes, invites closer attention to the "machinic subjection" required of bond issuers, investors, and beneficiaries. Currently, US municipal bonds are issued, debt bought and sold, exclusively through the electronic interface, which requires investors—or their proxies—to navigate its "Terms of Use" and to make calculations of risk on the basis of the information it proffers. Although the function of municipal bonds remains an issue of public funding, public works, and public debt, it is nevertheless technologically and machinically mediated such that municipal bond offerings, investment, and transactions are the result of clicking "Accept." As I suggest in the next section, municipal bonds and their differential work cannot be accounted for without attention to such interfaces: the material networks in which they emerge and enforce neoliberal expectations of individual risk calculation and management.

Low-Risk Rhetoric, Low-Risk Reputation

As an effect of the long history of municipal bonds and the shorter history of laws and technologies that support the bond market, in their contemporary forms in the United States, they have emerged as the principal way to fund local development and infrastructure, categorized as general obligation (or GO) bonds and revenue bonds, which have distinct debt caps and repayment structures.[4] Given municipal bonds' relations to taxes and public works, they not only invoke historical successes and stability to signify as a stable and worthy investment but also evoke the nation-state as a guarantor. That is, technically speaking, the federal government does not insure specific bonds or the municipal bond market; the instantiation of its regulatory board nonetheless suggests a tacit governmental endorsement, and the use of taxes—even though levied by municipalities—affirms their state sanction. What is more, the federal government purchases municipal bonds to stabilize the broader economy. In the spring of 2020, for example, in the midst of ongoing economic fallout related to COVID-19, the Federal Reserve Board established the Federal Liquidity Facility "to help state and local governments better manage cash flow pressures in order to continue to serve households and businesses in their communities." With specific requirements, the facility authorized the "purchase of up to $500 billion of short-term notes directly from U.S. states (including the District of Columbia), U.S. counties with a population of at least 500,000 residents, and U.S. cities with a population of at least 250,000 residents" (Board of Governors). Beyond providing a lifeline to municipalities themselves, this federal investment shores up trust in the municipal bond market, repudiating risk that might attach to it during unprecedented financial upheaval.

In the twenty-first century, municipal bonds thus rhetorically signify as one of the safest and most popular market products available to investors, due to their consistent return on investment, the "transparency" required of their governance (as overseen by the MSRB), and the shield from federal taxes they most often offer. Of the latter feature, the SEC explains, "Generally, the interest on municipal bonds is exempt from federal income tax. The interest may also be exempt from state and local taxes if you reside in the state where the bond is issued. Bond investors typically seek a steady stream of income payments and, compared to stock investors, may be more risk-averse and more focused on preserving, rather than increasing, wealth. Given the tax benefits, the interest rate for municipal bonds is usually lower than on taxable fixed-income securities such as corporate bonds ("Municipal Bonds"). Proposed to fund specific community or public needs, municipal bonds likewise enjoy the reputation of being pre-vetted because they are voted on by the constituents who will benefit from them. Whereas other investment products—stocks in a newly publicly traded company, for example—carry the inherent risk of a fickle marketplace, municipal bonds seemingly embody the will of voters. Moreover, not only municipal bonds but municipalities themselves are subject to rating, which assess them using a AAA+ to C scale (MSRB, "Credit Rating Basics"). This scale is designed to allow investors to make informed decisions about the municipal bonds in which they might invest on the basis of mathematically calculated and marked risk.

In addition to these factors that rhetorically secure the reputation of municipal bonds as a low-risk investment, US bankruptcy law also protects creditors of municipal bonds (those who buy bonds, those who "own" the debt) in particular ways. That is, whereas bankruptcy law for individuals and businesses might reduce the amount owed creditors (under chapters 7, 11, and 13 of the Bankruptcy Code), chapter 9 specifies that "a municipality debtor cannot, simply by filing bankruptcy, reduce debts to zero or make debt disappear" (Dabney et al. 7); it must "put forth a good-faith effort to repay creditors" (8). This requirement of good-faith effort minimizes the risk to investors by centering their interests in debt restructuring or relief, which, again, makes it an attractive financial product—a safe, (mostly) tax-exempt investment option for people interested in saving for retirement (via a 401k, for example), protecting savings, or preserving wealth more generally.

Taken together, the preceding descriptions represent municipal bonds *for* individual investors seeking secure, calculable benefits, while dissociating them from the rhetorical resonances of debt as a "moral hazard," a technical term adopted from the insurance industry to describe risk potential (including risk potential of municipal bonds). As indicated by scholarly literature on the term, there is some disagreement about whether the "moral" in "moral hazard" literally invokes morality or if it signifies financial risk without moralization (Rowell and Connelly; see also chapter 4). Despite disagreements about the morality implied by the *term* "moral hazard," however, investing in municipal bonds—which is to say, acting as a creditor for municipalities and their capital projects—assumes a preexisting financial (and, as I discuss shortly, technological) literacy and the moral uprightness of making wise financial decisions (decisions that will *pay off*). An individual who is investing in municipal bonds has the money with which to do so; they not only have made wise (individual) choices that have allowed them to accrue capital to invest but continue to do so by navigating governmental infrastructure to invest in a low-risk venture. Indeed, one characterization of municipal bonds is that they serve as insurance against inflation—protecting the accumulated wealth of individuals by accruing interest on money that would otherwise stagnate in purchasing power (Temel)—which further corroborates the financial literacy demonstrated by an investor who knows how to capitalize on their wealth.

As discussed in previous chapters, wealth accumulation and financial literacy are not only gendered and racialized but pathologized, projected in patterned ways onto individuals through policies and practices that not only disproportionately *support* white wealth generation and wealth holdings but simultaneously undermine wealth accumulation for people of color. Accounting for municipal bonds as fiscally sound investment products invokes this history and contributes back to rhetorical understandings of debt as an individual, moral choice based on mathematical calculation, effectively dismissing municipal bonds' more complex histories of use to shape asymmetrical development of municipalities. Indeed, as I illustrate in the next section, although reputed as an investment opportunity, bonds create and constrain infrastructure and development within municipalities, exacerbating inequities and multiplying precarities. Signifying as financial debts—that is, beholden to creditors—they are legitimized and moralized through normative understandings of *future* returns: a worthy bond (that is, a bond worth buying, a debt worth owning) is one that will *pay off* in the future. But the effects of municipal bonds are neither limited to investors who own them nor only lived in the future. Indeed, a closer look at their administration reveals how municipal bonds draw on the automation of an electronic market both to hail investors to take on supposedly low-risk debt and to offload such risk within municipalities to already "at-risk" populations. To explore this differential allocation of risk or, to put it otherwise, to identify where and to whom risk sticks, in the following sections, I consider how it emerges and attaches and with what effects. I do so by centering the "machinic" function of municipal bonds— tracing how they emerge and become meaningful through bureaucratic technologies and practices that obscure their divergent subjectivizing effects.

Defining Credit, Assigning Risk

Much like an individual credit score, a municipal rating is an algorithmic rendering of reputation and trustworthiness, a comparative calculation that designates municipalities as risky or worthy investments. Indeed, the MSRB confirms this comparison, as it explains in answer to the question "What is a credit rating?":

> Think about your own credit score. Credit scores and credit ratings are similar. Companies use credit scores (ranging from 300 to 850) to assess

people's ability and willingness to make car or mortgage payments. Investors in municipal bonds use credit ratings to assess creditworthiness, or the ability and willingness of the state or local government issuing the bond to pay investors their money back, plus interest. Credit ratings are symbols (e.g., AAA). Each symbol has a definition. Credit ratings address creditworthiness only. They are intended to reflect the rating agency's assessment of the likelihood of bond issuers, or any other responsible entity, paying investors as promised. ("Credit Rating Basics")

As framed by the MSRB, and akin to the moral significance of an individual credit score, the rating of a municipality indicates not only the ability but the *willingness* of a municipality to repay debts. Municipalities, in other words, take on moral and volitional attributes of an individual debtor who is either wise in their investments (and rated accordingly) or unwilling to repay (and, again, rated accordingly) but either way is considered an autonomous agent, whose choices reflect intention and *will*. Much like a credit score of an individual, this rating purposefully translates complex financial and economic histories into an easy-to-use metric.

This alphanumeric placeholder belies the sizeable number of people and groups involved in the function of municipal bonds, which is acknowledged in even the most basic explanations. In *The Fundamentals of Municipal Bonds*, produced by the Bond Market Association, for example, Judy Wesalo Temel explains, "Distinct roles are played by state and local government officials, public finance investment bankers, underwriters, sales peoples, traders, analysts, lawyers, financial advisors, ratings agencies, insurers, commercial bankers, investors, brokers, technology developers and vendors, the media, and regulators" (1–2). Despite the size and scope of this list, however, a credit rating does not stick to any of the actors or evaluate their competencies. Instead, credit ratings stick to the municipality itself, evaluating it as if it were an individual with a credit score, culpable for financial transactions and choices, including the choice to take on debt.

Describing the utility of ratings in determining the risk of bonds to investors, the MSRB qualifies them as "one factor when deciding to buy, sell or hold a municipal bond" or, in other words, "one tool in your toolbox and not the sole basis for buying, selling or holding a municipal bond" ("Credit Rating Basics"). Other factors include, as described by the SEC's "Investor Bulletin," call risk, credit risk, interest rate risk, inflation risk, and liquidity risk, as well as tax implications (when applicable) and the credibility and fees of bond brokers. Despite this range, however, the simplicity of the rating system makes it all the more persuasive as a catch-all determinant for assigning risk: the reduction of complexity to a simple AAA+ to C scale marks it as immanently usable and self-evident. Resonating with grading scales from a number of different contexts (including grades in school, grades of restaurants, and so forth), the bond-rating scale becomes not just one tool but the fundamental metric by which bonds—and bond risks—are evaluated.

Significantly, access to ratings of municipal bonds—which is technically public information—is protected by the MSRB's "Terms of Use" statement, which must be accepted by users before they can navigate either the MSRB website or EMMA itself. Serving as one machinic gateway to investor information about municipal bond risk, the statement rhetorically and legally assigns risk to individual investors, expressly repudiating its own liability:

> The website, content and services are provided "as is" and "as available," without any representations or warranties of any kind. The MSRB expressly disclaims all warranties, where express or implied, to the fullest extent permissible under the law, including the warranties of merchantability, fitness for a particular purpose, noninfringements and title. Your use of the website, content and/or services is at your sole risk, and you shall bear all risk, related costs and liability and be responsible for your use. The MSRB assumes no responsibility for any intentional or unintentional error, omission, inaccuracy, incompleteness, unavailability, interruption, delay, slow streaming, slow downloading speed, or unauthorized access in or with respect to the website, content, or services or for the consequences thereof. (MSRB, "Municipal Securities")

Of course, legal statements of this kind can be interpreted as perfunctory, the necessary bulwark against litigious users, and thus rhetorically insignificant in distributing risk. Certainly, though acting as a legal agreement, the 9,477 words that make up the "Terms of Use" are rarely read in their entirety, especially given the dense prose and repetitions of the text, even though the "Accept" button is often clicked.

As Lazzarato makes clear, however, this type of rote acceptance—following machinic instructions or prompts as de rigueur rather than as substantive—participates in the production of indebted subjectivity, requiring what he calls "dividuals" to "react appropriately, react quickly and without making errors, otherwise . . . run the risk of being momentarily excluded from the system" (*Making* 147). Accepting the "Terms of Use" to access information and invest in municipal bonds evades significance as a volitional act while, at the same time, assigning sole responsibility to the individual who accepts, who "shall bear all risk, related costs and liability" (MSRB, "Municipal Securities"). In other words, though investors may make calculated decisions about municipalities and municipal bonds in which they invest, they indicate their acceptance of risk through rote acceptance of the "Terms of Use." By doing so, they also tacitly accept the costs for municipal development as what the geographer Jamie Peck posits as a "clear manifestation of the 'push politics' characteristic of the austerity era," wherein, quoting a debt-focused task force of the US Governmental Accountability Office, "fiscal stress rolls downhill" (30).

To further clarify how risk is defined, or in other words, to whom it is assigned, the "Terms of Use" specifically identify who *cannot* be held legally accountable for the use of (or effects of use of) information on the MSRB website or EMMA, a sizeable and significant list:

> We, our affiliates, directors, officers, employees, agents, consultants, licensors and third party providers shall not be liable or responsible to you or anyone else for any losses, liabilities, damages, costs, expenses, suits, actions, proceedings or claims caused by, arising out of, relating to or in connection with: (a) acts, omissions, occurrences or contingencies beyond our or their reasonable control, including service interruptions or performance failures, such as those that result from the use of telecommunications facilities that are outside our control, including the Internet; (b) negligence, gross negligence or willful misconduct in procuring, compiling, interpreting, editing, writing, reporting or delivering any of the Content and, if any, the Services; (c) lost, stolen, late, corrupted, misdirected, failed, incomplete or delayed transmissions by anyone using the Website, including technical malfunctions, human error, computer viruses, lost data transmissions, omissions, interruptions, deletions, defects, hyperlink failures or line failures of any telephone network, computer equipment, software or any combination thereof; or (e) damage to your computer systems, equipment, software, data or other tangible or intangible property resulting from or sustained in connection with your use of the Website, Content and/or Services. (MSRB, "Municipal Securities")

Here the "Terms of Use" disclaim liability for not only human actions (beyond reasonable expectations) but the technical equipment, systems, operations, and functions that allow the website to function. The requirement of *using* the electronic interface and accepting its terms of use, then, is coupled with a denial of any responsibility for that technology or its failures. In this way, the statement seems to conceptualize use in the way Sara Ahmed does when she explains, "To be in a relation of use is to be in an environment with other things," because "use is *distributed* between persons and things" at the same time that it reattaches responsibility (for risk assessment) to individual, human users (*What's the Use?* 7).

Terms of Risk, Terms of Use

The questions that Ahmed proposes following the preceding articulations of use in *What's the Use? On the Uses of Use* are instructive for considering how municipal bonds, protected by specific, legal terms of use, distribute risk. She asks, "Who gets to use what? How does something become available to use?" (7). Turning these questions toward municipal bonds, we can ask not only "Who gets to use the technical information about municipal bonds?" as a question of technical accessibility and financial "literacy" but "How do municipal bonds become available for use?"—which foregrounds intended and elided audience and technical and material accessibility. Following Ahmed, we can also invert such questions to consider "What is used by municipal bonds?" Or, in other words, what commonplaces and rhetorics and relations justify municipal debt and its inequitable effects? The "Terms of Use" statement and portal to EMMA is directed toward those who use the site—(potential) investors and advisers looking to buy bonds and in so doing to serve as municipal creditors—but the *use* of municipal bonds themselves is framed in terms of community infrastructure and development: they are *used* to fund capital projects that (ostensibly) benefit municipal residents.

As an example illustrating the uses of municipal bonds from my current place of residence—Las Cruces, New Mexico—in 2018, voters were asked to vote on the following questions:

1. Shall the City issue general obligation bonds, payable from property taxes, in an amount up to $16,900,000 to construct improvements to parks, including sports fields and other related facilities?
2. Shall the City issue general obligation bonds, payable from property taxes, in an amount up to $9,800,000 to construct a new animal shelter facility and related improvements?
3. Shall the City issue general obligation bonds, payable from property taxes, in an amount up to $6,200,000 to construct replacement fire station facilities for Fire Station 3, including acquisition of necessary land?
4. Shall the City issue general obligation bonds, payable from property taxes, in an amount up to $2,700,000 to construct and improve recreational walking, jogging, and biking trails, including acquisition of necessary land? (City of Lac Cruces)

All four bond measures passed, with record voter turnout. Whereas voter turnout for local elections had been around 10 percent (Nevarez), each of these bond measures was voted on by over fifteen thousand people—bringing the percentage closer to 15 percent. Once these measures were passed, the process of bond issuance by the city began, such that searching EMMA for bond offerings within the state of New Mexico results in an $18 million "General Obligation Improvement Bond Series," available for investors. Rated by two companies—Moody's and Standard & Poor's—with Aa2 and AA- scores, respectively, the Official Bond Statement reinforces the investor's assumption of risk in (potentially) purchasing this bond: "In making an investment decision investors must rely on their own examination of the city and the terms of the offering, including the merits and the risks involved" (MSRB, "Supplement").

But the pro forma assumption of risk by the investor does not tell the whole story of how municipal bonds allocate risk or to whom it adheres. As General Obligation Bonds of Las Cruces, these bonds must be repaid by the municipality. In other words, the debt is *owned* by investors, but it is *owed* by Las Cruces, which must levy taxes or otherwise raise revenue to pay its debts. Although investors apparently assume the risk of not being repaid, then, municipalities risk not having the resources to repay and thus having to renege on other fiscal commitments (in a context in which, as I discuss in more detail shortly, bankruptcy law privileges the rights of investors). Neither the City of Las Cruces nor investors in its 2018 GO bonds probably foresaw the significant and ongoing economic consequences of the COVID-19 pandemic, for example, which compromises the stability of municipal tax revenue. But the obligation, or municipal bond debt, which *must* be repaid, will nonetheless supersede other commitments: public servants' salaries or cost-of-living increases, funding for public health programs and other social services, and so forth.

The risk to investors articulated by the MSRB and EMMA thus supplants discussion of risk to municipalities should they undertake debt, such that the rhetoric *of* municipal debt materializes risk exclusively for investors. To shift accounts to a rhetoric *in* debt invites questions of how, and with what effects, the social and machinic subjection of investors participates in the differential and misrecognized disbursal of risk. For although the terminology of risk associated with municipal bonds sticks to investors, the *consequences* of their risk assessments attach to and exacerbate those who are most vulnerable within communities. This can be illustrated by the assessment of the risks of climate change that have begun to shape the municipal bond market. In a study of the impact of climate change risk on municipal market and investor behavior, the finance scholar Marcus Painter found that "the market accounts for differences in credit quality when assessing climate risk," such that "investors appear to react to climate change news, showing that climate change is on the forefront of factors influencing investors' decisions" (481). One consideration among many, the idea that climate change shapes municipal *bond* risk (or financial risk to investors) deflects attention away from the differential exposure of municipalities and their residents to environmental hazards themselves. As confirmed by numerous studies across disciplines, while climate change itself is indiscriminate, it wildly exacerbates existing vulnerabilities for poor people, people of color, Indigenous people, undocumented people, and migrants (see, for example, Pezzullo; Rothstein), even producing an entirely new category of precarity: climate refugees. The effects of climate change—rising sea levels, superstorms, and droughts, for example—endanger not only capital projects or bond tax bases funding repayment, then, but the livelihoods and lives of the most precarious, who are most likely to be impacted by climate change.

Although bond assessment is articulated in terms of an individual reckoning of its merits and risks, considering the impact of climate change reveals how so-called individual decision-making reflects ideological investments and attachments. In other words, an individual belief (in climate change, for example) would necessarily shape how causes or corollaries factor into risk assessment, but individual risk assessment reflects the discursive availability, circulation, popularity, and political force of specific beliefs. Any "examination of the city" performed by an investor emerges within—and sticks back to—complex relations of material history, policy, polity, and ideology. When an investor "believes in" or pays attention to the damage of climate change, for example, they can use such belief to inform their decision about potential bond investments. Moreover, using such information can compound the reputation and climate-based risk of particular municipalities, directing investors away from communities that are overexposed to climate change because of their disproportionate risks. Importantly, this belief (or not) in climate change, which takes effect through interactions in the electronic market, fundamentally sponsors how communities might be funded and consequently how their residents are supported through the public projects on which they rely.

Using existing belief and bias to weigh municipal bond risk is well documented by Casey Dougal et al. in their study of racial discrimination in higher-education bond markets, where they found that "Historically Black Colleges and Universities (HBCUs) pay higher underwriting fees to issue tax-exempt bonds, compared to similar non-HBCUs" (570). Controlling for a number of other variables in their study (including ratings, insurance issuers, and location-based incentives), the authors demonstrate that the higher fees appear "to reflect higher costs of finding willing buyers," an effect that is "three times larger in the far Deep South, where racial animus remains the most severe" (570). As this example demonstrates, debt emerges spatially as an effect of trust in calculable bond ratings and acceptance of machine terms of debt offering and liability.

Dougal et al. conducted their research in direct response to the famed economist Milton Friedman's argument that the specific *products* within markets are interchangeable, such that "the transaction between the 'consumer' (a bond investor) and 'producer' (a municipality) is intermediated and impersonal, and the product (an interest payment) is, if it arrives, indistinguishable between payers" (571). Whereas Friedman argues that competition, more than substance, secures the marketability of products, the authors show that discrimination plays an active and vital role in the comparable prices of university bonds both in their initial offering and in the secondary bond market. Returning to the individual, legal language in which bonds are issued, this can be directly correlated with the mandate to investors that they take responsibility for the risk of their investments as well as their machinic acceptance of the "Terms of Use" of the technologies and interfaces that make investments available. Perceptions of economic risk, as discussed in chapter 1, are rhetorically *and* materially entangled in other kinds of risk. Thus, the racialized risk associated with Black people, neighborhoods, and economies *sticks* to HBCUs, undercutting the supposedly equalizing effects of high ratings scores and insurance guarantees in the context of a deeply racist history of segregation and oppression.

Marking Risk, Shifting Risk

Posited as unilateral, the allocation of risk to investors, or, put otherwise, the assumption of risk by investors, is nonetheless offset by the reputation of municipal bonds more generally. So even assessed with Aa2 or AA− ratings, multiple rungs below the highest bond rating, the bonds nonetheless signify as decidedly low risk compared with other types of bonds, stocks, or investment opportunities. Symptomatic of the risk of debt more generally, however, the ratings themselves are not meant to reflect past actions of the municipality but anticipate and project their futures. As explained in the "Supplement to Official Statement" of the General Obligation Bond in Las Cruces, "This Official Statement contains statements that are 'forward-looking statements' as defined in the Private Securities Litigation Reform Act of 1995. When used in this Official Statement, the words 'estimate,' 'project,' 'intend,' 'expect,' and similar expressions are intended to identify forward-looking statements. Such statements are subject to risks and uncertainties that could cause actual results to differ materially from those contemplated in such forward-looking statements. Readers are cautioned not to place undue reliance on these forward-looking statements, which speak only as of the date hereof" (MSRB, "Supplement" 3). The cautions that frame liability in this statement once again assign risk and risk assessment to investors, who must remember that calculations of risk are, themselves, risky—an attempt to anticipate rhetorical and material futures with no guarantee of their outcome. That is, because the statements cannot definitively project futures, they pass on the responsibility to the investors, who are encouraged, again, to use bond ratings as only "one tool in [their] toolbox" when making decisions about municipal bonds.

The accounting scholars B. Anthony Billings, Melvin Houston, and William H. Volz invoke the standards of financial accounting in their 2017 article in the *CPA Journal*, creating distance between the potential risk to investors and those who evaluate risk in the context of governmental units, which "are becoming more susceptible to the financial problems that have been more often suffered by private sector companies" (57). The risk of municipal default, they argue, should be mitigated by "prudent investors and creditors" who "can protect themselves from losses by analyzing financial statements and related disclosures of municipal units (57). Auditors, on the other hand, their targeted audience in the *CPA Journal*, are encouraged to "do their part in alerting investors, creditors, and officers of the troubled unit of a going concern problem" (57). But in "doing their part," auditors are nonetheless insulated from liability because, as the authors note, "auditors are not required to forecast a going concern problem; instead, they should base their opinions on matters arising in the audit that raise substantial doubt about the entity's going concern status" (57). As described by Billings, Houston, and Volz, then, auditors use expertise to alert investors to concerns, but it is the "prudent investor" who must ultimately "protect themselves" by practicing normative financial literacy to ground risk assessment.

Even with this requirement of individual investors to assess the risk of their potential investments, however, and unlike the student loans discussed in chapter 2, the fallout and lived consequences of potential default of municipalities (cities, counties, or states unable to repay their debts) does *not* only land on the individual assumed to be assessing risk (the investor). That is, while investors are technically—and legally—responsible to assume the risk of the financial decisions, and that risk can absolutely shape their economic livelihoods and futures, it is the lives and livelihoods of municipal residents and workers who necessarily bear the weight of loan default, insofar as public and social projects, programs, and services are the "belts" that can be tightened when expected revenues or taxes from capital projects are insufficient to repay bond investors. As Peck argues, "In the period since the Wall Street crash of 2008, the refurbished rationale for austerity measures is that the imposition of strict fiscal discipline and government spending cuts is the (only) way to restore budgetary integrity—thereby securing the confidence of the investor class, appeasing the jittery markets, and paving the way to growth" (28). This shifting of risk to those who most benefit from public programs, or, put otherwise, those who are most vulnerable within municipalities, correlates with a changing relationship between government and private investment sponsored by neoliberal logics and reasoning.

As recently as 1993, the legal scholars Randal C. Picker and Michael W. McConnell questioned why municipal bankruptcy did not result in the reorganization of municipalities (to parallel the expected restructuring of private companies following bankruptcy) and proposed that it *could* be used "as an instrument for more efficient organization" (427). By 2012, however, the economist James Crotty could premise an economic analysis of government debt on the commonplace that "we have reached what may be a crucial point in the evolution of the political economy of the USA.... A somewhat disparate right-wing coalition ... has demanded that the deficits be eliminated primarily by severe cuts at all levels of government in spending that either supports the poor and the middle class or funds crucial public investment in education, health care, infrastructure and technology" (79–80). In other words, contemporary governments, including local governments, now *are* fundamentally restructured in the face of inability to pay creditors: expected to adopt austerity measures in order to prioritize debt repayment and satisfy creditors.

Perceiving Risk, Containing Risk

To be sure, expectations of austerity and mandates to prioritize the repayment of creditors vary across municipalities; this is due, in no small part, to different bankruptcy laws and practices in effect in different states as well as demographics and political affinities. As Pengjie Gao, Chang Lee, and Dermot Murphy reveal in their comparative study of municipal bankruptcies between 1999 and 2010, whereas states with policies that "allow unconditional access to the Chapter 9 bankruptcy procedure ... [are] advantageous to debtors, because the Chapter 9 procedure can restructure the monetary obligations of the municipality, but cannot enforce the reorganization of the municipal" (404), by contrast, states with policies "that allow Chapter 9 only as a last resort" are "advantageous to creditors, because the state government provides implicit insurance for its local governments in times of distress to protect the overall creditworthiness of the state" (405). The authors conclude that the differences between these approaches to managing default—proactively intervening, allowing unfettered access to bankruptcy, or some combination—are motivated by and contribute back to different conceptions of risk and risk sharing, or contagion. They explain, "A major concern in municipal bond markets is the contagion effect in which a default event in one municipality is correlated with yield increases for bonds in other municipalities. The corporate bankruptcy literature attributes the contagion effect to a number of causes, such as counterparty default risk, updating of beliefs, and correlation risk" (419). Conceding that each of these factors contributes to potential risk contagion, they argue that "the updating of beliefs is particularly relevant" because "investors can change their risk perceptions of other municipalities within a state following a default in the same state, leading to higher yields for those municipalities" (419).

A higher yield on a bond offers potential for higher return on investment, but it simultaneously marks a riskier investment. The contagion effect that Gao, Lee, and Murphy describe thus shifts perception of risk by investors: one municipality in default (one city within a county, for example) is understood in relation to others (adjacent cities). States that actively intervene in municipal bond default seek to limit risk traveling or getting attached elsewhere; by shoring up one municipality, they hope that risk will not spread. As the authors put it, "While a default event in a Proactive state will lead to a change in the risk perceptions regarding the fundamentals of the local economy, the Proactive state's measures mitigate creditors' concerns that these weak fundamentals will affect their repayments from other municipalities in that state" (419). In their comparative analysis, the authors found "evidence of a contagion effect in Chapter 9 states, but not in Proactive states" (420).

The concern for contagion is enough to motivate some states to actively intervene in municipal default, tacitly acknowledging the interactions and interanimations of municipalities, but Crotty's argument about the shift to austerity in the United States suggests an increased moralization of municipal debt in individual terms, comparable to an individual deemed financially unwise or illiterate, unable to live within their means. This conceptualization of municipalities as individual actors follows Picker and McConnell's suggestion that there are two primary ways to conceptualize a city: "as a political subdivision of the sovereign state" or "as the agent of the private citizens who inhabit it" (427). While the former characterization theoretically invites shared responsibility in the face of contagious risk, the latter becomes the stand-in for its geographically bound residents, who are assumed as responsible to shoulder the costs of their debts. Indeed, residents who vote for public works, the logic suggests, should pay for such public works.

The effects of these divergent conceptualizations and the contemporary political economic tendency toward the latter can be seen in recent examples of municipal default, and Billings, Houston, and Volz's summaries of recent municipal bankruptcy filings reveal the stakes of each conceptualization. Of the largest municipal bankruptcy filing in US history, completed by Detroit, Michigan, in December 2014, the authors explain that the "the city was able to reject and renegotiate its debt load of $18 billion with its creditors, labor unions, and stakeholders" (55). The case was adjudicated and approved in US Bankruptcy

Court, and the presiding judge, Steven Rhodes, approved "Detroit's petition for bankruptcy ... based in major part on the evidence of the city's service delivery insolvency to its citizens, including what the court characterized as rampant crime, blight, poverty, and dysfunction" (56). Ostensibly sensitive to vulnerable populations in the city, however, the judge did "not hold pension obligations sacrosanct" (55–56), though he did indicate "to all interested parties that the taxpayers' interest in essential services must be a part of the debt adjustment process" (56). But even with the interest in the "dysfunction" of the city and "essential services," the end result was a plan based on "transferring certain assets to creditors to satisfy debts owed by the city" (56). For example, "Detroit reached a deal to pay Syncora, one of its largest creditors, a fraction of what it was owed while providing rights to city property and an extension of the company's lease to operate the Detroit-Windsor Tunnel. . . . Financial Guaranty Insurance Company, another creditor that was owed more than $1 billion, settled for about 13 cents on the dollar plus rights to develop the Joe Louis Arena waterfront property into a massive hotel development" (56). These examples and others, Billings, Houston, and Volz argue, show that "while the goal of providing essential services to residents may have been preserved, some of the other benefits expected by residents of a major city will now be privatized" (56). In the long term, of course, privatization means that once-public projects and infrastructure are no longer answerable to public interest or inquiry at all, as the terms of the bankruptcy replace the promise-to-repay debt with ownership or management of municipal assets. The authors also considered the "more immediate short term-impacts" on adjacent municipalities (Kalamazoo and Saginaw), which, doubtless concerned about the high-yield contagion, put off "planned securities offerings in the wake of Detroit's bankruptcy filing" (56).

Moralizing Municipal Risk

The case of Detroit's insolvency illustrates the moralization of defaulting municipalities as financial illiterates who cannot be trusted to make wise decisions about investment. This logic is implied when austerity measures are imposed on municipalities in debt, but it also takes very explicit legal and managerial forms—as in the case of the Emergency Manager Law passed in Michigan in 2011, which gave its governor the power to appoint a fiscal monitor to "failing" municipalities. As argued by Shawna J. Lee et al., such a law is racialized and classed in its application, meting out "disproportionate impact on vulnerable and oppressed populations, including racial and ethnic minorities, and families living in poverty" (5). Justified as the appropriate response to communities that "spend too much on themselves," such laws enact what Jason Stanley identifies as "strategic racism" operating through "technocracy," which emphasizes financial efficiency and financial responsibility above all else (40). Such a law rests on not only an "essential bias in favor of financial institutions" (Stanley 18) but a fundamental mistrust of community members, which "affects the ability of the urban poor and minorities to exert political power and, ultimately, to promote residents' health and wellbeing" (Lee et al. 5).

The bias toward financial institutions is evident not only in the selection of a financial manager who demonstrates normate financial literacy but in the scope of their power: in Michigan, the Emergency Manager Law (EM) specifically forbids "challenging contracts with bondholders" (Stanley 18). Moreover, the bias *against* the financial literacy, autonomy, and expertise of communities of color is called into relief by a statistical accounting of who in Michigan was affected by this law. In an analysis using US Census data, Lee at al. found that "EM laws disproportionally affect race and ethnic minority residents of urban areas with higher-than-average poverty rates," such that while "a startling 51% of African Americans residing in Michigan have come under the governance of EM laws at some point since 2008," only "2.4% of Whites statewide were ever directly under the governance of an emergency manager" during that time (4).

The overrepresentation of people of color governed by an emergency manager coincides with the overrepresentation of people of color in areas characterized by, in the words of Judge Rhodes, "crime, blight, poverty, and dysfunction" (as an effect of historical wealth and credit accumulation and denial). Classed and racialized, these terms equate issues of financial management with socioeconomic inequity and precarity while evading the complexities of municipal histories, demographics, and policies that produce crime, blight, poverty, and dysfunction. The development of Detroit as first a robust urban center that attracted thousands of workers during automotive booms to an economically depressed and abandoned Rust Belt city cannot be adequately represented without considering its long-standing practices of racial segregation, which shifted white workers and municipal investment first toward the city and then decidedly away from it—to suburbs inaccessible by public transportation and racially redlined to divide neighborhoods. The shift in population centers radically upended property values, resulting in, for example, nearly half of property owners in 2011 failing to pay property taxes (MacDonald and Wilkinson), which substantively contributed to municipal default.

Yet public accounts—based on financial accounting—of the bankruptcy frame unmet financial obligations in terms of individual choices and objective balance sheets. MunicipalBonds.com, perhaps targeting its explanation of the "root cause" of the bankruptcy to would-be bond investors, for example, cites reduced property and sales tax, population decline, "crippling" GO bond debt, and crime and abandonment (Sangha). This list elides both the conditions of possibility that contributed to these causes, including racialized housing policies, uneven development, union disintegration, and neoliberal trade, and the consequences of this combination of factors on the lives and livability of residents of Detroit in favor of a simple default of responsibility, reduced to the double-entry difference between what was owed and what was paid. Crime and abandonment are figured by the list as sources of municipal bond default rather than in terms of the lived reality of residents of Detroit. Simultaneously, crime and abandonment *stick* to people of Detroit, who are held responsible for the municipal default.

But whereas this rhetoric *of* municipal debt identifies how bankruptcy is articulated in terms of "crime, blight, poverty, and dysfunction," considering the emergence of this debt across temporal scales—the histories of Detroit that attracted investment via employment opportunities and urban development—reveals its work to *create* these very effects, spatializing creditworthiness and risk by attaching it to the bodies, lives, and communities of those who are presumed responsible for exodus from the city and its subsequent defaults. That is, attached to spaces and bodies, municipal bonds not only calculate risk to investors but calculate the (credit) worthiness of development projects: Which parts of cities merit bond investment in housing, street lighting, or water works? Which communities should have libraries, community centers, or public parks? These are both questions of who deserves these services *and* questions of whether they are likely to *pay off* for investors. Although assessing the risk of municipal bonds (for investors) is framed as a calculation that should be made by an individual "prudent investor" (Billings et al.) who uses credits ratings as one "tool" (MSRB) to evaluate their potential to produce acceptable yields, to safeguard wealth against inflation, or to fund retirement, in practice the (racialized) reputation of cities and their residents are key factors in identifying risk and creditworthiness.

In addition to eliding the temporal scales through which Detroit's municipal debts and subsequent bankruptcy occurred, a rhetoric *of* the municipal debt of

Detroit that assigns blame or moral hazard to the debtor—Detroit itself, its elected officials, its residents—also ignores the machinic production of debt through which dividuals (not individuals) are hailed to participate in a debt economy by voting *for* public works. Not only is Detroit famously critiqued for its gerrymandering and corruption (thus inviting mistrust and apathy toward voting in general; Alter), but those who vote on bond measures do so ostensibly expecting that proposed bond projects *will* be successful. Those who choose not to vote (or who are ineligible to vote on the basis of citizenship or other legal statuses) are conscripted into repayment via tax or austerity measures, interpellated into a political economic machine that requires no decision-making. As exemplified by the bond measures cited earlier (in Las Cruces), voters are asked if they support a *project*, not if they believe the bonds introduced to pay for such will inspire investment or if they believe those bonds will be repayable. Voting yes or no to a bond measure thus invokes the logic of machinic subject—participation by rote, complex risk assessment by vote.

Racialized Risk

Admittedly, with the largest bankruptcy in US history, the case of Detroit is not necessarily a representative model for how municipal bonds distribute risk. As Peck argues, "given that bankruptcy amounts, in effect, to a process of politically unmanaged subjection to budget-driven structural adjustment, it is . . . a rarely exercised option of last resort, for all its apparent appeal to some neoliberal hardliners" (29). As he explains, however—and recalling Sbragia's argument that legal restrictions actually *produce* creative financial solutions by serving as productive limits—state-level "balanced-budget requirements and/or legal limits on spending . . . further localize budget pressures, to pass down (or rather, *push*) cuts to local government. . . . Budget crises therefore trickle down" (28). Unlike those who identify the effects of municipal debt or default without mentioning its residents, Peck acknowledges labor unions and collective bargaining, pension plans, and public services, "including education, unemployment and disability insurance, corrections, welfare aid and health care for the poor" as recipients of the "trickle down" of budget pressures (27). Adding to this acknowledgment, accounting for rhetoric *in* debt also directs attention to the differential effects of budget pressures: cuts to public services radically target persons and groups that are already systemically disenfranchised and disproportionately vulnerable.

Despite filing the largest bankruptcy claim in the history of the United States, then, Detroit is not exceptional but paradigmatic in its exercise of racialized technocratic and colonial logics. As Jason Stanley succinctly puts it, "It is the logic of colonialism that is at work in Michigan's decisions to use its Emergency Manager law almost exclusively to displace the democratic structure of majority Black cities" (26). He further links the case of Detroit to "the logic of the Racial Contract" more specifically, invoking Charles Mills's germinal work to identify racial capitalism at work: "The Racial Contract is calculatedly aimed at economic exploitation. The whole point of establishing a moral hierarchy and juridically partitioning the polity according to race is to secure and legitimate the privileging of those individuals designated as white/persons and the exploitation of those individuals designated as non-white/subpersons" (qtd. in Stanley 26). Corroborated and cited over the past twenty years across a variety of disciplines, Mills's articulation of the racial contract upends the race ignorance of theories of the social contract to account for its white-supremacist underpinnings. Using this theory, we can also identify those underpinnings at work in Emergency Manager Laws and the relationships between municipalities and their creditors more broadly, which *stick* expertise to normative financial literacies *at the same time* that they stick fiscal—and moral—irresponsibility to communities of color, blaming mismanagement and overspending for the economic failures of cities rather than contextualizing them in more complex accounts of explicit segregation and neoliberal privatization.

Development Risk and Rehabilitation

In addition to being distributed by Emergency Manager Laws, the risks of municipal debt accrue and stick through other rhetorical and machinic means. Communities populated with renters, for example, might be assessed a lower credit rating than are more wealthy communities populated by home owners, reflecting a perceived risk that property taxes may not be paid in the poorer communities because of transience. Calculated under the cover of credit-agency neutrality and algorithmic accuracy, risk is, as discussed earlier, reduced to an alphanumeric representation. As Kathleen Daly Weisse, Julie Jung, and I argue, algorithmic abstraction—which suppresses complexity in the name of problem-solving—can serve as an animating force in racial neoliberal rhetorics. The low credit ratings of rent-based communities, for example, metonymically stand in for complex and asymmetrical histories of municipal development that took shape in the context of "racial segregation in housing... a nationwide project of the federal government in the twentieth century" (Rothstein xii). Policies and their legacies that range from explicit segregation and commonplace (redlined) real estate and lending practices to transportation routes and innovations intended to circumnavigate poor, minoritized urban centers result in neighborhoods defined by race and divested of resources. The same communities might not have political representation on city councils to agitate for bond measures that benefit their neighborhoods, which requires wealth adequate to fund campaigns. Conversely, bond measures intended to "rehabilitate" poor or neglected neighborhoods may have the effect of displacing their residents. As Jenny Rice argues, historically segregated neighborhoods can become opportunities for "development," annexing neighborhoods for white development under the guise of "urban renewal." The common sense of this argument itself is almost machinic in nature, readily mapping urban spaces via rhetorics of crime and blight as to become the obvious solution to the problem of neglected neighborhoods. Those who vote for development have little to consider; they remove municipal risk by removing the people to whom risk attaches.

Rice offers the specific example of Austin, Texas, to demonstrate this point. After reviewing the city's history of racialized housing and neighborhood policies and practices that successfully segregated the city, bifurcating the white West Side from the more diverse and economically depressed East Side, she relates the following account of the University of Texas seeking more land for its sprawling campus:

> Suddenly, land on the East Side looked more attractive than ever. Under the heading of "urban renewal," the city approached east Austin residents with the opportunity to sell their property back to the city. In the 1960s and 1970s, Austin launched an aggressive campaign for urban renewal. The city's claims were simple and unequivocal: urban renewal is good for everyone. In fact, urban renewal was sold to all Austinites as a solution to many problems. In a pamphlet dating back to the early 1960s titled "Rx for Cities: Urban Renewal," the city declared that urban renewal "offers the means to treat 'sick spots' of cities and urban areas." The pamphlet posed

blighted areas as a suffering human body whose future depends upon surgical removal. . . . By removing and clearing away entire neighborhoods, therefore, the whole body would be benefited. (134)

Although Rice does not investigate the specific municipal bonds used to fund this "renewal," her analysis reveals how the affective quality of spaces—embodied by the people of color who live there—can be used not only (as suggested earlier) as a reason *not* to invest in a city but, in the case of Austin, as a rationale for removal and renewal. Underwritten by a racialized logic that *sticks* creditworthiness and risk to people and spaces, this argument for development attempts to remove risk to investors by removing the people to whom financial risk most readily attaches. The "sick spots" of Austin are directly equated with the presence of Black, Brown, and poor bodies. Gargi Bhattacharyya explains this in terms of indebtedness more directly, suggesting that "what can be allowed for the life of the present and what has been relinquished already to the payments of the future reveals the histories of racialised and other dispossessions," whereby some people suffer "a depletion of terms of life in the present" and for others, it is "a means to asset-strip the necropolitans of the metropolis, ensuring that the future generations will continue to pay bonds taken to sustain life today" (175).

As Rice reveals, arguments to displace and dispossess are not accepted by all; indeed, in the case of Austin, "many people fought bitterly against losing their homes in the face of 'health benefits,'" through "a number of legal battles and public denouncements" (134, 35). Ultimately, however, the university released an official opinion paper reflecting its successful annexing of eight blocks of previously affordable housing: "On one hand, concluded the paper, affordable housing clearly provides a much-needed source of shelter for poor Austin residents. On the other hand, university development can serve as 'provision for the growth of a public institution that has a statewide and even national mission'" (Rice 135). The success of this proposition invites attention to Bhattacharyya's reminder that while debt depletes the present and the future for many people, "for others still, the terms of life remain available and, to the uneducated eye, life appears to continue 'as normal'"; for Chattacharyya, this is part of the "intoxicating promise" of debt (175).

Facilitating an analytic return to the central function of machinic subjection to create indebted subjects, Susan M. Turner argues that both proponents of development and its opposition draw residents into "legally required text-based processes via standardized texts embedded in those processes," which not only "shape residents' strategies" but produce "a powerful public knowledge and administrative 'regime'" (300). Writing in 2002 and based, in part, on her own experiences opposing the proposed development of a local wooded ravine (in Ontario, Canada), Turner considers how "texts that came to hand immediately provided the frame for how to speak about the project and [their] concerns" (300). In other words, participating in (or objecting to) neighborhood development requires literacies adequate to its legalese (M. Williams), but allowing it to progress unimpeded requires nothing—machinic acquiescence. Turner's work corroborates the technical and processual requirements of successful development advocacy, which not only necessitates time and organization but expertise and (normate financial and municipal) literacy to engage with technical and bureaucratic systems and processes. But even with these literacies, objections are difficult to register as development rhetorics map municipalities in terms of investment potential. In Austin, as Rice shows, the strident objections made to "renewing" university-adjacent land ultimately did not find purchase in the administrative regime of the city, in which the growth of the institution and its mission rhetorically outweighed the need for affordable shelter for Austin's poor. Or, in other words, the credit- (and debt) worthiness of the project outweighed concerns for livability of the residents.

Distributing Development, Distributing Debt

Whereas successful objections to bond measures that displace poor and vulnerable residents rely on sophisticated navigation of administrative processes, *accepting* bond measures—as discussed earlier—is as easy as voting yes.[5] To be sure, in the context of radically uneven development and resources within municipalities, which continue, as Rothstein notes, to be haunted by the legacies of explicit and tacit segregation as well as aging infrastructure and political divestment from public works, voting yes on municipal bonds seems the likeliest resource for increasing municipal equity and distributing responsibility. And indeed, bond measures often *pay off* for communities and investors alike: a win-win that uses debt to provide social services. Contra individual debt—student loans, medical debt, bail bonds, credit card debt, and auto loans—municipal bonds are distributed across communities and investors, all of whom have a stake in their success. As I have argued in this chapter, however, the individual, moral, and mathematical premises of debt continue to ground the uses and function of municipal debt. Individual investors accrue a reputation for drawing on financial literacies to calculate and assess the risk of municipalities and bond projects at the same time that they participate—by rote—in the bond marketplace. Agreeing to "Terms of Use" through which they adjudicate and accept risk, they nonetheless use simple alphanumeric renderings in place of complex histories and relations to understand the worth and worthiness of a city or project. Supported by laws that prioritize and protect creditors, investors are not imagined as debtors at all but as savvy, moral financial actors. Meanwhile, "failing" municipalities are framed as unwise financial actors who are not "living up to" their debt obligations. Such failure is transposed onto the bodies and choices of municipal residents, who are stripped of political power when public land, projects, and works are privatized, when elected officials are replaced by appointed fiscal managers, and when residents are forcibly displaced vis-à-vis eminent domain actions that prioritize urban development or renewal.

While a rhetoric *of* debt identifies how municipal bonds signify, in this chapter, I have tracked municipal bonds *in* debt to show how they emerge and stick risk to bodies through processes of social and machinic subjection. As Bhattacharya contends, these processes should not be conceptualized only in terms of "a flattening downwards that reduces all to the status of the formerly subjugated" but also "as another differentiating process" (17). By attending to the scales through which debt emerges, which include histories of development and exclusion, spaces of creditworthy or risky investment, and technocratic and bureaucratic texts and technologies, I have identified how municipal bonds produce differential relations to debt, allocating responsibility and risk in radically inequitable ways.

4

Community Risk, Actuarial Remainders, and Accounting for Medical Debt

While in popular and public discourses in the United States consumer debt is conceptualized as a foregone conclusion or matter of fact (see the introduction to this book), its effects are increasingly contested, as seen, for example, in calls for loan forgiveness, relief, or cancellation. Without denying debt as factually extant, those who call for debt forgiveness or cancellation propose that debt does not necessarily need to be a fact of life. The 2016 and 2020 US presidential campaigns, for example, included explicit calls and proposals from multiple candidates for student loan forgiveness and medical debt elimination. And the 2020 "pause" on federal student loan payments during the COVID-19 crisis contributed political firepower to arguments calling for their cancellation. Such arguments also undergird RIP Medical Debt, a charity organization founded by two (former) debt collectors and a (former) health care administrator that is explicitly premised on buying—and forgiving—unpaid medical bills. As articulated in Jerry Ashton, Robert Goff, and Craig Antico's polemic *End Medical Debt: Curing America's $1 Trillion Unpayable Healthcare Debt*, medical debt is "the enemy of everyone. That's not what we expect here in America" (36). This pithy claim reflects, perhaps, the authors' sense that medical debt is categorically distinct from other kinds of individual debt—"Medical debt is not like debt incurred by buying a big screen TV one cannot afford. It should not be treated the same way" (16)—neither wholly volitional nor irresponsible. And yet medical debt is distinct in, if not unique to, the United States: institutionalized in relation to medical institutions and practices and health care itself as the cost of doing business. That business, of course, is health insurance. Though run as a business, however, health insurance in the United States is also, as of March 23, 2010, with the passage of the Patient Protection and Affordable Care Act (ACA), the law of the land. Widely known as Obamacare, the ACA was intended to expand health insurance opportunities and availability beyond employer-based coverage, filling in the gaps that are too often met with medical debt. And yet, as suggested in a 2021 report in the *Journal of the American Medical Association* (*JAMA*), medical debt in the United States is estimated to be $140 billion. While this total number pales in comparison to total student loan debt in the United States ($1.76 trillion as of fall 2022), the dollar-for-dollar impact of medical debt can be much more challenging for those who hold it, in that it often accompanies debilitating medical events and strongly correlates with loss of work and aggregating financial hardships (Dobkin et al.).

The definition of medical debt is straightforward enough—"a debt arising from the receipt of health care services" (Law Insider)—and, like other forms of debt, rests on the taken-for-granted implication of individual responsibility. Explicated by Robert Goff (of RIP Medical Debt), it is the result of persons who are "unable to take personal financial responsibility for the economic results of medical efforts to restore (or try to restore) them to good health" (17). Affirming the individuating premises of (medical) debt, Goff nonetheless acknowledges that "personal medical debt does not stop with the debtor.... All of us pay for medical debt, if not our own, then the medical debt of others" (36). And indeed, such arguments helped carry the day for the Affordable Care Act, when medical debt was explicitly cited as a reason to expand Medicaid and federalize (in part, anyway) medical insurance options; an expanded market for Medicaid gives the government expanded negotiating power (to improve coverage, lower costs, and so forth). Even as insurance carriers themselves define health insurance, as behemoth Cigna does, as "a legal agreement between you and a health insurance company" that "includes a health plan that helps you pay for certain medical care and services, so you don't have to pay all the costs on your own," and, as BlueCross BlueShield does, in terms of helping "you pay for doctor visits, hospital stays, prescription drugs and important preventative care," health insurance is, of course, premised on collectivities. As the Stanford University Vaden Health Services explains, "The way it typically works is that the consumer (you) pays an upfront premium to a health insurance company and that payment allows you to share 'risk' with lots of other people (enrollees) who are making similar payments. Since most people are healthy most of the time, the premium dollars paid to the insurance company can be used to cover the expense of the (relatively) small number of enrollees who get sick or are injured. Insurance companies, as you can imagine, have studied risk extensively, and their goal is to collect enough premium to cover medical costs of enrollees." In the United States, this risk-sharing model of health insurance, where money is pooled and directed to pay the health care expenses for people in need—always in the context of the aforementioned agreement between individuals and their health insurance provider—participates in the conditions of possibility for significant medical debt, because while risk is ostensibly shared, economic responsibility for shares is once again articulated as individual, volitional, and moral. Not only do the *uninsured* incur debt when they are "unable to take personal financial responsibility for the economic results of medical efforts to restore (or try to restore) them to good health" (Ashton et al. 17), but so too do the *underinsured*: those whose agreements with health care providers are insufficient to cover the costs of care for their medical needs. Moreover, insurance that should be adequate to the health care costs and needs of an individual can fail to meet the financial exigencies of an unexpected medical event or crisis, and thus the *insured* can likewise find themselves with significant medical debt.

As health economists and historians make clear, and as I review in more detail in this chapter, the emergence of the US health care and insurance industries—which integrate premiums, out-of-pocket expenses, and other costs easily dispersed as medical bills (and thus debt) into their business models—was not inevitable. Indeed, assuming a business (or profit-based) model itself was just one option of many in the late nineteenth and early twentieth centuries, when industrialization (and its concomitant appetite for healthy workers) invited increased public attention to and debate about issues of health care. At the same time that wealthy individuals could bear the costs of health care *as* individuals (never mind the intergenerational wealth that made this possible), efficient production and economic might on a broader scale required health care for those who were unable to shoulder costs alone. Thus began practices of pooling resources in specific industries for workers to share in the costs of health care for the community. Contributing to "sickness funds"—the predecessor of health insurance—while in good health gave workers a safety net in case of illness or accident. The collected funds worked with the logic that not all workers would need them at the same time; they thus pooled not only resources but risk itself.

Health care in the United States has evolved into what the health policy historian Rosemary A. Stephens characterizes as beset by "Byzantine challenges of healthcare organization and financing" (vii), and it continues to reflect the resources and risk-sharing logics and practices of its antecedent forms. And built on then-nascent actuarial science, such logics and practices *account* for medical debt as the by-product *not* of inadequate mathematical models but of insufficient individual contributions, where money due is not matched by money paid. Indeed, as I argue in this chapter, while calculated risk *sharing* apparently grounds the relationship between contemporary health insurance policies and health care, it does not redistribute risks, whether they be health based or financial, but carefully redirects attention to individuals' "preexisting conditions" and medical and financial planning, wherein individual choices predict whether (or not) they will require credits for care (in the form of medical debt). The result of such accounting practices is that risk sharing becomes another way to exacerbate historical and contemporary inequities, requiring individuals to draw on specific, normative, and entangled health and financial literacies to forecast their own health and economic futures and allocating debt to the economically precarious under the banner of access to health care.

Moreover, I propose that the individuating premises on which US health insurance *as a market* are based allow medical debt to become the necessary rejoinder to "market failure." That is, whereas market tools and technologies are assumed to accurately predict and account for risk, matching needs with care, failure to match insurance with coverage *sticks* to individuals, requiring those with health and medical needs (all) to enter contractual obligations for care and assume responsibility for any expenses rendered in excess of the contract. In a context where actuarial science and technologies are not held to (full) account for the uncertainties of health care needs, presumably "fully informed and knowledgeable" (Donaldson and Gerard 18) medicalized subjects are expected to forecast their health and financial risks and futures and take responsibility for managing their *own* care under the banner of choosing "managed care" options. In this context, accounting for rhetoric in debt surfaces the implicit differentials meted out onto individuals, where increased (medical) debt and decreased health outcomes entangle with and exacerbate extant economic, health, social, and political vulnerabilities.

In the sections that follow, then, I once again invoke a methodology of accounting for rhetoric in debt to draw attention to the emergence and effects of medical debt across temporal and spatial scales. This work includes and incorporates rhetorical attention to the texts and discourses through which medical debt is terministically framed: public debates and laws, for example, which I consider later in this chapter. But I turn first to the history of health insurance and the accounting methods on which it is premised—actuarial science—to consider how and why medical debt has come to occupy distinct discursive territory in the US imaginary of health and economics that is premised on distinguishing between "planned" and "emergent" medical events. This actuarial, rhetorical distinction asymmetrically distributes financial and embodied risk, exacerbating lived inequalities and livability itself. This case study thus demonstrates how "individual" financial *and* health literacies are tied to spatial and ideological access, or what Harriet A. Washington calls "medical apartheid": not only differential access to medical care but asymmetrical need for medical debt. By drawing on a methodology of accounting for rhetoric *in* debt in this chapter, I collate close attention to texts—historical and contemporary—and their effects with broader, scalar conditions of possibility in which they emerge. I thus demonstrate not only the rhetorical work of medical debt but, once again, the affordances of a methodology adequate to the complexity of its objects (Royster).

Emergence of Insurance, Emergence of the Insured

In *The Blues: A History of the Blue Cross and Blue Shield System*, Robert M. Cunningham Jr. and Robert Cunningham III track the rise of what would become the "largest managed care network" (Stephens vii) in the United States to "an unlikely man to have started a revolution in medical economics" (Cunningham and Cunningham 4). In 1929, hired to rehabilitate the financial situation of Baylor's University Hospital, Justin Ford Kimball developed a hospital prepayment plan through which individuals could pay a monthly fee in case of, and in anticipation of, needed future medical care. Modeled in part on the idea of the "sick benefit fund" for teachers that he had administered in his previous role as a school superintendent, Kimball's hospital prepayment plan invited community members to "budget against future hospital bills" (Cunningham and Cunningham 5). By collecting money in advance, Kimball shifted hospital financing away from relying on either a consistent patient base (i.e., people reliably and consistently *using* hospital services) or charitable contributions (often required to bridge the gap between costs of care and available funding), creating a more sustainable economic model. James E. Stuart, a future leader in the Blue Cross organization, described the plan in these terms: "The Plan was hospital prepayment in its simplest and purest form. There was no third party. The hospital collected the money directly, underwrote the risk directly, guaranteed the benefits and had the means of control of the utilization under its thumb" (qtd. in Cunningham and Cunningham 5).

The apparent simplicity of the plan, however, required accurate data on which to make decisions about price, cost, and use: How many people use the hospital, for what services, and how often? How many people needed to sign up to cover the costs of those who used it? How much would individuals need to prepay to cover the services used? Importantly, these were the questions that motivated Kimball, who admitted that his interest in the problem of health care was "primarily actuarial" (Cunningham and Cunningham 6). This focus aligned well with ongoing local, regional, and national discussion of health care possibilities, coming "after nearly three centuries of widely scattered and diverse experiments to solve problems of cost and access in health care" (8). The actuary-science historians Steven Haberman and Trevor A. Sibbett track this history to the 1792 publication of *Observations on Reversionary Payments*, written by the Welsh mathematician and moral philosopher Richard Price, which "set up the first hypothesis about the rate of sickness and calculated tables of contributions to provide weekly allowances during incapacity for work by reason of sickness or accident" (2).

Rooted in experiments with "sickness funds" in Great Britain, the seeds of actuary science began to root (and later flower) in the United States in a variety of industries in the later nineteenth and early to mid-twentieth centuries. Sickness funds operated with low overhead costs and key restrictions, and their goal, as articulated by the historian John E. Murray, "was consistent with the principles of insurance: to protect the insured from the shock of an unexpected adverse event" (7). From their inception, he continues, "restrictions were intended to exclude those who had already experienced the adverse event of ill health or who expected to experience illness in the near future" (8). Successful as they were in accomplishing their goal to protect the insured individual against financial shock, even in the face of the financial upheaval and uncertainty of the Great Depression, sickness funds were ultimately replaced by commercial insurance because, as Murray explains, "they could not withstand . . . the development of a technologically superior alternative, namely, actuarially sound group health insurance" (218).

In the United States, the development of this actuarial technology—or statistical models adequate to the task of making insurance plans financially sound—emerged alongside political and ideological struggles over questions of how health care should be funded. As Beatrix Hoffman recounts in her historical account *The Wages of Sickness: The Politics of Health Insurance in Progressive*

America, "When Progressives first proposed government-sponsored health insurance in 1915, their vision of protecting working people from the economic burden of sickness seemed well within reach" (1). Just five years later, however, a disparate collection of stakeholders, led by the American Medical Association (AMA) but including commercial insurance companies, labor organizations, and employers, "joined together in an unprecedented and highly effective alliance against compulsory health insurance" (3). Allied against government-sponsored insurance on economic grounds, these groups also rejected encroachments on their autonomy (3). As Hoffman explains, "The story of the Progressive Era health insurance campaign demonstrates that America's limited welfare state was born not simply of preexisting structural constraints but of political and ideological struggles and turbulent historical changes" (5). Indeed, as an example, she cites fissures in women's groups over the support of this item in the Progressive agenda, some enthusiastic about maternity benefits with leave and sick pay and others nervous about how these benefits might be exploited by men, who would send their wives to work to capitalize on this benefit (4). Apprehensions of this sort foreshadowed what would become (and remain) a significant principle on which actuarial risk prediction rests, moral hazard: "a change in the attitude of consumers and providers of health care which results from becoming insured against the full costs of such care" (Donaldson and Gerard 35). More generally, the terms and rhetoric of the Progressive-era debate continue to structure the possibilities for contemporary health care.

Viable Actuarial Models, Moral Hazard

In the context of complex political tides shaping the persuasive potential of arguments for government-sponsored health insurance, then, commercial insurance became viable as it developed actuarial technology capable of making health care profitable, using statistical models and inferences to accurately assess how the insured would *use* benefits *as a group*. As Murray argues, "the concentration on the political role played by these insurers has obfuscated their role in a critical episode in the history of technology" (219). In this history, actuarial science became charged with accounting for the complexity of the relationships between individual and groups, considering how uncertainty on the level of individual illness or accident could emerge in precise and predictive statistical models. As Cam Donaldson and Karen Gerard further explain, "For the individual, illness is unpredictable. In general terms it may be possible to predict the prognoses associated with various chronic conditions and to predict in probabilistic terms how people of varying ages, circumstances, and pre-existing conditions will fare in terms of their health status. But at the level of the individual, future health status is likely to be uncertain" (32). From the time of the Progressive debates to the mid-1930s, then, insurers—eager to monetize the possibilities of the *need* for health care—focused on developing actuarial science and technologies that could account for group health and risk, entangled as it was in individual behavior and risk and necessary to develop insurance commercially (Murray 219).

As Murray explains, working with "sickness tables" was crucial but insufficient to this goal, capable as they were of accounting for the likelihood of the insured getting sick but incapable of projecting "the incentive consequences of sick pay benefits" or how individuals might change their behaviors (and thus risk profiles) on the basis of their access to insurance (219). As actuarial science and technology advanced, then, it shifted from accounting for probability of sickness, illness, or accident *in general* to how these probabilities interfaced with key premises about behaviors of the insured. In other words, to be predictive and profitable, risk projections needed to account for the effect of insurance itself on how individuals (statistically speaking) would make choices. Building in the assumptions of moral hazard, that the insured would be *more* likely to "overconsume" health care services and *less* likely "to adopt healthier lifestyles" (Donaldson and Gerard 35), actuarial science could better forecast how commercial insurance might be economically sustainable and profitable on a large scale.

Moral hazard is not a concept unique to health insurance or contemporary with the emergence of commercial health insurance. As the economic and social historian Robin Pearson argues, the late nineteenth century invited numerous industries to "bridge the gap" between personal trust—on which business *had* run—and "the emergence of new commercial relations where moral hazard was mass produced and where a commanding knowledge of personal reputations was virtually impossible" (1). Shifting away from personal trust and seeking actuarial methods capable of projecting *group* risk, however, commercial insurance was (and continues to be) hyperarticulated with assumptions about sovereign-individuals-cum-economic-actors, their knowledges, agencies, and behaviors, as is fundamental to mainstream or classical economic models.

Donaldson and Gerard confirm the relation between insurance models and mainstream economics, noting, "In mainstream economics, individuals are the unit of analysis. Individuals are seen as sovereign. That is they have preferences, evaluate choices and act" (16). The effect of this classical or mainstream model on shaping the health care market, they continue, is that

> by definition, fully informed and knowledgeable consumers will weigh up the costs and benefits of health care relative to other goods. They will spend that amount of money on health care which maximizes their well-being. This will result in the appropriate amount of resources being allocated to health care overall and to different types of health care (what is termed in economics language allocative efficiency). At the same time, health care producers, seeking to maximise profits, will produce consumers' most highly valued types of health care at least cost, so behaving in a technically efficient manner. This combination of technical and allocative efficiency... ensures that consumers' well-being is maximized at least cost to society. (18)

As Donaldson and Gerard make clear, however, the premise of "fully informed and knowledgeable consumers" of health care is impossible due both to the asymmetry of information available to medical providers versus consumers and to the fallibility of doctors as agents of health care (44–45). Among other reasons, they attribute the "market failure" of commercial insurance—or the inability of the market to communicate and regulate health care supply and demand without intervention—to this faulty premise of "fully informed and knowledgeable consumers." More specifically, "the market fails to inform the consumer of the contribution of health care to health status" (45).

Interestingly, whereas individuals are *the* unit of analysis of classical models of economics, assumed discrete, sovereign, and agential, they emerge in much more complex terms in actuarial science. That is, ultimately charged with predicting the potential cost of care (and attendant economic responsibility) of individuals, actuarial science must begin with data about *groups* of people and the qualities that make them into a viable, representative "class." Such data include, for example, "credit reports, econometric time series, geographic information systems, and census data" (Frees et al. 3). Collated into statistics and models and interpreted algorithmically, these data are the ground for the predictive modeling that is central to actuarial science. As the actuary researchers and practitioners Edward W. Frees, Richard A. Derrig, and Glenn Meyers explain, "Predictive modeling involves the use of data to forecast future events. It relies on capturing relationships between explanatory variables and the predicted variables from past occurrences, and exploiting those relationships to predict future outcomes" (9). While "exploitation" is used here to denote a technical process that links pasts and futures, it also (rhetorically) speaks to the uneasy relationships between pasts and possible futures. Existing asymmetries in past health outcomes, for example, ground predictions for what might be expected in the future. And integrated into technical models, they take on the ethos of scientific reliability and detachment—data in and data out.

Within actuarial science, then, individuals—including their health needs, realities, and behaviors—become data points to inform statistics and models before they become customers and consumers of insurance products in need of health care. Moreover, as discussed earlier, though behaviors calculated in terms of moral hazard are integral to the calculus of profitable insurance, they are forecast in terms of likelihoods and propensities within a group or class. Conversely, risk profiles are gathered via statistical representation of a class (risk of heart attack, risk of needing maternity care) and meted out in insurance rates and possibilities, packages, and products available to *individuals*, who—in ideal circumstances—can choose the insurance products or packages that best match their needs and circumstances. Even given the choice, however, individuals are tasked with calculating risk that is not fully accounted for by the most sophisticated actuarial methods; for those without the means to cover the difference, the consequence is medical debt.

Emergent Disparities, Emergent Options

Of course, the emergence of actuarial science and technology and the insurance plans they made possible cannot be divorced from broader sociopolitical contexts of their use and effects, including, as mentioned earlier, issues of gender parity but also what the public health scholar Jenna M. Lloyd refers to as "histories of class and racial exclusion in health care reform" (66). Paradigmatic in this history is, of course, what Harriet A. Washington terms "medical apartheid," "the history of ethically flawed medical experimentation with African Americans" (20–21), which rendered Black Americans not patients of health care but subjects of medical curiosity and exploitation. Contributing key scientific and medical insights to medical advancement without consent, compensation, or acknowledgment but with horrifying and predictable medical complications and consequences, including death, this constituency was not only radically excluded from historical practices of health care but continues to, in the words of W. Michael Byrd and Linda A. Clayton, experience "slave health deficit," what Lloyd explains as "health inequities rooted in chattel slavery and perpetuated by institutionalized racism in medicine and other institutions" (61).

Emerging not only alongside but entangled with this history of racial exclusion and racialized access to and treatment by health and medical institutions, health insurance policies and coverage themselves contribute to inequitable health outcomes along racial lines. Lloyd explains that during World War II, even as political conditions allowed unions to successfully argue for health care in collective bargaining, for example, "the expansion of private insurance through union contracts and employer benefit packages during and after the war largely benefited white workers" (67). Moreover, employer-based insurance expanded alongside rhetorics of self-reliance and individual accountability. Introducing the edited collection *Subprime Health: Debt and Race in U.S. Medicine*, Nadine Ehlers and Leslie R. Hinkson quote Republican Senator Robert Taft, who in 1949 declared, "It has always been assumed in this country that those able to pay for medical care would buy their own medical service, just as under any system, except a socialistic system, they buy their own food, their own housing, their own clothing, and their own automobiles" (xxi). Such framing, of course, denies any inequities in access to care, framing it as a choice made by and responsibility of individuals and moralizing it as an individual consumer *choice*. But even the programs intended to support *all* individuals reinscribed racial inequity. When Medicare and Medicaid were created during the presidency of Lyndon Johnson, for example, political compromises over their implementation reveal race-based attitudes about worthiness. As Lloyd explains, "While Medicare for all people over the age of sixty-five was a universal entitlement, states had tremendous latitude in the benefits they would offer and how many people would be covered under Medicaid. Medicaid thus represented a concession to Southern states that had failed to extend even minimal health and social services to poor and Black residents" (68).

As these and other moments of (historical and contemporary) emergence of and political struggle over health insurance reveal, the industry and its practices cannot be disarticulated from larger social relations. But this is not only a history of the emergence of an industry. Rather, the emergence of health insurance in the United States tells the story of (medical) debt. Thus, differential patterns in Medicaid access for southern states in the 1960s foreshadow differential expansions of Medicaid with the passage of the ACA in 2010 and give way, as reported in 2021, to significantly different amounts of medical debt between residents of southern and other states (Kluender et al.). Such patterns are not accidents of political history but embedded in the relationships that stick debt differentially to racialized subjects and narrate the difference in terms of individual fiscal and health literacies and behaviors.

Individualized Insurance, Managed Care Options

The significance of Senator Taft's remarks about medical costs being the responsibly of an individual is considerably heightened in a contemporary moment marked by an aggressively neoliberal (political) economy. As Ehlers and Hinkson argue, "What Taft raised here was an ideology of personal responsibility for medical care—a viewpoint that has been a continuing thread in national policy related to medical health care in the decades since his claim, and a sentiment that is only augmented within the contours of neoliberalism. Personal responsibility characterizes the neoliberal era, which has revived and intensified laissez-faire individualism and which has subjected almost every aspect of life to the logic and imperatives of the market" (xii). The hypothesis that individuals are best suited to make choices about their health insurance needs is perhaps nowhere more evident than in the marked shift toward, and increase in, "managed care" options for health insurance, which move away from simple prepayment for health care services and toward plans with specific consumer options. While this shift happened over some decades in the twentieth century with developments in actuarial technologies and health care legislation, Donaldson and Gerard, writing in 2005 in *Economics of Health Care Financing*, confirm, "The greatest change in the US health care market over the past two decades ... has been the move to the private sector from the domination by private care insurance to 'managed care,' as embodied most notably in the proliferation of HMOs and preferred provider organizations (PPOs)" (9). The National Council on Disability explains, "Today, such prepaid health plans are commonly referred to as Health Maintenance Organizations (HMOs)," a term that was "not coined until 1970, with the aim of highlighting the importance that prepaid health plans assign to health promotion and prevention of illness."

Unlike earlier plans that served as safety nets in the case of accident or illness, HMOs made a rhetorical and substantial turn toward market-based options for health care, ostensibly giving consumers choices about where and how to manage their own care. Assisted by the passage of the Health Maintenance Organization Act (in 1973), its attendant stimulus monies and requirements (for employers, for example), and a "relaxed regulatory environment," health care moved away from hospitals toward "group practices and open outpatient centers specializing in diagnostic imaging, wellness and fitness, rehabilitation, surgery, birthing, and other services previously provided exclusively in hospital settings" (National Council on Disability). When this lax regulatory environment in the 1980s and increasing costs passed to employers and—by extension—their employees resulted in significant denials for health care coverage in the 1990s, "nearly 900 state laws governing managed health practices were enacted," and consumers became more apprehensive about a market-based approach to health insurance (National Council on Disability). Despite this seeming turn in public opinion in the 1990s, by the time George W. Bush delivered his second inaugural address in 2005, he touted a "vision of an ownership society," which referred to "not only the ownership of homes, businesses, and retirement savings, but also that of health insurance" (James Robinson 1199).

This emphasis on ownership continues to be reflected today in the marketing rhetoric of "managed care" by health insurance companies, which explain it as a "model to limit costs, while keeping quality high" (Cigna), with plans based in contracts "with healthcare providers focused on prevention and care management, which helps produce better patient outcomes and healthier lives" (Intermountain Healthcare). As Donaldson and Gerard summarize, "Managed care embodies several features, such as: greater competitiveness amongst funders in attracting enrollees; more active 'management' of providers by these funders (through the use of protocols and negotiation of lower fees and prices); and some might say, greater restrictions on the range of services, providers, and other aspects of care made available" (9). While health care providers and economists articulate the "management" of care as a feature of insurance options, it is individual consumers who must manage normative economic and health literacies to make choices about which plans are financially viable and fit their needs. In this way, "ownership" is not only offered to but required of individuals as they interpret information, parse options, and make decisions that impact their economic and health-related well-being. In the United States, managed care plans are rhetorically organized in terms of relationships between premiums (what customers pay for in *advance* of care), copays (what customers pay for at the time of care), and out-of-pocket expenses (which fall outside the "coverage" offered by the plan). When options for plans are available, then, individuals are tasked with weighing anticipated health care needs and possible medical exigencies against predicted income streams and other financial obligations.

Managing Care, Managing Literacies

Corroborating the requirement for individuals to negotiate health and financial literacies and assisting in this decision-making in the contemporary moment, HealthCare.gov offers background information for "how to pick a health insurance plan," introduced with "3 Things to Know Before You Pick a Health Insurance Plan": (1) "The 4 'Metal' Categories," which explains cost-sharing options of different types of plans; (2) "Your Total Costs of Healthcare," which explains the differences between and relationships among premiums (i.e., monthly fees) and deductibles (i.e., out-of-pocket costs); and (3) "Plans and Network Types—HMO, PPO, POS, and EPO." While explanations are ostensibly simple and thus potentially (rhetorically) accessible to a variety of users of the website, they belie the requirement of complex risk calculations. Introducing the "metal" categories—or types of plans—for example, HealthCare.gov describes "Bronze" in the following terms:

- *Lowest* month premium
- *Highest* cost when you need care
- Bronze plan deductibles—the amount of medical costs you pay yourself before your insurance plan starts to pay—can be thousands of dollars a year.
- *Good choice if*: You want a low-cost way to protect yourself from worst-case medical scenarios, like serious sickness or injury. Your monthly premium will be low, but you'll have to pay for most routine care yourself. (emphasis in original)

This plan is contrasted with Silver, Gold, and Platinum plans, the last of which is described in the following terms:

- *Highest* monthly premium
- *Lowest* costs when you get care

- Deductibles are very low, meaning your plan starts paying its share earlier than for other categories of plans.
- *Good choice if:* You usually use a lot of care and are willing to pay a high monthly premium, knowing nearly all other costs will be covered. (emphasis in original)

By framing these plans in terms of simple choices ("good choice if"), these descriptions not only ignore the complex and entangled literacies required to make them (and the histories implicated in each) but the material requirements of each. The "Platinum" plan, for example, marketed to consumers who "usually use a lot of care," requires consumers to forecast their needed care *and* have the means necessary to pay for it. Perhaps hailing those who pair a history of consistently high income with a chronic health condition, this description leaves out any who do not—or cannot—combine those variables: those who cannot pay a high premium but require significant, consistent care or those who may be able to pay a high premium but cannot project their need for care. Of these two possibilities, both require financial literacy and assessment, but the former disqualifies people without adequate financial means for their health care needs (those who cannot afford a high monthly premium), while the latter penalizes those who cannot adequately forecast health care needs (and thus pay into a plan that they do not need).

The literacies required to make decisions that will *not* result in medical debt are not only challenging in their own right—that is, navigating information, understanding financial possibilities and risk, and assessing health care needs, risks, and contexts—but all the more so in their commingling, which cannot be accounted for by simple arithmetic or with regard to the capacity of an individual to interpret information and use it to make decisions. The idea of an individual making decisions independently discounts, as mentioned earlier, complex relationships between patients and the medical and health insurance industries (as I discuss in more detail shortly) as well as the role of a doctor or health care practitioner's interpretation or advice. Explaining this in economic terms by way of comparison, Donaldson and Gerard write,

> In other production processes, like food production, some regulatory processes may be applied, such as in monitoring standards of products. But, in such cases, the consumer is still judged to be the best judge of his/her own welfare. This is not necessarily so in health care because of the

technical relationship between health care and improvements in health. Basically, consumers desire improvements in or maintenance in health status. However, improvements in health status cannot be purchased in the market. The consumer is forced to purchase health care in order to achieve an improvement in health. Health care itself is normally of no value but is linked to health improvements via a "technological" relationship about which doctors know more than consumers. (44–45)

Donaldson and Gerard further contextualize the entanglements of individual health literacy and doctors' knowledge and expertise with respect to doctors' positionality within the health care system: positioned to advise their patients, doctors cannot be "perfect agents" who simply or "objectively supply information" because they retain their own interests and needs, distinct from that of the patient/consumer (46). This is not to say that doctors always or intentionally prioritize their own interests and needs above those of their patients but that they do not work outside of their own economic realities and networks of interpretation. Moreover, even shelving financial conflicts of interest, doctors do not have totalizing knowledge of the relationships between health care and improvements in health.

In addition to discounting the role of a doctor in contributing to or facilitating the health literacy of a patient/consumer, an individual interpretation of literacy also elides how it is situated in broader contexts of possibility and meaning. In the United States, the Health Resources and Services Administration explicitly defines "health literacy" as "the degree to which individuals have the capacity to obtain, process, and understand basic health information needed to make appropriate health decisions" and cites low health literacies among "older adults," "minority populations," "those who have low socioeconomic status," and "medically underserved people." Even accounting for these patterns in relational terms—for example, acknowledging that health care providers may "use words patients don't understand" or the "cultural barriers to health care"—this definition *sticks* literacy and its (differential) effects to individuals as a learnable, demonstrable "skill." As Dawn S. Opel argues in "Challenging the Rhetorical Conception of Health Literacy," the health care industry's "skill-based" conception of literacy, which "reinforces the notion of health literacy as an independent and self-sufficient act," cannot account for the relational aspects of health and health care and leaves "little room for caregiving and socially constructed notions of health and wellness" (138). Focused on aging and older adults' relationships to health care, Opel reviews literature that correlates "low health literacy" and the likelihood to "incur more medical costs" and directs attention to the problematics of framing health literacy in individual terms: "health literacy, narrowly defined as 'the ability to understand and act on health information,'" she explains, "is a problematic lens . . . as it locates the problem with the individual, alone" (137).

As discussed in previous chapters (in terms of financial literacy), literacy cannot be divorced from the political and ideological contexts in which it arises. Moreover, as literacy scholars attest, it does not reflect individual skill in a defined area but emergent relations and normative expectations of a range of practices and behaviors. In the words of Paul Prior, literate activity "is not located in acts of reading and writing, but as cultural forms of life saturated with textuality, that is strongly motivated and mediated by texts. Given this perspective, it becomes particularly important to examine the concrete nature of cultural spheres of literate activity" (qtd. in Opel 138). The spheres of activity for performing health literacy in the United States are bound to its finance-scapes: health care is a for-profit industry, in which health insurance is purchased by consumers and mediates access to care and medical practitioners, facilities, and technologies. Reading, understanding, and making meaning of health care options thus requires cooperating financial literacies and resources. As articulated in an ongoing, multistate study of "the intersection of healthcare and financial decision making across the lifespan," "The consumer-driven approach of decision-making assumes that the simple provision of information will be sufficient to affect consumer choice, [but] the process of using data to inform choice is actually quite complex" (NIMSS).

With health care costs in the United States outpacing any other country (globally) while health outcomes lag behind much of the developed world, the health care industry is rhetorically framed in public discourse in terms of financial crisis. But Opel disrupts the scapegoating of individual literacies in this crisis rhetoric by identifying the pattern wherein the "low health literacy of older adults is implicated as a convenient explanation" for the crisis (140). But as she confirms, this "invocation of poor health literacy of individuals is also designed to mask the increasingly bureaucratic imbroglio of American health care. There are very few people that do not have difficulty navigating the American healthcare system, so much so that an Institute of Medicine discussion paper redefined health literacy to be both related to an individual's competencies and to the complexity of the system" (140). Despite this recognition of the systemic complexities that circumscribe health literacies and possibilities for successfully navigating the health care industry by one institute, however, the rhetorical framing of both health care and financial literacies as individual competencies has dire and differential consequences for anybody whose health care plans are inadequate to their health care needs. Medical debt is the fiscal remainder in this equation, but its impact cannot be accounted for on a balance sheet. As I review in the following section, it impacts individuals, families, generations, and communities with regard to health, wellness, employment, and financial futures, legislating and reinscribing asymmetrical vulnerabilities under the rubric of (self-)managed care.

Financial and Health Literacies in/as Health Savings Accounts

A recent development in managed care that more tightly yokes health and financial literacies together is the financial product referred to as a Health Savings Account (HSA), metonymically representing rhetorical expectations for how people with health care needs are figured by the health care "market." In the words of the health economist James Robinson, HSAs not only mark a "philosophical shift in emphasis from collective to individual responsibility for the management and financing of care" but "form the core of the emerging 'consumer-directed' insurance plans, imposing greater cost sharing on enrollees but permitting broader choices than the health maintenance organization (HMO) plans of the managed-care era" (1199–1200). Technically speaking, HSAs allow a subset of the insured (those with qualifying plans) to set aside money for anticipated health care costs or health care exigencies without tax implications: it is thus "a financial vehicle, akin to an individual retirement account, to which contributions may be made with pretax dollars and from which balances may be withdrawn to pay medical claims, again without payment of tax" (James Robinson 1200). HSAs are only allowed for high-deductible plans, or "generally a health plan ... that only covers preventative services before the deductible"; the money can be used on "qualified medical expenses," predefined by the plan, and might include not only costs that supersede medical coverage but "deductibles, copayments, coinsurance, and some other expenses." The stated value of the HSA is that it may effectively "lower ... overall health care costs," but this is as an effect of "using untaxed dollars" (National Council on Disability). In other words, it is a viable plan for those who not only have economic means sufficient to set aside money for health care costs but for whom doing so will lower their effective tax. Those who do not have the capital to save, the income bracket to benefit, and the need for a high-deductible plan may have the option for an HSA but will gain no financial advantage from it. And indeed, it is marketed as a tax "advantage," an economic prize for those who meet its criteria.

No doubt impacting millions of Americans who do fit this profile, the rhetoric of Health Savings Accounts has broader impact still on how health care is conceptualized in the United States as/in relation to health and financial literacies and medical debt. As a "savings account," HSAs participate in the moralization of projecting financial and health futures. Someone who accurately anticipates health care needs and risks and sets aside or saves money to cover associated costs while simultaneously lowering their own tax liability is not only displaying normative financial literacies but taking responsibility for their own fiscal and embodied health. Thus, an ethos of responsibility sticks not only to the choice itself but to those whose financial circumstances enable them to make the choice. The inverse is also true as "risky" rhetorically frames not only choices but those who ostensibly choose them (Scott, *Risky Rhetoric*).

Robinson points out the danger of HSAs becoming the model for health insurance, acknowledging that "although some persons can and will function effectively as consumers of health services—pursuing information about quality, comparing prices, and balancing care received today against care that may be needed tomorrow—others will fare less well" (1201). As indicated later in this chapter, these "others who fare less well" are predictable, emerging as a class *in relation* to histories, practices, policies, and patterns that (materially and discursively) differentiate between those who can purchase health (care) vis-à-vis a savings plan and those who must go into debt.

In shifting toward individual responsibility and ownership, HSAs also shift away from the community logics on which insurance and its antecedents had been historically based, wherein risk was shared across a community and in which "unspent" monies were redirected back to the insurance pool—the "financial benefit going to sick enrollees who claim in excess of their premium payments." As Robinson explains, however, "contributions to the HSA remain the property of each enrollee," which "increases enrollees' responsibility for costs incurred in their own care but decreases their responsibility for costs incurred in the care of strangers" (1201). This fundamental shift does not eliminate the need for risk sharing and insurance pools; in the United States, the costs of care directly to individuals are all but prohibitive. But the rhetoric of the HSA nonetheless centers "the individual citizen as the appropriate setter of health care priorities," casing insurance assessment and actuarial methods in individual responsibility and financial fortitude and planning (James Robinson 1201).

Planned Savings, Unplanned Debt

In addition to shifting away from or undermining community care models, the idea of accurate financial projection related to health needs and outcomes also bifurcates planned versus exigent medical events, mapping risky behavior onto bodies along economic, gendered, and racialized lines (Scott, *Risky Rhetoric*). A middle-class heterosexual couple that signs up for a high-deductible plan in preparation for planned maternity care, for example, becomes a paragon of financial literacy and healthy behavior. Meanwhile, a woman without sufficient maternity coverage for an "unplanned" pregnancy rhetorically signifies as financially irresponsible and morally culpable. But even in the context of two people with identical Health Savings Accounts, the significant difference in maternal care across racial lines means that a Black or Brown pregnancy patient may incur more costs if or when medical practitioners recommend more invasive care options (see also Lloyd).

That pregnancy can be framed in terms of "planned" or "unplanned" itself is, of course, a symptom of the moralization of health literacies. While much scholarship and activist rhetoric acknowledge the consequences of this moralization on differentially legislating women's bodies, denying access to education, birth control, and abortion services to low-income and racialized bodies, less explicit has been a scholarly focus on how rhetorics of health projection interface with rhetorics of financial literacy to exacerbate this moral accounting or how both are indebted to the temporal emergence of actuarial technologies and health insurance arrangements that yield significant debt. Moreover, as reported by the journal *Health Affairs* in 2020, "out-of-pocket" spending for maternity care for women even with employer-based insurance is significant, having increased substantially in the seven years following the adoption of the ACA (from an average of $3,069 to $4,569—or 67 percent). That is, while the ACA mandated employer-based plans to "cover" preventative care, maternity care was relegated to an "out-of-pocket" expense born by customers (Moniz et al.). The logics and rhetoric of health insurance and medical debt suggest that such women might have chosen, instead, a different health insurance plan, but with 98 percent of the 657,061 women surveyed paying some out-of-pocket costs, clearly this "choice" did not exist. HSAs thus become the wise financial plan for those who plan to need maternity care. As noted, however, HSAs only benefit those whose tax liability is reduced by contributing to the account.

Distinguishing between so-called planned and unplanned medical costs using normative financial logics—where "planned" signifies as financial literacy—both elides the specific contexts in which medical debts emerge and corroborates prevailing narratives of the debt (as individual, moral, and volitional). Indeed, as proposed by the 2003 report of the Access Project investigating the health and health care access in three communities, in "The Consequences of Medical Debt," for example, "unlike other forms of debt, medical debt is often involuntary, the result of an event over which one has little or no control" (2). But even in a direct effort to contest the volitional premises of *medical* debt, the report corroborates debt itself as a choice. That is, while the report does single out the exigencies for medical debt as distinct, contextualizing it in the business model of health care and the specific needs of the "customers" of health care and specifying health care customers as uniquely vulnerable (given their need for medical care), it nonetheless invokes a distinction between planned and unplanned debt, affirming the former as moral, wise, and creditworthy and the latter as irresponsible—or at least lacking in financial foresight. Even when emphasizing that medical expenses "are often sudden and unplanned and, particularly for people without health insurance, may bring large financial burdens that are involuntary in the sense that they are not the result of a traditional consumer choice," the report reinscribes debt as the consequences of individual financial "choice" (2).

Consumers, of course, do make choices, both in anticipation of planned *and* unplanned health care needs and expenses and, importantly, *in relation* to other debts, expenses, and resources. In a study of the relationships between cancer diagnoses and wealth, for example, Arpit Gupta et al. find that the financial destabilization that follows cancer diagnoses must be contextualized in relation to "understanding how households manage the credit instruments available to them" (6). Savings accounts, they explain, are only useful "if households have not incurred substantial debt" because the high interest rates of debt undermine the benefit of the low-interest-rate yields of savings plans (6).

Further contextualizing medical expenses in relation to other economic indicators, in the *American Economic Review*, Carlos Dobkin et al. study "the economic consequences of hospital admissions," guided by the premise that despite the significant expansion in insurance coverage for American adults created by the expansion of the ACA, "we know remarkably little about their exposure to economic risk from adverse health events" (309). Their findings—based on twenty years of data about insured adults admitted to the hospital—include significant evidence of persistent, even increasing impacts of hospitalizations. Notably, the economic consequences of such hospital admissions "increase out-of-pocket medical spending, unpaid medical bills, and bankruptcy, and reduce earnings, incomes, access to credit, and consumer borrowing" (309). Focused on the adult population that does not qualify for Social Security retirement income (and thus depends on continuous employment), this study makes evident the ongoing consequences of a hospital admission—even for the insured—which includes a decline in earnings "at least three times that of the out-of-pocket medical spending increase" (310). Or, in other words, the money required to cover the cost of care *not* paid by insurance is only one piece of the economic picture.

Although neither of these studies centers medical debt proper, they both expose the entanglement of unpaid medical expenses with myriad economic factors: insurance, employment, savings, credit, and other debts. Like other forms of debt, it is not the *amounts* that necessarily make medical debt onerous or debilitating but its relation to debtors. As reported in a survey of people struggling to pay medical bills, nearly one-quarter of respondents had bills of less than $1,000, while 60 percent described their finances as either barely adequate or inadequate to meeting basic expenses (Hamel et al. 8). Meanwhile, of respondents who did not struggle to pay medical bills, over 75 percent reported living comfortably, often with "a little left over for extras" (8). Perhaps an obvious conclusion of the study—that people with medical debt are more likely to be subject to economic precarity on a larger scale—these trends nonetheless point to the cyclical patterns of debt, whereby the inability to pay a debt results, predictably, in the inability to pay a debt. Measured via metrics of responsibility and literacy, however, even small debts signify as personal "struggles," an indication that someone should have chosen a better insurance option, engaged in preventative health measures, or set aside money in case of emergency.

In fact, many cases of outstanding medical bills do encourage people with health care needs to alter their behavior in response to economic precarities, reflecting what Judy Z. Segal identifies as the machinations at work in North American (US and Canadian) rhetorics of health care, where problems "are typically framed in public discourses as, in the first instance, economic problems" (119). She argues that "the fact that the 'health care crisis' is most often represented in public discourse as a crisis of money itself forecloses, by its own terms, the very policy debate it promises to engage" (120). This shapes not only public discourse but individual behavior, as people seek or avoid *health* care based on *economic* calculations. In Michelle H. Moniz et al.'s study of the costs of maternity care, for example, they found that these "financial burdens place women at risk of delaying or deferring maternity care" (22). Avoiding needed health care, of course, can create cascading health care problems (for women and babies). As Elizabeth Sweet argues in "Debt-Related Financial Hardship and Health," "When medical care and treatment are skipped because of being in debt, it may worsen existing physical and mental health issues that require regular or long-term management, or may lead to new health problems by delaying necessary intervention when an issue first arises" (5). Yet again, however, the decision to forgo care (as a calculation of economic necessity) reveals differential relations to debt, whereby some people have access to its affordances and others only to its risks.

Bad Options, Bad Debt

Corroborating and complicating the mediating influence of debt on health care choices and their consequences in the *Journal of Health and Social Behaviors*, Lucie Kalousova and Sarah A. Burgard explain:

> Indebtedness could increase the likelihood of foregoing care because it may constrain the use of financial resources, but the association could vary depending on the type of debt under consideration. Extant studies have suggested that unpaid credit card balances generate stress, so individuals may allocate resources to pay it back at the expense of other things they need. However, other forms of debt could signal positive financial standing, because the ability to take on some kinds of debt depends on credit worthiness and collateral. Many individuals with substantial debt due to a sizeable home mortgage loan are capable of servicing this kind of secured debt because they earn high incomes or have sufficient assets. Debts that simply reflect credit worthiness and are affordable given financial resources should not be associated with foregoing needed medical care. (205)

Those who would forgo medical care in relation to debt—including medical debt—then, are those for whom debts stick as *bad debt*, which is to say, as a risk to financial institutions. "Bad debt" is akin to "moral hazard," technical terminology used to describe a specific, and ostensibly neutral, phenomenon. That is, whereas insurance literature is quick to qualify the "moral" qualifier in "moral hazard" as only reflecting the *economic* consequences of risk behaviors and decision-making that are altered by the presence of insurance, the qualifier "bad" in "bad debt" is used in accounting to denote debt deemed unrecoverable. Debt marked as "bad," in other words, is treated in a specific way. For tax purposes in the United States, for example, bad debt is written off as an "expense" on a balance sheet, a predicted and predictable aspect of any business that extends credit to customers. Bad debt associated with unpaid medical bills accounts for (as of March 2020) 52 percent of all debts sent to collections (Debt.org, "Medical Debt").

The terminology of "bad debt" is somewhat of a misnomer in the health insurance industry, however. That is, while unrecoverable debts are indicated in the accounting methods of the industry, they do not necessarily reflect direct financial losses to (or expenses of) health insurance providers. Lloyd invokes the dissenting opinion of Supreme Court Justice Ruth Bader Ginsberg (in the case of *National Federation of Independent Business v. Sebelius*) to explain the idea that in the health care and health insurance industries, debts are not *absorbed* but *distributed*: "Health care providers do not absorb these bad debts" for unpaid care for the uninsured, she explains. "Instead, they raise their prices, passing along the cost of uncompensated care to those who do pay reliably: the government and private insurance companies" (Ginsberg, qtd. in Lloyd 63). Notably, it is accounting practices and conventions that allow the so-called *unrecoverable* debt to be written off as a loss or expense, even when such losses (in the short term) enable health care providers to justify increased costs and, by extension, profits. Though ultimately contributing to the financial success of the health care system, however, these "bad debts" nonetheless *stick* to debtors—those who would not or could not predict risk or manage finances adequate to avoiding debt. Lloyd draws out the implications of this distributed debt onto the beliefs about "bad debtors," who are positioned as "free riders." Rhetorically, that is, those who do not have health insurance "become a threat to the insured and to the broader health care system because of their failure to function as paying bodies in a circuit of services, exchange, and accumulation" (63). But whereas functionally medical debt is spread throughout the social body, people without insurance or with unpayable medical debt are marked as drains on the economy and the reason health care costs are high: the culprits in the dysfunction of health care and health insurance.

Individuated Options, Individualized Debt

Mapped onto individual decision-making, the entanglement of medical care needs with financial contexts, which range from creditworthiness and the extension of credit as good debt to the denial of credit and presence of bad debt, shapes not only how individuals or households make decisions about managing their own health care (by pursuing or forgoing it) but how they make decisions about other expenses, including housing. As Jessica E. Bielenberg et al. explain in their study of the relationships between medical debt and homelessness in the *Journal of Health Care Organization*, for example, most of the people surveyed (sixty homeless persons in the Seattle area) reported debt, with two-thirds of respondents citing medical debt and half of those attributing medical debt to being homeless (1). Representing those both with and without health insurance (about half each), the homeless persons surveyed who identified problems paying their medical bills "experienced a more recent episode of homelessness 2 years longer than those who did not have such trouble, even after controlling for race, education, age, gender, and health status" (1). The authors further note that "people of color who had trouble paying medical bills reported almost 1 year more homelessness than whites" (1). Certainly indicating a host of systemic failures, these patterns in the relationships between medical debt and homelessness also invite attention to its significance in shaping the lives and livability of those whose health needs outpace their economic means for health care. As Maurizio Lazzarato reminds us, the function of debt is "to make an enterprise of oneself (Foucault)—that means taking responsibility for poverty, unemployment, precariousness, welfare benefits, low wages, reduced pensions, etc., as if these were the individual's 'resources' and 'investments' to manage, as 'his' capital" (*Making* 51). As embodied by those whose medical debts result in homelessness, the individuating and responsibility-making of debt is lived out daily as faulty "choices" about "resources" that result in no less than loss of housing. Moreover, the presence of insurance for half of respondents who cited medical debt as a significant contributing factor to homelessness bespeaks the inability of actuarial methods to calculate risk for the insured. And indeed, it is (economic) risk to the insurance provider that is the subject of calculation.

The inseparability of medical debt from its contexts of emergence and use means it intensifies extant economic patterns and precarities as well as health outcomes themselves. Considering the relationship between debt and health in general terms in a 2016 study, "The High Price of Debt: Household Financial

Debt and Its Impact on Mental and Physical Health," Elizabeth Sweet et al. draw damning conclusions from a study of eighty-four hundred young adults: "In testing multiple indices of debt, we found high household debts relative to assets to be the most consistent and robust predictor of health outcomes. We also found that a high subjective assessment of indebtedness was the strongest predictor of blood pressure, suggesting that psychological dimensions of debt may be particularly salient when it comes to cardiovascular health" (99). Verifying these trends in 2020, Sweet identifies that patterns of changes in behavior (financial and health related) for people with debt correlated with "worse self-rated health, and higher depressive symptoms, anxiety, and perceived stress" (1). Whereas Sweet et al. and Sweet offer compelling evidence of the inverse relationship between all forms of household debt and health, other studies provide a more acute picture of how medical debt in particular shapes health and medical-care-seeking behaviors and outcomes.

For example, in a 2004 study of Baltimore's urban poor published in the *Journal of General Internal Medicine*, Thomas P. O'Toole, Jose J. Arbelaez, and Robert S. Lawrence, characterizing research subjects as either un- or underinsured, found that "over two thirds of those who either had a current medical debt or had been referred to a collection agency reported that it *caused them to seek alternative sites of care or to delay or avoid seeking subsequent care* when needed" (775, emphasis added). They correlated this finding with "aggressive debt restitution practices," whereby "more and more physicians and clinical groups are referring outstanding medical bills to collection agencies much earlier than previously noted" (772). Collection agencies that pursue medical debt, even after it has been *accounted for* as bad debt (again, debt assumed uncoverable), make pennies on the dollar of what is "owed." And yet a whole industry is built on the recollection of so-called bad debt, turning it into income and profit for those who collect it.

Differentiating Debtors

To be sure, it is not only aggressive collection practices that influence health-related behaviors of people with medical debt. As discussed in the *Journal of the American Medical Association* in 2021, "medical debt may compromise seeking or receiving appropriate medical care that may lead to delayed diagnosis of health conditions or exacerbations in preexisting conditions and may potentially contribute to increased risk of premature mortality" (Mendes de Leon and Griggs 228). Moreover, the authors cite "clear evidence for a link of personal debt and financial hardship with poor mental health, which in the case of medical debt could worsen the adverse effects of medical conditions on mental health or vice versa" (228). Careful to qualify these statements with the admission that "little information is available on the downstream health effects of medical debt," the public-health scholars Carlos F. Mendes de Leon and Jennifer J. Griggs nonetheless conclude that "there is solid evidence regarding the association of wealth with important health metrics, such as mortality and disability, and the likelihood of recovery after illness. In addition, the sudden loss of wealth (such as what may occur after serious illness and because of medical bills not covered by health insurance) has been associated with a significant increase in mortality risk" (228).

The positive correlation between medical debt and adverse health—including mental health—means that demographic distinctions in medical debt holdings also indicate demographic differences in health outcomes. A 2016 report conducted jointly by the Kaiser Family Foundation and the *New York Times*, "The Burden of Medical Debt," reveals some of these distinctions, with the following groups more likely than their counterparts to have problems paying medical bills: women, young adults under thirty, adults with children in the house, residents in southern states, people without college degrees, and Black and Hispanic people (Hamel et al. 2). But the "strongest predictors" revealed in the study were not demographics themselves but differences in "income, insurance status, and all 3 measures of health status (being in fair or poor health and having a disability or chronic condition)" (2). Discrepancies, then, among gender and race, for example, are better attributed to the "underlying differences in income and insurance status between these groups and their counterparts" (3).

The report validates findings from the *American Journal of Public Health* published the same year, which considered the overrepresentation of medical debt among older African American adults compared with their white counterparts. While lower socioeconomic indices qualify proportionally more African American older adults for Medicare and Medicaid, "which should alleviate out-of-pocket spending for healthcare" (Wiltshire et al. 1086), barriers to access to these programs combine with significant economic and social obstacles to result in "2.6 times higher odds of medical debt" for African Americans than whites. Jaqueline Wiltshire et al. attempted to disarticulate "economic measures" from "self-rated health status and other covariates," controlling for each in an attempt to isolate the other. They found that "perceived health status explained about 35% of the racial/ethnic disparity in problems paying medical bills, and economic factors explained an additional 39%" (1089). They also found that "older African Americans were more likely than were Whites to be contacted by a collection agency and to borrow money, whereas older Whites were more likely to use savings because of medical bill problems" (1089).

The differential correlates of Wiltshire et al.'s research ground the study in tacit acknowledgment of the relationships between health and financial outcomes and the requirement for normative literacies. Accordingly, they cite "the burden of the eligibility and enrollment process," "the lack of awareness of eligibility," and "racially segregated, low-wage jobs that offer no retiree health benefits [resulting in] . . . avoidance of medical services and nonadherence to prescribed medications because of costs" as some reasons that the disparity in debt between African American and white adults in the United States is so high (1086). At issue, then, is not only an availability of insurance programs—like Medicare or Medicaid—designed for older adults generally but their entanglement in longer histories and larger systems of inequity and the requirement for health care recipients to navigate these histories and systems. While Medicare and Medicaid may be adequate to the needs of an older adult with a personal history of good health, that history also indicates past health insurance (probably employment based) and medical care; education or experience navigating the insurance enrollment processes and medical bureaucracy; geographically accessible health care; and, crucially, functional interactions with health and medical professionals themselves.

Harriet A. Washington's exposé of the historical mistreatment and exploitation of African Americans by the medical industry reveals the requirement of normative health care literacies as adding insult to injury: expecting the medically disenfranchised to rhetorically, ideologically, and, ultimately, economically invest in an industry that emerged as viable on the backs of uncredited and hyperexploited bodies. Moreover, as Dorothy Roberts points out, differential, racialized access to and treatment by the medical and health care industry is ongoing and implicated in contemporary sociopolitical and economic contexts. She argues that "race-based" approaches to medicine, though explicitly designed to invoke race-consciousness and to call attention to differential health outcomes, actually subvert attention to the systemic causes and potential solutions to medical inequities. In her words, "race-based medicine helps to promote a biological explanation for racial inequities that obscures their sociopolitical causes and requires individuals and market-based solutions rather than social change" (538). These market solutions mean that, in the words of Nadine Ehlers and Leslie R. Hinkson, "race-based medicine creates new debts and compounds old ones" (ix).

As an example of market-based solutions leading to new debts, Hinkson examines the correlation between the costs of hypertension medicine and treatments and the demographic patterns of prescription in data collected from 1988 to 1994. With new—and expensive—treatments for hypertension emerging during that period, Hinkson's analysis reveals that "in terms of direct monetary costs, Black women were disproportionately prescribed what was at the time the newest, most expensive drug" (17). And noting the significant difference in earnings between Black women and their white counterparts (in 1992, during her study, Black women made sixty-four cents on the dollar of white men, while white women made seventy-eight cents), Hinkson found that "not only were Black women being prescribed the most expensive drug to control their hypertension at the time but they were also the least financially able to absorb this cost" (18). While such a pattern might be narrated in terms of the affordances of race-based medicine and their alleged ability to better target and address specific needs of particular bodies and groups, Hinkson notes that the medicine being prescribed was still experimental and thus that "the drugs' efficacy and safety was still tenuous" (18). Moreover, centering her study on prescriptions related to a disease with a markedly higher correlation with Black patients, Hinkson reminds us that such a correlation itself must be circumscribed in terms of historical, social, and cultural covariates rather than assumed to be a mere matter of fact for Black bodies. Ehlers and Hinkson invoke the journalist Troy Duster's account of the overrepresentation of hypertension in the Black community to illustrate the point: "If you follow me around Nordstrom, and put me in jail at nine times the rate of whites, and refuse to give me a bank loan, I might get hypertensive" (qtd. in Ehlers and Hinkson xix). One problem with race-based medicine in the United States, then, especially in the context of market-driven medical access and care, is that race is used as a metonym for embodied difference and billed accordingly.

Differential Exposure, Differential Debt

Disarticulating differential health patterns from racialized bodies and acknowledging race in terms of its rhetorico-material production direct attention to significant factors of health disparity. In addition to differential access to insurance, care, and caregiving, for example, Ehlers and Hinkson cite Rinaldo Walcott's terminology of "zones of death" to account for the increased likelihood of minorized communities living "in areas where hazardous waste sites, industrial pollution, and lead exposure are prevalent." They continue, "Landfills and transfer stations, power plants, incinerators, and major highways are more commonly situated in communities of color, creating health risks for minority populations" (xiii). In *Toxic Tourism: Rhetorics of Pollution, Travel, and Environmental Justice*, Phaedra C. Pezzullo affirms that places subject to what she calls "toxic assault" "tend to occur in or on communities that historically have been segregated from elite centers of power" and to be concentrated in "neighborhoods of people of color and low-income communities" (5). Such concentrations are not coincidental but policy driven, reflecting, for example, histories of segregation, racialized housing ordinances, and differential municipal spending and debt (see chapter 3) as well as explicit legal statutes. As Winona LaDuke documents in *All Our Relations: Native Struggles for Land and Life*, American Indian tribes and communities have been systematically exposed to toxins via historical and ongoing land incursions that first relegated tribes and peoples to specific areas and then abused them with industrial and nuclear waste.

An increase in the likelihood of exposure does not disrupt dominant discourses of personal responsibility that frame medical debt, which accumulates for individuals who are presumed to *have* (read: own) health care needs and *have* medical bills. Moreover, the *presence* of toxic exposures or other health risks coincides with the *absence* of medical or heath care centers, which shutter when "bad debt," or bills that cannot be repaid, becomes overwhelming. In response to the correlation of overrepresentation of medical care due to a combination of toxic exposure, costs and inaccessibility of care and healthy food, and violence, this absence has found some response via practices of "medical hot spotting." Designed to account for the overrepresentation of health needs in low-income communities and communities of color, medical hot spotting, as explained by Ehlers and Shiloh Krupar, coordinates medical data, data from geographic information systems, and "spatial profiling" to identify neighborhoods that would benefit from preventative care and other programs. The authors explain how medical hot spotting, driven by and dependent on market logics, however, emerges in relation to the "expense" of these communities, who are understood to be financially burdensome and to overwhelm resources with their medical needs. In their words, an "incentive of medical hot spotting is the aim of minimizing health care expenditure, specifically to lower what is known as uncompensated care debt" (32). Rhetorically, the recipients of this care are reinscribed as financially irresponsible—a fiscal drain on communities. The effect of this framing is that "the most vulnerable are positioned as 'bad' or 'failed' citizens because they are presented as a drain on the U.S. health system and on society at large" (32). Modeled on crime-prediction mapping technologically—itself implicated in racial profiling (see Eubanks; Weisse et al.)—medical hot spotting inverts causal relations between income and race and health, misidentifying the actions and behaviors of low-income and minoritized individuals, households, and communities as the causes of poor health and increased health care need.

Further contextualizing the inverse relationship between medical care and medical debt for African Americans in particular and minoritized groups in general, Ehlers and Hinkson argue that "what ties race-based medicine and debt together is the health debt that has accumulated throughout the African American community over the course of four centuries" (ix). Referencing "foregone health and medical resources," "disproportionate disease burdens," asymmetrical debt accumulation, and the "corporeal, financial, and psychological costs that minorities have to bear as a consequence of their otherness," the authors conclude that race-based medicine "operates in and through a web of debt and indebtedness" (ix). Such debt accumulates for and sticks to individuals and households hailed as consumers of health care. But the relationship between race and debt does not end there. Building on Roberts's work critiquing race-based medicine, Lloyd considers how debt itself is used as rhetorical cover to protect and reproduce medical inequities across race and class. She recounts the actions of seventy-nine Republicans in the US House of Representatives who, in contesting the ACA in 2013, signed a letter rejecting raising the US Treasury's debt ceiling, arguing that it would bankrupt the country and undermine health care. For these congresspeople, the financial health of the country supersedes the physical health of constituents, who are presumed responsible for their own debts. The effect, as Lloyd contends, is that "efforts to block expanded access to health care under the ACA explicitly perpetuate existing social and health injustices, and thereby sanction premature death" (59). Ultimately, she argues that such struggles end up "dividing the worthy and unworthy along racial and class lines," which reveals how "some people's premature deaths can accumulate for others as wealth, health, and political power" (58). While correlating the debts and deaths for some with wealth and accumulation for others would seem to reveal an imbalanced ledger, it accords with accounting logics in which so long as debts are paid, it does not matter who is held to account.

Actuarial Remainders

Ultimately, this division between worthy and unworthy is not only mapped onto individual bodies. Instead, as Ehlers and Hinkson argue, "In a circular operation, this set of choices regarding health care feeds into and compounds the history and present of racial inequality formed by the workings of structural racism and practices of neglect, dispossession, and abandonment" (xii). In other words, asymmetrical, actuarialized histories of health and wealth emerge in differentiated access to and care for individuals who are, in turn, required to demonstrate health and financial literacies to best predict their (individuated) needs. The gulf between need and care is cast as a problem of individual financial planning and bridged by medical debt.

Whereas accounts of medical debt may represent it as the remainder in a calculation where money owed has not been squared with money paid, accounting for this rhetoric *in* debt considers the conditions of possibility for medical debt to emerge as an individual, mathematical calculation, directing analytic attention to interfacing histories and discourses that rhetorically manage risk, sticking it to the bodies and lives of the most precarious by way of economic rationality and health literacy. This is a rhetoric not only *of* medical debt but *in* debt, insofar as histories of actuarial technologies, medical subjectivities, and economic responsibilities map rhetorical possibilities and futures writ large. In the conclusion, then, and supported by this and previous chapter case studies that lay bare the consequences of rhetoric in debt, I pursue this argument more directly, considering how it might be leveraged to reenergize and remap relations among economics and rhetoric to offer more complex accounts of differential debt and to intercede in its insidious work.

Conclusion | Rhetorical Futures in Debt

My internet-assisted research and writing practices mean that I am daily sent Google alerts of debt-related news articles, which paint a picture of an unprecedented global debt crisis emerging from the COVID-19–instigated market slowdown and resulting stimulus packages. Targeted social media ads that algorithmically interpret my interest in debt also mean that I am daily offered debt-relief advice, products, and services. My favorites are headed by narratives of individuals or couples paying off incredible amounts of debt in just a few months by following "one simple rule" (I am not yet sure what that rule is: it is kept behind a paywall). My Amazon algorithm offers me critical social theories and popular press publications that range from explaining finance concepts to selling financial advice, the latter of which is heavily geared toward making smart investments and avoiding debt. During the writing of this book, I engaged with my medical provider a number of times to resolve what appeared to be unpaid bills but represented merely the fiscal difference between what the medical provider calculated as my share of costs versus what my insurance plan was willing to pay. Via my institutional email address, I was sent a survey requesting my input on the design for a new "gateway to campus" bond funded to the costs of $1 million, while my college was asked to reduce its operating budget by the same amount. Meanwhile, my state's balanced-budget requirement was used by the state congress to justify pulling funding from my university's permanent budget, the amount removed equal to that awarded from a one-time Coronavirus Aid, Relief, and Economic Security (CARES) Act payment at the beginning of the COVID-19 pandemic (in spring 2020). The combined effect: I am surrounded by debt, swimming in debt, and yet, as my university faces another budget crisis (in a long line of them) threatening jobs, programs, and research, inevitably meted out on the most vulnerable on campus—staff, part-time instructors, graduate students—we are denied debt.

As I have argued throughout this book, debt does not merely exist as a line of credit available to the financially worthy and literate. Rather, debt, credit, worth, and financial literacy emerge in relation, sticking to bodies and confirming subjectivities in normative ways and across levels of scale. And yet, framed by a commonplace rhetoric of debt-as-existing, as an individual, moral, and calculable choice, a denial of credit to a university in a state whose primary tax revenue (oil and gas) was fundamentally compromised by a pandemic is interpreted as making good sense: it is the moral choice given the university's designation as *not for profit*, where spending on credit might not *pay off*, where administrators should learn to live within their means, tighten their belts, or pursue private partnerships to fund worthy projects (my program in rhetoric and professional communication, for example, is being encouraged to find "revenue streams" that replace a graduate assistant model of graduate funding). It also suggests that we cannot be trusted with debt—our future is not secure enough to underwrite our current needs.

I have also argued throughout this book that the effects of imagining rhetoric and debt separately, where the former merely describes the latter and the latter is assumed to exist independently, are distributed in radically inequitable ways—across bodies and lives, across cities and states, across whole nations. Following colonial, racialized, and gendered histories of value, debt signifies as the extension of credit for the financially literate, those who have significant wealth holdings, historical wealth accumulation, and normed financial practices. Although offered as an indication of worthiness and trust in financial decision-making of individuals, then, debt simultaneously confirms (and reaffirms) acceptable subject positions and practices—who and what matters—legislating and moralizing normative economic relations across levels of scale. Debt serves up "choices" required for economic participation and advance: student loans sponsor employment opportunities; bail bonds are often the only available option to avoid being jailed before a court date; mortgages pave the way for home ownership and wealth accumulation; municipal bonds distribute city amenities and services to its residents; medical bills accompany urgent, emergent, and planned medical services. But its moralistic backhand can be toxic. The onetime student with significant student loan debt and unstable employment should not have taken it out; the family who needs bail bonds to release a loved one from jail should have a savings account (and the loved one should make better life choices); the home owners whose mortgage is higher than the market value of their home should have known better; the city whose residents could not pay their property taxes should not have proposed new capital projects; the person whose body needs medical attention and care should have money set aside in an HSA.

More than just evaluating these so-called choices, these rhetorical rebukes are meted out in terms of affective discipline and livability. In other words, when debt is reduced to a moral calculation of risk made through rational cost-benefit analysis and normative financial literacy, austerity measures become the appropriate response to significant debt. According to this logic, individuals with debt should not only live with the consequences of debt but *feel* the weight of their choices—shamed in segregated lunch lines at school, required to prove worthiness for public assistance, stripped of public and social services. The affects of debt do not only stick punitively, however, reinforcing the immorality of what Darrick Hamilton and William A. Harity Jr. call "bad debt," but buttress credit, or "good debt," as the required means for economic participation. As Maurizio Lazzarato succinctly puts it, "Debt is the technique most adequate to the production of neoliberalism's *homo economicus*" (*Governing* 70).

The persuasive and encompassing rhetoric *of* debt as an individual and moral choice, I have further argued throughout this book, emerges through technologies and practices of accounting that reduce debt to a numerical and mathematical calculation. In other words, when debt is conceptualized numerically, it can be accounted for mathematically, a simple calculation of money lent and money due. By reducing debt to a matter of calculation, however, such accounting practices ignore its complex and violent histories in colonization, slavery, segregation, discrimination, and oppression. Under the rubric of financial accounting as a rational, positivist calculation, debt is simple, merely extant. In order to reframe and intercede in this reductive logos and its violent effects, then, I have proposed and mobilized a methodology capable of accounting for rhetoric in debt. Surfacing the enthymematic reasoning that leads to the conclusion that debt merely exists, I have followed scholars of rhetoric, affect, risk, and scale to offer a counterproposal: it emerges across spatial and temporal scales, entangled with normative rhetorics of individuality and morality, numeracy and rationality. With this inverted premise, I have theorized a methodology capable of tracking the emergence of debt across scales and exposing its differential effects. Mobilizing this methodology as a method has allowed me not only to wrestle debt from some of its commonplaces and resituate it temporally and spatially but to identify avenues for intervention, which I pursue in more detail in this conclusion, because, as discussed in the introduction, technologies (or methodologies) do not merely record who and what matters but fundamentally participate in and sponsor terms of materiality.

Alternative Debts

To be sure, there are other ways to talk about debt that shift attention away from economic exchange and toward more affirmative relations. Indebtedness *often* bespeaks relations irreducible to economic exchange: a debt that can be neither paid off nor expressed in monetary terms. It would seem vulgar, for example, to attempt to express my indebtedness to academic mentors using a monetary calculation. Whereas I probably could identify a percentage of their salary or perhaps a percentage of mine to "repay" the time they spent on me, no dollar amount could accurately express what their "investment" made possible (my student loan payments, my mortgage, my career, this book, my sense of self, my own mentoring practices). Nor would I want it to. To represent such relationships with a dollar amount would, ironically, cheapen them; to calculate the hourly rate of this labor would misrecognize its nonmonetary qualities and value. Yet my graduate school experience—like many others—was also sponsored in part by student loan debt (my own and my mentors'), a risky choice for a humanities degree, a choice not guaranteed to "pay off," economically anyway. And my time in a doctoral program was during the worst economic downturn since the Great Depression, marked by municipal failings and ensuing austerity measures that ravaged state governments and public universities. While such economic debts do not change my feeling of (nonmonetary) indebtedness as fundamentally sponsoring my graduate work and future possibilities as a scholar in my own right (and, indeed, give me even more pause as I consider the complicated contexts in which my own mentors were working to support my peers and me), they do not, either, eliminate the ways in which economic debts sponsored and shaped the same experience. One does not replace the other. Nor does one exist independently of the other. Moreover, the idea that some labor cannot be reimbursed because it cannot be quantified reproduces economic disparities along normative lines. Emotional labor and care work, for example, are denied as labor but nonetheless inequitably required of people of color and women, sans compensation.

To categorically deny the economics of mentoring relationships by admitting that such work cannot be adequately *represented* in terms of money simultaneously denies any claims for financial compensation.

The dangers of this logic are evident in many care and service industries, where the requirements of affective labor are met with affective—rather than monetary—compensation: teachers, social workers, medical assistants, and day-care providers are compensated with *feelings* of pride in their work, social contribution, and moral uprightness rather than strong wages or benefits. This is not to say that affective labor is never met with monetary compensation. Lawsuits that pursue damages for "pain and suffering," for example, lay claim to affective debts that must be serviced monetarily. Insurance providers likewise address pain and suffering monetarily. Here "pain and suffering" is not so much "repaid" as acknowledged by way of a monetary reward. Of course, the calculations for adequate compensation in such cases might *feel* dehumanizing as often as they *feel* appropriate: What is the appropriate award for loss of life or chronic pain? How can such debts be repaid?

Perhaps the starkest example invoking debt and financial repayment in the case of a debt wholly irreducible to money is the argument for reparations for slavery. Indeed, such arguments capitalize on the violent logics of capitalism itself to lay claim to the unpaid debts of slavery, which not only funded the historical and current wealth of the United States and its white citizens but undermine the wealth accumulation and well-being of Black persons and communities in the United States to this day. Although the atrocities of slavery and its afterlives can never be addressed in their entirety through money, which once again equates people with—or reduces people to—the exchange or market value of their labor, arguments for reparations invoke money as (one) necessary acknowledgment of the ongoing effects of slavery. In a popular and anthologized *New Yorker* essay, Te-Nahisi Coates affirms, "Perhaps no number can fully capture the multi-century plunder of black people in America. Perhaps the number is so large that it can't be imagined, let alone calculated and dispensed" (207). While he continues by arguing that "wrestling with these questions matters as much as—if not more than—the specific answers that might be produced" and that such wrestling would be "more important than any single check cut to any African American" (207), others are more insistent that literal repayment cannot be supplanted by scholarly conversation or debate.

In *Rethinking Racial Capitalism*, Gargi Bhattacharyya summarizes "interrelated models" that ground debates about reparations as follows:

- A calculation of the contemporary value of the breached promises of forty acres and a mule for each freed slave
- A calculation of the value created by the forced labor of slaves, and a calculation of contemporary monetary value of this injection of free labor
- A calculation of the continuing economic loss represented by the impact of slavery on nations of the Caribbean
- A calculation of the continuing economic loss represented by the loss of human capital to countries of Africa
- A calculation of the "price" of the injury to enslaved peoples and a calculation of the contemporary value of such compensation for injury to feelings. (92)

Each of these calculations, Bhattacharyya argues, "suggests something of how we might *account* for the impact of past racialised dispossession and exploitation on the racialised patterns of economic life daily." She continues, "Most interestingly, each approach suggests a method of *calculation*, with the strong implication that all such matters can be accounted for, despite the passing of time and the uncertainty of accounting processes" (92, emphasis added).

The uncertainty that Bhattacharyya indicts accords with Coates's recognition that calculation itself is one significant obstacle in ongoing debates about reparations: the question of how atrocity and deprivation can be calculated proves a stumbling block to making the case for its possibility. This failure of imagination is directly linked, following Bhattacharyya, to a failure of accounting—or, to put it otherwise, to an overwhelming trust in accounting systems and technologies inadequate to the complexity and horror of the material. For Caitlin Rosenthal, by contrast, the inability of accounting to account for the horrors of slavery is unsurprising, given that slavery was itself "a laboratory for the development of accounting" (4). Whether a failure or a feature of accounting, however, debts of slavery cannot be calculated when the terms of calculation are inadequate to the complexity of the issue. Because slavery cannot (or should not, anyway) be represented in a double-entry system, calculation seems impossible. In this way, the case for reparations—as literal repayment of the debts of slavery—subverts logics of debt and accounting by dramatizing their failures. Slavery cannot be reduced to monetary debt and repayment. And yet refusing to discuss monetary claims denies the long-term economic impacts of slavery and the real, ongoing effects of economic privations. One does not replace the other. Nor does one exist independently of the other. They are entangled with each other. As Coates puts it, "We cannot escape our history. All our solutions to the great problems of health care, education, housing, and economic inequality are troubled by what must go unspoken" (206).

The case for reparations, then, marshals the unstated premises of debt—that it is individual, moral, calculable—to draw attention to the yet unacknowledged costs and consequences of slavery. To put it otherwise, it is when it is *given* that debt is conceptualized as the calculable responsibility of individuals to repay for past credits or advances that reparations must be repaid. By this logic, individuals must (collectively) repay the long-overdue debt: a financial and moral reckoning. Ironically, the call to equate and redress slavery with financial compensation exposes debt as wholly irreducible to money. But the goal of the call for reparations is not a simple identification or recognition of its irony because monetary compensation, no matter how inadequate, *would* help address the continuing legacies—including economic injustices—of slavery.

Leveraging the unstated premises of debt in this way, I submit, allows Coates, Bhattacharyya, Rosenthal, and others to surface its complex history and differential work. Unlike the increasingly popular demands to *cancel* debt, this argument for reparations acknowledges the messy imbrication of rhetoric *in* debt. A vocal proponent of the call to cancel debt for all, the late David Graeber justified it on the grounds that debt is "the perversion of a promise" (391). Framed in this way, *promising* is a moral act, its perversion immoral. The only appropriate response, according to Graeber, is thus to "wipe the slate clean," which would allow us to reconceptualize how we make promises or "what we truly owe" each other (391). The appeal of starting over, so to speak, is that it ostensibly cancels the stranglehold of historical inequities on present and future opportunities and flourishing. The clean slate is promised as the great equalizer, allowing promises to become something different from a perverse relationship to credit, finance, and global capitalism writ large. Indeed, wiping the slate clean should dispel the disproportionate hold of debt on the flourishing and futures of racialized, minoritized, and otherwise-dispossessed groups.

But influenced by Coates, I submit that wiping the slate clean also, even if unwittingly, erases the histories of debt, denying its emergence and differential effects with the idealistic goal of erasing differences for all. And given that Graeber is so insistent on telling the (five-thousand-year) history of debt, tracing its forms across time and spaces, his proposal to cancel debt cannot *but* be read as a cancellation of history. Erasing and denying history, ugly and implicated in violence as it is, does little to illuminate the unstated premises on which debt rests. Moreover, clearing the ledgers, wiping them clean, does not interrupt the accounting technologies and processes through which individuals (read: debtors) are produced, moralized, and managed. Individuals are not questioned as rational economic actors responsible for decisions about the future; rather, starting with a clean slate, individuals' embodied actions and practices are once again misrecognized as pathological, disarticulated from the complex webs of meaning in which they emerge.

Lazzarato, offering his own critique of Graeber's proposal, contends that "Graeber thinks that debt is merely exchange that has yet to come to an end, presupposing the equality of parties" (*Governing* 84). By contrast, Lazzarato insists that "in finance capitalism, debt is infinite, unpayable, inexpiable, except through political redemption . . . and never through monetary reimbursement" (84). Indeed, "political domination and economic exploitation" (88) are assured when debts are never ending, when credit is always required: "we go from one debt to another, take out credit and repay it, and so on" (89). In this context, given that "the debt of today's capitalism is unpayable, unreimburseable, and infinite," Lazzarato proposes, "we must change the sense of the unpayable by quite simply *not paying*" (89, 90, emphasis added). Despite the seeming similarities with Graeber's call to "wipe the slate clean," Lazzarato asserts a fundamental difference in their conceptualizations of debt; for him, it is "through a *political act*, a refusal, that we will break the relation of the domination of debt" (89, emphasis added). Rather than erasing history by wiping the slate clean or lamenting the apparent inescapability of debt, Lazzarato follows Deleuze to suggest that "there is no need to fear or hope, but only to look for new weapons" (qtd. in Lazzarato, *Governing* 90).

Building on Lazzarato's call for a *political* act rather than an economic reimbursement—or even a clean slate—I suggest that it must also be a *rhetorical* act. Or, rather, to conceptualize the political acts of refusal necessary to divest from logics of and (following Lazzarato) governmentality by debt, we need methodologies capable of accounting for rhetoric in debt. In the remainder of this conclusion, then, I discuss how the methodology of accounting that I propose and practice in this book can both facilitate more just material practices of rhetorical inquiry and contribute to more equitable economic and accounting theories and practices.

More than a Metaphor: Rhetoric in Debt

Articulating a methodology of accounting for rhetoric in debt at the interdisciplinary crossroads of social, cultural, and critical theories of rhetoric, economics, and accounting and the conceptual crossroads of affect, risk, and debt ostensibly invites an almost ready-made genealogy in the Western canon. Who better to drive inquiry into the emergence and effects of debt than Marx, Derrida, Deleuze and Guattari, and Lazzarato? And indeed, my own education and citation practices are indebted to this work, "reverberating," as Kyle P. Vealey and Alex Layne put it, with their profound influence on rhetoric, economics, and the humanities writ large (54). While the conceptual affordances and provocations of this genealogy are vast, however, they simultaneously elide key questions of the imbrication of debt in conquest, colonization, and racialized and gendered oppression, which more explicitly invoke histories of trade and development grounded in people and land as colonial property, always already available to fund capital projects.

Motivated by a feminist commitment to differential embodiment, then, I sought out the theories and scholarship from a variety of disciplines responsive to questions of how and for whom debt emerges and matters, where and how it sticks. Moreover, reminded by Vealey and Layne that "the reverberations of scholarly work not only shape the future but also construct a comprehendible narrative of the past through our practices of citation" (70), I considered how the enthymematic analysis I conducted, the methodology I theorized and mobilized, and the interdisciplinary scholarship I relied on to parse (some of) the complexities of debt might highlight its uneven emergence, its sticky attachments, its differential work. The reverberations of this research compelled me to consider how the case studies of debt I centered in this project *must* contextualize the discourses *of* debt across temporal and spatial scales, marking their emergence within histories of credit (and debt) allocation and denial. In other words, by considering the emergence of rhetorics *of* debt, I identified rhetoric as always already *in* debt, not only coincident but coemergent—not merely a vehicle to describe differential debt but intimately entangled in the production and work of debt to authorize who and what counts, who and how they matter.

My selection of three US-centered case studies both constrains the implications of this work and invites further study. As demonstrated by each chapter, materializing the scalar boundaries through which debts emerge is paramount to my articulation of accounting for rhetoric *in* debt; thus, articulating my own cases vis-à-vis national boundaries was productive—in surfacing certain *kinds* of debts and debtors, histories and elisions—as well as limiting, insofar as I mostly partitioned off questions of transnational finance and trade that are so fundamental to contemporary issues of debt and differential mattering. And indeed, temporal and spatial scales through which debt emerges can hardly be contained by national boundaries. As I suggested in the introduction to this book, however, working to "generate descriptions of localized interaction" (Jung) renders accounts of debts that are otherwise unavailable and, I further propose here, invites additional research that articulates and uses different boundaries to continue to better understand and track rhetoric in debt. As scholars in rhetoric and critical and financial accounting and debt studies take up the charge to consider rhetoric *in* debt, then, I see opportunities to track debt and its affects across national boundaries, in order to better account for the transnational flows of monies, peoples, resources, credit, and debt that participate in differential conditions of possibility. This work would be well supported, too, by reducing scalar boundaries to focus on local interactions: within specific regions, cities, and even institutions.

As scholars of rhetoric seek to interrupt and intervene in patterns and practices of differential mattering, it is imperative that our methodologies build in accounting practices adequate to the complexity of our debts and our (rhetorical) complicity with those debts. It is equally important that they foreground the inequitable distribution of rhetoric and debt, sensitive not only to theoretical and technological accounts of debt but to their uneven effects on communities, bodies, and lives. Accounting for differential mattering, in other words, cannot be conducted through the expansion of rhetorical theory or the refining of accounting technologies but through methodologies that center histories and realities of debt for all, when it is only good for some. Further, such methodologies cannot, as suggested earlier, ignore, deny, or erase the push politics (Peck) or ideological pull of calculation and equivalency but must imagine our rhetorical and economic inheritances as fundamentally entwined in order to imagine them otherwise. In short, rhetoric cannot be cast as a critical heuristic independent of the historical, social, cultural, and economic relations in which *it* emerges. Indeed, as discussed in the introduction to this book, accounting itself is neither ahistorical or arhetorical but the product of histories, discourses, and relations that produce rhetorical equivalencies compressed into numerical equivalencies. Likewise, rhetoric is neither afinancial nor aeconomic but emerges always already in relation to both (Hanan). Erasing this entanglement only denies its history and consequences. To contend with these relations, by contrast, invites a form of interdisciplinary rhetorical accounting that is sensitive to history, to complicity, and to interanimations. This form of accounting not only highlights the construction of our ledgers but materializes our suppressed premises, seeking out the sticking points through which individuals—people, numbers, debts—emerge as stand-ins for rhetoric *in* debt.

Notes

Introduction

1. Translating *homo economicus* as the "economic man" or the "indebted man" is haunted by the troubled lexical and rhetorical relationships between gendered pronouns and generalizations in the English language, whereby "man" or "mankind" stands in for people more generally. But this metonymy also bespeaks gendered assumptions about economic actors, whereby "man" is the presumed referent for economic participation and literacy (see also chapter 1).

2. As the political economist Martijn Konings writes of the US context, for example, in the 1960s and '70s "household debt became a prominent way to secure participation in the American dream, and the baby boomer generation borrowed money for homes, cars, college, and consumption" (107). This increase in credit, borrowing, and debt did not merely "entail comfortable enjoyment of the conveniences of consumer capitalism, but an anxiety driven integration into disciplinary mechanisms of credit and debt in a context of stagnant wage growth and rising unemployment" (107). In the United States in 2019, for example, total consumer debt was recently calculated near $14 trillion, which includes mortgage debt ($9.4 trillion), student loan debt ($1.7 trillion), auto debt ($1.3 trillion), and credit card debt (nearing $1 trillion), each of which increases each successive fiscal quarter (Fay). As reported by the big-data conglomerate Experian, student loan debt itself saw "an increase of 116% in 10 years" as of the first quarter of 2019 (Tatham). Calculated as distinct from consumer debt, medical debt is reported to negatively affect 137 million Americans, contributing to nearly 66 percent of bankruptcy cases in the United States (Konish). In the midst of the global crisis of COVID-19, these numbers have surged.

3. Indeed, in *The Art of Gratitude*, Jeremy David Engels traces neoliberal governance to the rhetoric of debt and indebtedness.

4. Using individual debt to describe debt at larger levels of scale is predicated on what Paul Krugman identifies as a bad metaphor, which "equates the debt problems of a national economy with the debt problems of an individual family." Whereas an individual family might seek financial stability by paying off debt, applying that logic to the economy on a broad scale would result in massive instability: "if everyone simultaneously slashes spending in an attempt to pay down debt ... everyone's income falls—my income falls because you're spending less, and your income falls because I'm spending less. And, as our incomes plunge, our debt problem gets worse, not better" (Krugman).

5. Lazzarato reminds us that "capitalism (and its power) is above all defined as absolute control over what is possible and what is impossible" and that the "first watchword of neoliberalism has been 'there is no alternative'" (*Governing* 23).

6. As the anthropologist Caitlin Zaloom explores in her study of college costs and loans for the US middle class, for instance, whereas college education seemingly offers autonomy and an "open future" to children, it is parents' finances that are required to assess which students qualify for debt (and for how much they qualify). Despite being issued in individual students' names, such debt depends on normative intergenerational relationships wherein parents' financial obligations and assets directly correlate with children's financial opportunities and

futures, and thus individuals within families *feel* the weight of moral responsibility: parents feel guilt for not saving enough for their children's college, anxiety about their own financial futures, and moral obligation to do everything they can to provide opportunities for their children; children feel guilt for their choices of college (metonymically figured in terms of costs) and pressure to make debt feel worthwhile. These feelings of debt are concatenated with individual, moralized choices: individuals, whether students or their parents, take responsibility for fiscal choices and futures by taking on—and paying off—debt.

7. As Oliver and Shapiro note, such differences in opportunity emerge from specific and racialized policies in the United States that extend back to slavery (37) and homesteading and land-grant laws (38), as well as to New Deal eligibility for Social Security benefits (38), Federal Housing Authority policies and practices (39), the Internal Revenue Service's tax code (42), and "barriers that denied blacks access to quality education, job training opportunities, jobs, and other work-related factors" (37). The effect of the programs, policies, and legacies produces what Oliver and Shapiro refer to as "the sedimentation of racial inequality," which acknowledges that the "disadvantaged status of contemporary African Americans cannot be divorced from the historical processes that undergird racial inequality" (50).

8. Oliver and Shapiro evidence as much when they cite the "economic detour" made by Black entrepreneurs who, denied entry or participation into white markets, developed expertise to "create their own opportunities for capital formation and business development" (47–48). As explained by Darrick Hamilton and William A. Darity Jr. in their study "The Political Economy of Education, Financial Literacy, and the Racial Wealth Gap," the (rhetorical) framing of racialized wealth disparities centers "poor financial choices and decision making on the part of largely Black, Latino, and poor borrowers" and a "culture of poverty thesis," which indicts borrowers for "undervaluing and low acquisition of education." They explicitly reject this reasoning, arguing, "*This framing is wrong*—the directional emphasis is wrong. It is more likely that meager economic circumstance—not poor decision making or deficient knowledge—constrains choice itself and leaves borrowers with little to no other option but to use predatory and abusive alternative financial services" (59, emphasis added). Without an explicit invocation of rhetoric, Hamilton and Darity explain how the language used to describe differential wealth accumulation pathologizes it, relying on "the implicit notion that the racial wealth gap is a matter of financial literacy, choice, and agency, as opposed to inheritance and structure. It does not offer sufficient attention to the intergenerational and iterative role of wealth creation" (60). The conceptualization of (financial) literacy that they reject here is one in which literacy is reduced to an individual, volitional, and moral capacity measured against normative standards (of whiteness).

9. In parts of the postbellum South, for example, Indigenous land that was colonized and claimed as property by Europeans was denied ownership to any but white persons, while Black farmers were indebted to white landowners as a condition of sharecropping. As tenants, these Black farmers owed a portion of each crop to their landlords, which continuously indebted them to white landlords. As summarized by Ta-Nehisi Coates describing Mississippi in particular, "Black farmers lived in debt peonage, under the sway of cotton kings who were at once their landlords, their employers, and their primary merchants. Tools and necessities were advanced against the return on the crop, which was determined by the employer. When farmers were deemed to be in debt—and they often were—the negative balance was then carried over to the next season. A man or woman who protested this arrangement did so at the risk of grave injury or death" (165). Such debts were passed on not only seasonally but intergenerationally—as successive generations were shaped and governed by their parents' debts—and across communities: the indenture and debt of individuals effect how they relate to others, economically, socially, and affectively.

10. Sharpe details the specific case of a ship, the *Zong*, as an example of this dehumanizing representation. Overloaded with enslaved persons from the time it set sail, the *Zong* threw between 132 and 142 of those persons overboard during the course of the passage and later claimed insurance monies for them. Because the enslaved persons were recorded as property and not people, however, compensation was addressed through an insurance claim rather than criminal proceedings (for murder).

11. Responding to the use of numerical representations of debt that underwrite its significance as mathematical, universal, and ahistorical, and further problematizing accounting as self-evident, James Alfred Aho identifies the moral, religious, and rhetorical emergence of double-entry bookkeeping, in which debits, debts, or money "owed" (and recorded on the left) are visually represented through numerical values and made to equal credits (recorded on the right), as responsible for the ascendance of debt as mathematical. Aho rejects the reputation of DEB as "simply another mathematical technology," tracking how the "calculative practice emerged from the moral milieu of the late Middle Ages; how Roman Catholic moral theology insinuated itself into commerce via sacramental confession; and how both commerce and morality were changed as a result: morality becoming, as it were, commercialized (more accommodating to the merchant), and commerce 'Christianized'" (*Bookkeeping* 1). The accounting scholar Paolo Quattrone corroborates as much when he contextualizes the disarticulation of "ownership and management" in the nineteenth century in the West, during which accounting "became an instrument of measurement rather than of judgment: a tool for representation rather than one for reflection."

12. As Lamia Karim explains in her book that explores the effects of microfinance on women in Bangladesh, for example, neoliberalism "creates the need to evaluate development as a quantifiable process, such as the decline in fertility rates, number of loans distributed, students enrolled in primary schools, or number of children immunized" (xxv). These acts of quantification are in place to support larger, ideological projects, which "generate new social meanings and identities" and "have profound implications for the ways postcolonial actors think of themselves in this world, and of the possible kinds of selves they believe they can be and of the actions they believe they can perform" (xxv). Indeed, it is when fertility rates, number of loans, level of education, and ratio of immunization are evaluated in Western terms of acceptability that loans are deemed secured for the Bangladeshi women Karim studies. It is not merely math, then, but Western math that is used to calculate risk.

13. In a study that Karim cites about the effects of loans—or debt—on Bangladeshi women, for example, "only 10 percent of women controlled the use of the loans; 72 percent of women said that after enrollment they were 'occasionally' given more importance in family decision making; 28 percent of the women faced physical violence from another member of the family, usually the husband, and 60 percent of these female respondents noted an increase in physical torture" (xxx).

Chapter 1

1. To clarify, acknowledging the entanglements of rhetoric and economics does not *require* heterodox approaches. As McCloskey argued in her 2009 "Rhetoric Matters," "the problem is that economists in their rhetoric have become shameless" (29). For McCloskey, then, the issue is how economics, including orthodox approaches, are *framed* rhetorically and ethically.

2. As a rejoinder to Dana Cloud's positioning class politics as an "objective fact," Greene asserts that "social categories do not exist independently of class and class does not exist independently of other categories of self-definition," which include nation, sexuality, gender,

and race ("Rhetoric and Capitalism" 197). And contravening James Arnt Aune's call to "account for the sexual division of labor," Greene argues that "there remains the conceptual problem associated with the racialization and 'ethnicization' of the division of labor" (192).

3. Rachel Riedner, for example, examines human-interest stories that focus on benevolent gift-giving and individual economic triumph over poverty without acknowledging historical or material complexities, not only exposing the economic rhetoric of such stories (in their specificity) but using them to evidence her broader claim: "stories tell us how neoliberal political economic values are written into everyday life—their 'modes of composition, its rhetoric, its metaphors, its language, its fiction'" (*Writing* xi). As another example, and citing Worsham explicitly in a more recent exploration of the "normative intimacies" required of academic job seekers in rhetoric and composition, Jennifer Sano-Franchini corroborates the entanglements of rhetoric, labor, and affect in reproducing institutional norms. "Analyzing the ways in which candidates are hailed to perform particular normative intimacies during the academic job search," Sano-Franchini argues, "can make clearer how emotions are politicized within the broader context of academia and how that politicization is wrapped up with larger rhetorical exigencies" (101).

4. Indeed, Lazzarato finds similarity between Marx's description (from an 1844 economic manuscript) of the "affective environment in which the relationship between creditor and debtor occurs in both public and private sectors [and which] is ruled by hypocrisy, cynicism, and distrust" and "the modern-day Welfare State" (*Making*, 129).

5. "With neoliberalism, the creditor-debtor relation redefines biopolitical power, since the Welfare State not only intervenes in the 'biology' of the population (birth, death, illness, risks, etc.), it requires ethico-political work on the self, an individualization involving a mix of responsibility, guilt, hypocrisy, and distrust. When social rights (unemployment insurance, the minimum wage, healthcare, etc.) are transformed into social debt and private debt, and beneficiaries into debtors whose repayment means adopting prescribed behavior, subjective relations between 'creditor' institutions, which allocate rights, and 'debtors,' who benefit from assistance or services, begin to function in a radically different way" (Lazzarato, *Making* 130).

6. I follow the feminist philosopher Sandra Harding to distinguish between "methodology" as a "theory and analysis of how research should proceed" and "method" as a "technique for (or way of proceeding in) gathering evidence" (3).

7. Whereas the figure of the bricoleur draws on a "complex networks of theories" (Frost and Haas 92) to navigate corresponding complex rhetorical relations and practices, Kyle P. Vealey and Alex Layne use the figure of indebtedness explicitly to prioritize relations in their feminist methodology of "rhetorical reverberations," which "consciously recognizes [their] knowledge and work as always *indebted* to ways others have made sense of the world" (71, emphasis added). Taken together, these articulations of rhetorical methodologies pave the way for accounting for rhetoric in debt by *both* drawing on a range of theories adequate to understanding debt in its complexity *and* attending to the emergence of debt always in relation to the rhetorics through which it is articulated, whether acknowledged or not.

8. As Royster and Gesa E. Kirsch make clear in *Feminist Rhetorical Practices*, the resonances and relations of rhetorical inquiry or analysis cannot be separated from their objects; in their words, we need to be "deliberate about developing and sustaining throughout the analytical process a more conscious and explicit habit of thinking about our work as part of, rather than disconnected from, other rhetorical enterprises around the world" (145). This is vitally important to building a methodology adequate to accounting for rhetoric *in* debt, which rejects rhetoric *and* debt as a priori or static concepts, insisting, instead, that they emerge *in relation* (see also Greene, "Another Materialist Rhetoric"; Hanan).

9. Chaput helpfully differentiates affect from emotion vis-à-vis sensation: "I reserve the term 'affect' to reference the physiological energies inhabiting the world; I use 'sensation' to

mark the bodily recognition of this energy; and I rely on 'emotion' to denote the rationalizing of that sensation" (4).

10. In September 2019, for example, encouraged by would-be investors, Apple "issued $7 billion in corporate bonds ... even though it has more than $200 billion of cash on hand" (Reinicke). Across financial media, this debt was interpreted as a savvy exploitation of low interest rates, sure to bolster the growth and reputation of the widely respected corporate financial structure of the company.

11. Colombini demonstrates the impossible, normative expectations of financial literacy in her analysis of "hardship letters," a rhetorical prostration expected in the face of mortgage foreclosure: "Threats like bankruptcy, foreclosure, and eviction call upon millions of adults to employ a complex of super-academic literacy skills, including seeking, cultivating, and applying genre knowledge as they craft and deploy consequential discourse" (241). Not focused explicitly on the affective milieu of such expectations, her analysis nonetheless reveals how neoliberal requirements for performances of financial literacy are symptomatic of "the more enduring and overarching rhetorical demands that political economy levies on citizens," which increasingly individuate responsibilities and consequences.

12. To be fair, Lazzarato states explicitly that "capitalism is not a *structure* or a *system*: it develops, transforms, plans, integrates more or less well-adapted procedures according to imperatives of exploitation and domination" (*Making* 107). But he continues, "The power of capitalism, like the world it aims to appropriate and control, is always *in the process of being made*" (107). As articulated, Lazzarato seems to be denying that capitalism is a *closed* system. And Jung's invocation and explanation of complex systems theory resonates with Lazzarato's account of capitalism and—by extension—debt.

Chapter 2

1. In August 2022, the "Biden-Harris Administration Student Debt Relief Plan" was signed into law, which was designed to "cancel $10,000 of student debt for low- to middle-income borrowers" (The White House). Via a White House press release, the plan was justified in terms of its economic threat, explicitly acknowledging that while student loan debt is "a significant burden on America's middle class, ... for the most vulnerable borrowers, the effects of debt are even more crushing" (The White House).

2. Women made up only 32 percent of postsecondary enrollments in 1950 but 57 percent in 2008. In 1967, only 13 percent of Black eighteen- to twenty-four-year-olds enrolled in college, compared with 32 percent in 2008; and in 1972, 13 percent of Hispanic eighteen- to twenty-four-year-olds enrolled, compared to 26 percent in 2008 (Mullen 4).

3. Of course, Millman's definition of "cultural capital" invokes Pierre Bourdieu's germinal definition of the concept.

4. As reported by *Inside Higher Ed*, LGBTQ adults are also more likely to have student loans than non-LGBTQ adults are, an understudied aspect of the gendering and differential impact of student debt (Gravely).

Chapter 3

1. Zaloom uses the case of a first-year college student selected for FAFSA "verification" to highlight the difficulties of both the form and the larger processes in which it is embedded. The student was admitted to and enrolled in college with a specific plan from her divorced

parents detailing their contributions and was required to provide additional information to satisfy additional requirements of the verification process, which added significant stress and discord to the student's semester and family relationships (77–79).

2. Interestingly, in this context, the need for public works and internal improvements and the responsibility of state governments to act as guarantor for bonds were not a partisan issue, despite significant political disputes that characterize the era: "Considering that national politics during the antebellum era emphasized disputes between the Whigs and Democrats on economic issues, it is noteworthy that state politics did not reflect fundamental disagreements over internal improvements. Politics in that area involved intrastate sectional conflicts over where improvements should be built. However, the basic argument that the state should use improvements as an instrument of economic-development policy was not seriously or widely challenged. At its inception, state intervention generally had bipartisan support" (Sbragia 31).

3. Hildreth and Zorn cite, in particular, the profound effect of the 1986 Tax Reform Act (TRA '86), which they call a "watershed event in the market for municipal securities" (128). Whereas prior to the act, "virtually all interest on state and local government debt was exempt from federal taxation," they explain, "once enacted, only particular types of debt were eligible for this federal subsidy and only certain investors could avail themselves of this tax break" (128). Corroborating Sbragia's argument that restrictions propel market innovation, Hildreth and Zorn track the emergence of "derivative products developed to meet the wide variety of financing needs of state and local government issuers" following the passage of TRA '86 (135). They explain that because these "types of debt issues are extremely complex and challenge even the most sophisticated issuers to manage their financial liability risks," regulation increased accordingly, such that "state governments have responded with prescriptive rules while the government finance profession has adopted recommended practices" (135).

4. The funding of local development and infrastructure includes "elementary and secondary school buildings; streets and roads; government office buildings; higher education buildings, research laboratories, and dormitories; transportation facilities, including bridges, highways, roads, airports, ports, and surface transits; electric power-generating and -transmission facilities; water tunnels and sewage treatment plants; resource recovery plants; hospitals, healthcare and assisted living facilities, and nursing homes; [and] housing for low- and moderate-income families" (Temel 1).

> GO bonds are backed by the full faith and credit of the issuing entity and are thereby guaranteed. There is usually a limit set on the amount of GO indebtedness an entity can issue at any one time. This limit is often referred to as the debt limit or debt cap. Revenue bonds do not carry the same guarantee as GO bonds do and are not typically limited by debt cap statutes. While GO bonds are usually paid from ad valorem revenues such as the general tax pool, revenue bonds are funded from specific fees, taxes, or assessments on the item they are supporting. For example, revenue bonds issued to fund a toll road might be repaid using the tolls collected on that road. GO bonds therefore carry lower interest rates because of the full faith and credit guarantee, whereas revenue bonds have higher rates since their repayment is dependent upon the success or failure of the project they support. (Butler et al. 2877)

5. Of note, the ease of voting yes is itself predicated on assumptions of citizenship, functional voter registration, and accessible voting, none of which can be assumed for all residents of a municipality. Moreover, voting districts that are drawn to benefit specific parties can undermine the power of those who can successfully vote.

Works Cited

Abraham, Matthew. "Rhetoric and Composition's Conceptual Indeterminacy as Political Economic Work." *College Composition and Communication*, vol. 68, no. 1, 2016, pp. 68–97.
Access Project. "The Consequences of Medical Debt: Evidence from Three Communities." Feb. 2003, https://www.healthcareconsumers.org/files/med_consequences.pdf.
Addo, Fenaba R., Jason N. Houle, and Daniel Simon. "Young, Black, and (Still) in the Red: Parental Wealth, Race, and Student Loan Debt." *Race and Social Problems*, vol. 8, no. 1, 2016, pp. 64–76.
Ahmed, Sara. *The Cultural Politics of Emotion*. Routledge, 2004.
———. *On Being Included: Racism and Diversity in Institutional Life*. Duke UP, 2012.
———. *What's the Use? On the Uses of Use*. Duke UP, 2019.
Aho, James Alfred. *Bookkeeping and Confession: The Religious, Moral, and Rhetorical Roots of Modern Accounting*. State U of New York P, 2005.
———. "Rhetoric and the Invention of Double Entry Bookkeeping." *Rhetorica: A Journal of the History of Rhetoric*, vol. 3, no. 1, 1985, pp. 21–43.
Akers, Beth, and Matthew M. Chingos. *Game of Loans: The Rhetoric and Reality of Student Debt*. Princeton UP, 2018.
Alter, Charlotte. "Detroit Voting Machine Failures Were Widespread on Election Day." *Time*, 13 Dec. 2016, https://time.com/4599886/detroit-voting-machine-failures-were-widespread-on-election-day/.
Antoniades, Andreas, and Ugo Panizza, editors. *Global Debt Dynamics: Crises, Lessons, Governance*. Routledge, 2019.
Arthur, Chris. "Debt and Financial Literacy Education: An Ethics of Capital or the Other?" *The Debt Age*, edited by Jeffrey R. Di Leo, Peter Hitchcock, and Sophia A. McClennen, Routledge, 2018, pp. 176–96.
———. "Financial Literacy Education as Public Pedagogy for the Capitalist Debt Economy." *Topia: Canadian Journal of Cultural Studies*, vols. 30–31, 2013–14, pp. 147–63.
Asen, Robert. "Neoliberalism, the Public Sphere, and a Public Good." *Quarterly Journal of Speech*, vol. 103, no. 4, 2017, pp. 329–49.
Ashton, Jerry, Robert Goff, and Craig Antico. *End Medical Debt: Curing America's $1 Trillion Unpayable Healthcare Debt*. Hoku, 2018.
Aune, James Arnt. "An Historical Materialist Theory of Rhetoric." *American Communication Journal*, vol. 6, no. 4, 2003, pp. 1–17.
———. *Selling the Free Market: The Rhetoric of Economic Correctness*. Guilford, 2001.
Bateman, Milford, Stephanie Blankenburg, and Richard Kozul-Wright, editors. *The Rise and Fall of Global Microcredit: Development, Debt and Disillusion*. Routledge, 2019.
Baum, Sandy. *Student Debt: Rhetoric and Realities of Higher Education*. Palgrave, 2016.
Bay, Charlotta, Bino Catasús, and Gustav Johed. "Situating Financial Literacy." *Critical Perspectives on Accounting*, vol. 25, no. 1, 2014, pp. 36–45.
Beck, Ulrich. *World at Risk*. Polity, 2007.
———. *World Risk Society*. Polity, 1999.

Berger, Lawrence M., and Jason N. Houle. "Rising Household Debt and Children's Socioemotional Well-Being Trajectories." *Demography*, vol. 56, no. 4, 2019, pp. 1273–1301.

Berlant, Lauren. *Cruel Optimism*. Duke UP, 2011.

Beverungen, Armin, Casper Hoedemaekers, and Jeroen Veldman. "Charity and Finance in the University." *Critical Perspectives on Accounting*, vol. 25, no. 1, 2014, pp. 58–66.

Bhattacharyya, Gargi. *Rethinking Racial Capitalism: Questions of Reproduction and Survival*. Rowman and Littlefield, 2018.

Bielenberg, Jessica E., Marvin Futrell, Bert Stover, and Amy Hagopian. "Presence of Any Medical Debt Associated with Two Additional Years of Homelessness in Seattle Sample." *INQUIRY: Journal of Health Care Organization*, vol. 57, 2020, pp. 1–10.

Billings, B. Anthony, Melvin Houston, and William H. Volz. "How to Navigate Municipal Bankruptcy." *CPA Journal*, May 2017, pp. 52–57.

Bird, Michael Yellow. "Terms of Endearment: A Brief Dictionary for Decolonizing Social Work with Indigenous Peoples." *Indigenous Social Work Around the World: Towards Culturally Relevant Education and Practice*, edited by Mel Gray, John Coates, and Michael Yellow Bird, Ashgate, 2008, 275–92.

Black, Jason Edward. *American Indians and the Rhetoric of Removal and Allotment*. U of Mississippi P, 2015.

BlueCross BlueShield Minnesota. "How Health Insurance Works." https://www.bluecrossmn.com/members/shop-plans/individual-family-health-plans/how-health-insurance-works. Accessed 12 Oct. 2022.

Board of Governors of the Federal Reserve System. "Municipal Liquidity Facility." 10 July 2020, https://www.federalreserve.gov/monetarypolicy/muni.htm.

Bohoslavsky, Juan Pablo, and Kunibert Raffer. "Introduction: We Need to Learn from Experience." *Sovereign Debt Crises: What Have We Learned?*, edited by Juan Pablo Bohoslavsky and Knubert Raffer, Cambridge UP, 2017, pp. 1–11.

———, editors. *Sovereign Debt Crises: What Have We Learned?* Cambridge UP, 2017.

Bousquet, Marc, Tony Scott, and Leo Parascondola, editors. *Tenured Bosses and Disposable Teachers: Writing Instruction in the Managed University*. Southern Illinois UP, 2004.

Brodskey, Richard E. "Something Called the Municipal Securities Rulemaking Board: Unexamined Issues of Constitutionality." *American University Business Law Review*, vol. 8, no. 1, 2019, pp. 23–65.

Brown, Wendy. *Undoing the Demos: Neoliberalism's Stealth Revolution*, Princeton UP, 2015.

Bruner, M. Lane. *Democracy's Debt: The Historical Tension Between Political and Economic Liberty*. Humanity Books, 2009.

Burke, Kenneth. "Terministic Screens." *On Symbols and Society*, U of Chicago P, 1989, pp. 114–25.

Butler, Alexander W., Larry Fauver, and Sandra Mortal. "Corruption, Political Connections, and Municipal Finance." *Review of Financial Studies*, vol. 22, no. 7, 2009, pp. 2873–2905.

Butler, Judith. *Precarious Life: The Powers of Mourning and Violence*. Verso, 2006.

Byrd, W. Michael, and Linda M. Clayton. "The 'Slave Health Deficit': Racism and Health Outcomes." *Health/PAC Bulletin* 21, no. 2, Summer 1991, pp. 25–28.

Calafell, Bernadette M. "Rhetorics of Possibility: Challenging Textual Bias Through the Theory of the Flesh." *Rhetorica in Motion: Feminist Rhetorical Methods and Methodologies*, edited by Eileen E. Schell and K. J. Rawson, U of Pittsburgh P, 2010, pp. 104–17.

Carruthers, Bruce G., and Wendy Nelson Espeland. "Accounting for Rationality: Double-Entry Bookkeeping and the Rhetoric of Economic Rationality." *American Journal of Sociology*, vol. 97, no. 1, 1991, pp. 31–69.

Chakravartty, Paula, and Denise Ferreira da Silva. "Accumulation, Dispossession, and Debt: The Racial Logic of Global Capitalism—An Introduction." *American Quarterly*, vol. 64, no. 3, 2012, pp. 361–85.
Chaput, Catherine. *Market Affect and the Rhetoric of Political Economic Debate*. South Carolina UP, 2019.
Chaput, Catherine, M. J. Braun, and Danika M. Brown, editors. *Entertaining Fear: Rhetoric and the Political Economy of Social Control*. Peter Lang, 2010.
Chaput, Catherine, and Crystal Broch Colombini. "The Mathematization of the Invisible Hand: Rhetorical Energy and the Crafting of Economic Spontaneity." *Arguing with Numbers: The Intersections of Rhetoric and Mathematics*, edited by James Wynn and G. Mitchell Reyes, Penn State UP, 2021, pp. 55–81.
Charland, Maurice. "Constitutive Rhetoric: The Case of the Peuple Québécois." *Quarterly Journal of Speech*, vol. 73, no. 2, 1987, pp. 133–50.
Christie, Hazel, and Moira Monroe. "The Logic of Student Loans: Students' Perceptions of the Costs and Benefits of the Student Loan." *British Journal of Sociology of Education*, vol. 24, no. 5, 2003, pp. 621–36.
Cigna. "How Health Insurance Works." https://www.cigna.com/individuals-families/understanding-insurance/how-health-insurance-works. Accessed 10 Dec. 2021.
City of Las Cruces. "Go Build: General Obligation Bonds—Building Your Future." https://www.clcbond.org. Accessed 31 July 2020.
Cloud, Dana L. "Book Review: Rhetoric and Economics: Or How Rhetoricians Can Get a Little Class." *Quarterly Journal of Speech*, vol. 88, no. 3, 2002, pp. 342–58.
———. *Reality Bites: The Rhetorical Circulation of Truth Claims in US Political Culture*. Ohio State UP, 2018.
Clough, Patricia, with Jean Halley, editors. *The Affective Turn: Theorizing the Social*. Duke UP, 2007.
Coates, Ta-Nehisi. *We Were Eight Years in Power: An American Tragedy*. One World, 2017.
Codagnone, Cristiano, Athina Karatzogianni, and Jacob Matthews, editors. *Platform Economics: Rhetoric and Reality in the Sharing Economy*. Emerald, 2019.
Cohen, Patricia Cline. *A Calculating People: The Spread of Numeracy in Early America*. Routledge, 1999.
Colombini, Crystal Broch. "Composing Crisis: Hardship Letters and the Political Economics of Genre." *College English*, vol. 80, no. 3, 2018, pp. 218–46.
Conley, Dalton. *Being Black, Living in the Red*. U of California P, 2010.
Connolly, William E. "Materialities of Experience." *New Materialisms: Ontology, Agency, Politics*, edited by Diana Coole and Samantha Frost, Duke UP, 2010, pp. 178–200.
Coultard, Glen. *Red Skin, White Masks: Rejecting the Colonial Politics of Recognition*. U of Minnesota P, 2014.
Critical Perspectives on Accounting. Home page, edited by Jane Andrew, Christine Cooper, and Yves Gendron, https://www.journals.elsevier.com/critical-perspectives-on-accounting. Accessed 16 July 2020.
Crotty, James. "The Great Austerity War: What Caused the US Deficit Crisis and Who Should Pay to Fix It?" *Cambridge Journal of Economics*, vol. 36, no. 1, 2012, pp. 79–104.
Cunningham, Robert M., Jr., and Robert Cunningham III. *The Blues: A History of the Blue Cross and Blue Shield System*. Northern Illinois UP, 1997.
Dabney, H. Slayton, Patrick Darby, Daniel G. Egan, Marc A. Levinson, George B. South III, and Emily J. Tidmore. *Municipalities in Peril: The ABI Guide to Chapter 9*. 2nd ed., American Bankruptcy Institution, 2012.

Debt.org. "Medical Debt and Collections." https://www.debt.org/medical/collections/. Accessed 10 Dec 2021.

———. "Students and Debt." https://www.debt.org/students/. Accessed 28 July 2020.

———. "Timeline of the U.S. Federal Debt Since Independence Day 1776." https://www.debt.org/faqs/united-states-federal-debt-timeline/. Accessed 7 Oct. 2022.

"Deficit Spending." *Encyclopedia.com*, https://www.encyclopedia.com/economics/encyclopedias-almanacs-transcripts-and-maps/deficit-spending. Accessed 28 July 2002.

Deleuze, Gilles, and Félix Guattari. *A Thousand Plateaus: Capitalism and Schizophrenia*. U of Minnesota P, 1987.

Derrida, Jacques. *Spectres of Marx: The State of Debt, The Work of Mourning, and the New International*. Routledge, 2006.

Dingo, Rebecca. *Networking Arguments: Rhetoric, Transnational Feminism, and Public Policy Writing*. U of Pittsburgh P, 2012.

———. "Re-evaluating Girls' Empowerment: Toward a Transnational Feminist Literacy." *Circulation, Writing, and Rhetoric*, edited by Laurie E. Gries and Collin Gifford Brooke, Utah State UP, 2018, pp. 135–51.

Dingo, Rebecca, Rachel Riedner, and Jennifer Wingard. "Toward a Cogent Analysis of Power: Transnational Rhetorical Studies." *JAC*, vol. 33, nos. 3–4, 2013, pp. 517–28.

Dobkin, Carlos, Amy Finkelstein, Raymond Kluender, and Matthew J. Notowidigo. "The Economic Consequences of Hospital Admissions." *American Economic Review*, vol. 108, no. 2, 2018, pp. 308–52.

Dolmage, Jay Timothy. *Academic Ableism: Disability and Higher Education*. U of Michigan P, 2017.

———. *Disabled upon Arrival: Eugenics, Immigration, and the Construction of Race and Disability*. Ohio State UP, 2018.

Donaldson, Cam, and Karen Gerard. *Economics of Health Care Financing: The Visible Hand*. 2nd ed., Palgrave Macmillan, 2005.

Donovan, Donal, and Antoin E. Murphy. *The Fall of the Celtic Tiger: Ireland and the Euro Debt Crisis*. Oxford UP, 2013.

Dougal, Casey, Pengjie Gao, William J. Mayew, and Christopher A. Parsons. "What's in a (School) Name? Racial Discrimination in Higher Education Bond Markets." *Journal of Financial Economics*, vol. 134, no. 3, 2019, pp. 570–90.

Douglas, Alexander X. *The Philosophy of Debt*. Routledge, 2016.

Duerringer, Christopher M. "Research in the Rhetoric of Economics: A Critical Review." *Review of Communication*, vol. 18, no. 4, 2018, pp. 284–300.

Dwyer, Rachel E. "Credit, Debt, and Inequality." *Annual Review of Sociology*, vol. 44, 2018, pp. 237–61.

Dwyer, Rachel E., Randy Hodson, and Laura McCloud. "Gender, Debt, and Dropping Out of College." *Gender and Society*, vol. 27, no. 1, 2013, pp. 30–55.

Dwyer, Rachel E., Laura McCloud, and Randy Hodson. "Debt and Graduation from American Universities." *Social Forces*, vol. 90, no. 4, 2012, pp. 1133–55.

Edbauer, Jenny. "Unframing Models of Public Distribution: From Rhetorical Situation to Rhetorical Ecologies." *Rhetoric Society Quarterly*, vol. 35, no. 4, 2005, pp. 5–24.

Edwards, Mike, and Jessica Reyman. "Open Access and the Economics of Scholarship in Rhetoric and Composition Studies" *Rhetoric Review*, vol. 37, no. 2, 2018, pp. 212–25.

Ehlers, Nadine, and Leslie R. Hinkson. "Race-Based Medicine and the Specter of Debt." *Subprime Health: Debt and Race in U.S. Medicine*, edited by Nadine Ehlers and Leslie R. Hinkson, U of Minnesota P, 2017, pp. vii–xxxi.

Ehlers, Nadine, and Shiloh Krupar. "'When Treating Patients like Criminals Makes Sense': Medical Hot Spotting, Race, and Debt." *Subprime Health: Debt and Race in U.S. Medicine*, edited by Nadine Ehlers and Leslie R. Hinkson, U of Minnesota P, 2017, pp. 31–54.

Engels, Jeremy David. *The Art of Gratitude*. State U of New York P, 2019.

Enoch, Jessica. *Domestic Occupations: Spatial Rhetorics and Women's Work*. Southern Illinois UP, 2019.

Erie, Steven P. "How the Urban West Was Won." *Urban Affairs Quarterly*, vol. 27, no. 4, 1992, pp. 519–54.

Eubanks, Virginia. *Automating Inequality: How High-Tech Tools Profile, Police, and Punish the Poor*. Picador, 2018.

Fay, Bill. "Key Figures Behind America's Consumer Debt." *Debt.org*, https://www.debt.org/faqs/americans-in-debt/. Accessed 5 Aug. 2020.

Federal Student Aid. "Coronavirus and Forbearance Info for Students, Borrowers, Parents." https://studentaid.gov/announcements-events/coronavirus. Accessed 28 July 2020.

FICO. "What's in My FICO Scores?" *myFICO*. https://www.myfico.com/credit-education/whats-in-your-credit-score. Accessed 16 July 2020.

Flores, Lisa A. "Between Abundance and Marginalization: The Imperative of Racial Rhetorical Criticism." *Review of Communication*, vol. 16, no. 1, 2016, pp. 4–24.

———. *Deportable and Disposable: Public Rhetoric and the Making of the "Illegal" Immigrant*. Penn State UP, 2020.

Flynn, David T. "Credit in the Colonial American Economy." *EconomicHistory.net*, 16 Mar. 2008, https://eh.net/encyclopedia/credit-in-the-colonial-american-economy/.

Food and Nutrition Service, US Department of Agriculture. "Proposed Rule: Revision of Categorical Eligibility in the SNAP." 24 July 2019. https://www.fns.usda.gov/snap/fr-072419.

Foucault, Michel. *The Birth of Biopolitics: Lectures as the Collège de France 1978–1979*. Edited by Michel Sennellart, translated by Graham Burchell. Picador, 2008.

Frees, Edward W., Richard A. Derrig, and Glenn Meyers. *Predictive Modeling Applications in Actuarial Science*, vol. 1. Cambridge UP, 2014.

Friedman, Zach. "DeVos: Here's Why We Want to End Student Loan Forgiveness Program." *Forbes*, 8 Mar. 2020, https://www.forbes.com/sites/zackfriedman/2020/03/07/student-loans-forgiveness-devos/#79b32b04184c.

Frost, Erin A., and Angela M. Haas. "Seeing and Knowing the Womb: A Technofeminist Reframing of Fetal Ultrasound Toward a Decolonization of Our Bodies." *Computers and Composition*, vol. 43, 2017, pp. 88–105.

Fu, Jessica. "Lots of American Families Are Struggling with Student Lunch Debt. What's the Solution?" *Chalkbeat*, 25 Apr. 2019, https://www.chalkbeat.org/2019/4/25/21108020/lots-of-american-families-are-struggling-with-student-lunch-debt-what-s-the-solution.

Fuller, Matthew B. "A History of Financial Aid to Students." *Journal of Student Financial Aid*, vol. 44, no. 1, 2014, pp. 42–68.

Gao, Pengjie, Chang Lee, and Dermot Murphy. "Municipal Borrowing Costs and State Policies for Distressed Municipalities." *Journal of Financial Economics*, vol. 132, no. 2, 2019, 404–26.

Goldrick-Rab, Sara. *Paying the Price: College Costs, Financial Aid, and the Betrayal of the American Dream*. U of Chicago P, 2016.

Grabill, Jeffrey T., and W. Michelle Simmons. "Toward a Critical Rhetoric of Risk Communication: Producing Citizens and the Role of Technical Communicators." *Technical Communication Quarterly*, vol. 7, no. 4, 1998, pp. 415–41.

Graeber, David. *Debt: The First 5,000 Years*. Melville, 2011.

Gravely, Alexis. "Study: LGBTQ Adults More Likely to Have Federal Student Loans." *Inside Higher Ed*, 28 July 2021, https://www.insidehighered.com/quicktakes/2021/07/28/study-lgbtq-adults-more-likely-have-federal-student-loans.

Greene, Ronald Walter. "Another Materialist Rhetoric." *Critical Studies in Mass Communication*, vol. 15, no. 1, 1998, pp. 21–40.

———. "Rhetoric and Capitalism: Rhetorical Agency as Communicative Labor." *Philosophy and Rhetoric*, vol. 37, no. 3, 2004, pp. 188–206.

Grewal, Inderpal, and Caren Kaplan. "Global Identities: Theorizing Transnational Studies of Sexuality." *GLQ*, vol. 7, no. 4, 2001, pp. 663–79.

Gupta, Arpit, Edward R. Morrison, Catherine R. Fedorenko, and Scott Ramsey. "Leverage, Default, and Mortality: Evidence from Cancer Diagnoses." Columbia Law and Economics Working Paper No. 514, Columbia Business School Research Paper No. 15-35, 2015, pp. 1–58.

Haberman, Steven, and Trevor A. Sibbett. Introduction to Richard Price, "Observations on Reversionary Payments." *Health and Sickness Insurance*, vol. 9 of *History of Actuarial Science*, edited by Steven Haberman and Trevor A. Sibbett, Pickering & Chatto, 1995, p. 2.

Hamilton, Darrick, and William A. Darity Jr. "The Political Economy of Education, Financial Literacy, and the Racial Wealth Gap." *Federal Reserve Bank of St. Louis Review*, vol. 99, no. 1, 2017, pp. 59–76.

Hamel, Liz, Mira Norton, Karen Pollitz, Larry Levitt, Gary Claxton, and Mollyann Brodie. "The Burden of Medical Debt: Result from the Kaiser Family Foundation / New York Times Medical Bills Survey." Henry J. Kaiser Foundation, Jan. 2016, https://www.kff.org/wp-content/uploads/2016/01/8806-the-burden-of-medical-debt-results-from-the-kaiser-family-foundation-new-york-times-medical-bills-survey.pdf.

Hanan, Joshua S. "From Economic Rhetoric to Economic Imaginaries: A Critical Genealogy of Economic Rhetoric in U.S. Communication Studies." *Communication and the Economy: History, Value and Agency*, edited by Joshua S. Hanan and Mark Hayward, Peter Lang, 2014, pp. 67–93.

Hanan, Joshua S., and Catherine Chaput. "Theories of Economic Justice in the Rhetorical Tradition." *Oxford Research Encyclopedias*, 22 Nov. 2016, https://oxfordre.com/view/10.1093/acrefore/9780190228613.001.0001/acrefore-9780190228613-e-148.

Hanan, Joshua S., and Mark Hayward, editors. *Communication and the Economy: History, Value and Agency*. Peter Lang, 2014.

Harding, Sandra. "Introduction: Is There a Feminist Method?" *Feminism and Methodology: Social Science Issues*, edited by Sandra Harding, Indiana UP, 1987, pp. 1–14.

Harvey, David. *A Brief History of Neoliberalism*. Oxford UP, 2005.

Haynes, Cynthia. *The Homesick Phonebook: Addressing Rhetorics in the Age of Perpetual Conflict*. Southern Illinois UP, 2016.

HealthCare.gov. "How to Pick a Health Insurance Plan: 3 Things to Know Before You Pick a Health Insurance Plan." https://www.healthcare.gov/choose-a-plan/comparing-plans/. Accessed 10 Dec. 2021.

Health Resources and Services Administration. "Health Literacy." https://www.hrsa.gov/about/organization/bureaus/ohe/health-literacy/index.html. Accessed 10 Dec. 2021.

Herring, William Rodney. "Neither Pistols nor Sugar Plums: The Rhetoric of Finance and the 1720 Bubbles." *Advances in the History of Rhetoric*, vol. 21, no. 2, 2018, pp. 147–62.

———. "The Rhetoric of Credit, The Rhetoric of Debt: Economic Arguments in Early America and Beyond." *Rhetoric and Public Affairs*, vol. 19, no. 1, 2016, pp. 45–82.

Herring, William Rodney, and Mark Garrett Longaker. "Rhetoric as Economics: Samuel Newman and David Jayne Hill on the Problem of Representation." *Rhetoric Review*, vol. 31, no. 3, 2012, pp. 236–53.

Hesford, Wendy S. *Spectacular Rhetorics: Human Rights Visions, Recognitions, Feminisms*. Duke UP, 2011.

Hesford, Wendy S., Adela C. Licona, and Christa Teston. "Rhetorical Recalibrations and Response-abilities." *Precarious Rhetorics*, edited by Wendy S. Hesford, Adela C. Licona, and Christa Teston, Ohio State UP, 2018, pp. 1–17.

Hildreth, W. Bartley, and C. Kurt Zorn. "The Evolution of the State and Local Government Municipal Debt Market over the Past Quarter Century." *Public Budgeting and Finance*, vol. 25, no. 4s, 2005, pp. 127–53.

Hinkson, Leslie R. "The High Cost of Having Hypertension While Black in America." *Subprime Health: Debt and Race in U.S. Medicine*, edited by Nadine Ehlers and Leslie R. Hinkson, U of Minnesota P, 2017, pp. 3–30.

Hoffman, Beatrix. *The Wages of Sickness: The Politics of Health Insurance in Progressive America*. U of North Carolina P, 2001.

IFRS. "IASB Clarifies Its Definition of Material." 31 Oct. 2018, https://www.ifrs.org/news-and-events/2018/10/iasb-clarifies-its-definition-of-material/.

Intermountain Healthcare. "What Is Managed Care? And How Does It Make Healthcare Better?" *Intermountain Healthcare Blog*, 21 Apr. 2021, https://hcpnv.com/blog/what-is-managed-care-and-how-does-it-make-healthcare-better/.

Investopedia. "Municipal Bonds." https://www.investopedia.com/terms/m/municipalbond.asp. Accessed 12 Oct. 2022.

Issar, Siddhant. "Listening to Black Lives Matter: Racial Capitalism and the Critique of Neoliberalism." *Contemporary Political Theory*, vol. 20, no. 1, 2021, pp. 48–71.

Jackson, Brandon A., and John R. Reynolds. "The Price of Opportunity: Race, Student Loan Debt, and College Achievement." *Sociological Inquiry*, vol. 83, no. 3, 2013, pp. 335–68.

Jackson, Matthew. "The Enthymematic Hegemony of Whiteness: The Enthymeme as Antiracist Rhetorical Strategy." *JAC*, vol. 26, nos. 3–4, 2006, pp. 601–41.

Joseph, Miranda. *Debt to Society: Accounting for Life Under Capitalism*. U of Minnesota P, 2014.

Jung, Julie. "Systems Rhetoric: A Dynamic Coupling of Explanation and Description." *Enculturation*, vol. 17, 2014, http://enculturation.net/systems-rhetoric.

Kalousova, Lucie, and Sarah A. Burgard. "Debt and Foregone Medical Care." *Journal of Health and Social Behaviors*, vol. 54, no. 2, 2013, pp. 204–20.

Karim, Lamia. *Microfinance and Its Discontents: Women in Debt in Bangladesh*. U of Minnesota P, 2011.

Katz, Steven. "The Ethic of Expediency: Classical Rhetoric, Technology, and the Holocaust." *College English*, vol. 54, no. 3, 1992, pp. 255–75.

Klamer, Arjo, Deirdre McCloskey, and Robert M. Solow. Preface. *The Consequences of Economic Rhetoric*, edited by Arjo Klamer, Deirdre McCloskey, and Robert M. Solow, Cambridge UP, 1988, pp. vii–x.

Kluender, Raymond, Neale Mahoney, Francis Wong, and Wesley Yin. "Medical Debt in the US, 2009–2020." *Journal of the American Medical Association*, vol. 326, no. 3, 2021, pp. 250–56.

Knutson, Brian, and Gregory R. Samanez-Larkin. "Brain, Decision, and Debt." *A Debtor World: Interdisciplinary Perspectives on Debt*, edited by Ralph Brubaker, Robert M. Lawless, and Charles J. Tabb, Oxford UP, 2012, pp. 167–80.

Konings, Martijn. *The Emotional Logic of Capitalism: What Progressives Have Missed.* Stanford UP, 2015.
Konish, Lorie. "137 Million Americans Are Struggling with Medical Debt. Here's What to Know If Your Need Some Relief." *CNBC*, 10 Nov 2019, https://www.cnbc.com/2019/11/10/americans-are-drowning-in-medical-debt-what-to-know-if-you-need-help.html.
Krippner, Greta R. *Capitalizing on Crisis: The Political Origins of the Rise of Finance.* Harvard UP, 2011.
Krugman, Paul. "The Austerity Agenda." *The New York Times*, 31 May 2012, https://www.nytimes.com/2012/06/01/opinion/krugman-the-austerity-agenda.html.
Kundnani, Arun. "The Racial Constitution of Neoliberalism." *Race & Class*, vol. 63, no. 1, 2021, pp. 51–69.
LaDuke, Winona. *All Our Relations: Native Struggles for Land and Life.* South End, 1999.
Lakoff, George, and Mark Johnson. *Metaphors We Live By.* 1980. U of Chicago P, 2003.
Law Insider. "Medical Debt." https://lawinsider.com/dictionary/medical-debt#. Accessed 12 Oct. 2022.
Lazzarato, Maurizio. *Governing by Debt.* Translated by Joshua David Jordan. Semiotext(e) 17, 2013.
———. *The Making of the Indebted Man.* Translated by Joshua David Jordan. Semiotext(e) 13, 2011.
Lea, Stephen E. G., Avril J. Mewse, and Wendy Wrapson. "The Psychology of Debt in Poor Households in Britain." *A Debtor World: Interdisciplinary Perspectives on Debt*, edited by Ralph Brubaker, Robert M. Lawless, and Charles J. Tabb, Oxford UP, 2012, pp. 151–66.
Lee, Shawna J., Amy Krings, Sara Rose, Krista Dover, Jessica Ayoub, and Fatima Salman. "Racial Inequality and the Implementation of Emergency Management Laws in Economically Distressed Urban Areas." *Children and Youth Services Review*, vol. 70, 2016, pp. 1–7.
Legal Information Institute. "Definition of Disability." U.S. Code 42, Chapter 162, §12102. https://www.law.cornell.edu/uscode/text/42/12102. Accessed 5 Dec. 2021.
Lepore, Jill. *These Truths: A History of the United States.* Norton, 2018.
Lindquist, Julie. *A Place to Stand: Politics and Persuasion in a Working-Class Bar.* Oxford UP, 2002.
Lloyd, Jenna M. "Obamacare and Sovereign Debt: Race, Reparations, and the Haunting of Premature Death." *Subprime Health: Debt and Race in U.S. Medicine*, edited by Nadine Ehlers and Leslie R. Hinkson, U of Minnesota P, 2017, pp. 55–82.
Lou, Michelle. "75% of US School Districts Report Student Meal Debt. Here's What They're Doing to Combat the Problem." *CNN*, 17 May 2019, https://www.cnn.com/2019/05/17/us/unpaid-school-lunch-debt-trnd/index.html.
MacDonald, Christine, and Mike Wilkinson. "Half of Detroit Property Owners Don't Pay Taxes." *Detroit News*, 21 Feb 2013, https://www.detroitnews.com/story/news/local/detroit-city/2018/06/13/detroit-property-owners-tax-delinquency/700005002/.
Mantzari, Elisavet, and Omiros Georgiou. "Ideological Hegemony and Consent to IFRS: Insights from Practitioners in Greece." *Critical Perspectives on Accounting*, vol. 59, 2019, pp. 70–93.
Martin, Randy. *Financialization of Daily Life.* Temple UP, 2002.
Massumi, Brian. *Parable of the Virtual: Movement, Affect, Sensation.* Duke UP, 2002.
MaterialityTracker.net. "Financial Thresholds." https://www.materialitytracker.net/standards/financial-thresholds/. Accessed 16 July 2020.
McCloskey, Deirdre N. "Rhetoric Matters: Ethical Standards in a Humanist Science of Economics." *Challenge*, vol. 52, no. 4, 2009, pp. 25–31.

———. *The Rhetoric of Economics*, 2nd edition. U of Wisconsin P, 1985.
———. "The Rhetoric of Finance." *The New Palgrave Dictionary of Money and Finance*, 1992, pp. 350–52.
McGee, Michael Calvin. "'The Ideograph': A Link Between Rhetoric and Ideology." *Quarterly Journal of Speech*, vol. 66, no. 1, 1980, pp. 1–16.
McKerrow, Raymie. "Critical Rhetoric: Theory and Praxis." *Communication Monographs*, vol. 56, no. 2, 1989, pp. 91–111.
Mearman, Andrew. "Who Do Heterodox Economists Think They Are?" *The American Journal of Economics and Sociology*, vol. 70, no. 2, 2011, pp. 480–510.
Mendes de Leon, Carlos F., and Jennifer J. Griggs. "Editorial: Medical Debt as a Social Determinant of Health." *Journal of the American Medical Association*, vol. 326, no. 3, 2021, pp. 228–29.
Merskin, Debra. "The Show for Those Who Owe: Normalization of Credit on Lifetime's 'Debt.'" *Journal of Communication Inquiry*, vol. 22, no. 1, 1998, pp. 10–26.
Millet, Catherine M. "How Undergraduate Loan Debt Affects Application and Enrollment in Graduate or First Professional School." *The Journal of Higher Education*, vol. 74, no. 4, 2003, pp. 386–427.
Millman, Marcia. *Warm Hearts and Cold Cash: The Intimate Family Dynamics of Family and Money*. Free Press, 1991.
Moniz, Michelle H., A. Mark Fendrick, Giselle E. Kolenick, Anca Tilea, Lindsay K. Admon, and Vanessa K. Dalton. "Out-of-Pocket Spending for Maternity Care Among Women With Employer-Based Insurance, 2008–15." *Health Affairs*, vol. 39, no. 1, 2020, pp. 18–23.
Mountford, Roxeanne. "From Labor to Middle Management: Graduate Students in Writing Program Administration." *Rhetoric Review*, vol. 21, no. 1, 2002, pp. 41–53.
Mullen, Ann L. *Degrees of Inequality: Culture, Class, and Gender in American Higher Education*. Johns Hopkins UP, 2012.
Municipal Securities Rulemaking Board (MSRB). "Credit Rating Basics for Municipal Bonds on EMMA." https://www.msrb.org//media/Files/Education/Credit-Rating-Basics-for-Municipal-Bond-Investors.ashx??. Accessed 31 July 2020.
———. "Municipal Securities Rulemaking Board's Website Terms of Use." Electronic Municipal Market Access, 25 Oct. 2021, https://emma.msrb.org/AboutEmma/User Agreement.
———. "Supplement to Official Statement." $18,000,000 City of Las Cruces, New Mexico General Obligation Improvement Bonds Series 2019, 12 Feb. 2019, Electronic Municipal Market Access, https://emma.msrb.org/IssueView/Details/ES392401.
———. "Terms of Use." https://emma.msrb.org/IssuerHomePage/. Accessed 31 July 2020.
Murray, John E. *Origins of American Health Insurance*. Yale UP, 2007.
National Center for Education Statistics. "Tuition Costs of Colleges and Universities." https://nces.ed.gov/fastfacts/display.asp?id=76. Accessed 28 July 2020.
National Council on Disability. "Appendix B: A Brief History of Managed Care." https://www.ncd.gov/policy/appendix-b-brief-history-managed-care. Accessed 10 Dec. 2021.
National Information Management and Support System (NIMSS). "NC2172: Behavioral Economics and the Intersection of Healthcare and Financial Decision Making Across the Lifespan." https://www.nimss.org/projects/view/mrp/outline/18455. Accessed 10 Dec. 2021.
National Public Radio. "Comment Period Ends for Proposal that Would Cut SNAP Benefits for Millions." 1 Nov. 2019, https://www.npr.org/2019/11/01/775078148/comment-period-ends-for-proposal-that-would-cut-snap-benefits-for-millions.
Neilson, Brett, and Ned Rossiter. "From Precarity to Precariousness and Back Again: Labour, Life and Unstable Networks." *The Fibreculture Journal*, vol. 5, 2005, https://five.fibre

culturejournal.org/fcj-022-from-precarity-to-precariousness-and-back-again-labour-life-and-unstable-networks/.

Nevarez, Jessica. "Las Cruces Residents Still Have Time to Vote in Go Bond Election." *Las Cruces Sun News*, 3 Aug. 2018, https://www.ktsm.com/local/las-cruces-news/las-cruces-residents-still-have-time-to-vote-in-the-go-bond-election/.

Newcomb, Matthew J. "Feeling the Vulgarity of the Numbers: The Rwandan Genocide and the Classroom as a Site of Response to Suffering." *JAC*, vol. 30, no. 1–2, 2010, pp. 175–213.

Newfield, Christopher. "Student Debt and the Social Functions of Consolidation College." *The Debt Age*, edited by Jeffrey R. Di Leo, Peter Hitchcock, and Sophia A. McClennen, Routledge, 2018, pp. 197–213.

Nissen, Sylvia, Bronwyn Hayward, and Ruth McManus. "Student Debt and Wellbeing: A Research Agenda." *Kōtuitui: New Zealand Journal of Social Sciences Online*, vol. 14, no. 2, 2019, pp. 245–56.

Noble, Safiya Umoja. *Algorithms of Oppression: How Search Engines Reinforce Racism*. New York UP, 2018.

Ohlsson, Claaes. "The Rhetoric of Financial Literacy." *Journal of Interdisciplinary Economics*, vol. 24, no. 1, 2012, pp. 55–75.

Oliver, Melvin L., and Thomas M. Shapiro. *Black Wealth / White Wealth: A New Perspective on Racial Inequality*. Routledge, 1995.

O'Neil, Cathy. *Weapons of Math Destruction: How Big Data Increases Inequality and Threatens Democracy*. Broadway Books, 2016.

Opel, Dawn S. "Challenging the Rhetorical Conception of Health Literacy: Aging, Interdependence, and Networked Caregiving." *Literacy in Composition Studies*, vol. 6, no. 2, 2018, pp. 136–50.

O'Toole, Thomas P., Jose J. Arbelaez, and Robert S. Lawrence. "Medical Debt and Aggressive Debt Restitution Practices: Predatory Billing Among the Urban Poor." *Journal of General Internal Medicine*, vol. 19, no. 2, 2004, pp. 772–78.

Painter, Marcus. "An Inconvenient Cost: The Effects of Climate Change on Municipal Bonds." *Journal of Financial Economics*, vol. 135, no. 2, 2020, pp. 468–82.

Papaconstantinou, George. *Game Over: The Inside Story of the Greek Crisis*. George Papaconstantinou, Create Space, 2016.

Pearson, Robin. "Moral Hazard and the Assessment of Insurance Risk in Eighteenth- and Early-Nineteenth-Century Britain." *Business History Review*, vol. 76, no. 1, 2002, pp. 1–35.

Peck, Jamie. "Pushing Austerity: State Failure, Municipal Bankruptcy, and the Crises of Fiscal Federalism in the USA." *Cambridge Journal of Regions, Economy and Society*, vol. 7, no. 1, 2014, pp. 17–44.

Pezzullo, Phaedra C. *Toxic Tourism: Rhetorics of Pollution, Travel, and Environmental Justice*. U of Alabama P, 2007.

Picker, Randall C., and Michael W. McConnell. "When Cities Go Broke: A Conceptual Introduction to Municipal Bankruptcy." *University of Chicago Law Review*, vol. 60, no. 2, 1993, pp. 425–95.

Poovey, Mary. *A History of the Modern Fact: Problems of Knowledge in the Sciences of Wealth and Society*. U of Chicago P, 1998.

Prasad, Monica. *The Land of Too Much: American Abundance and the Paradox of Poverty*. Harvard UP, 2012.

Price, Margaret. *Mad at School: Rhetorics of Mental Disability and Academic Life*. U of Michigan P, 2011.

Quattrone, Paolo. "The Forgotten History of Accounting Words." *Financial Management*, 30 Nov. 2019, https://www.fm-magazine.com/issues/2019/dec/history-of-accounting-words.html.

Raju, Chandra Kant. "Decolonising Mathematics." *Alternation*, vol. 25, no. 2, 2018, pp. 12–43.
———. "A New Mathematics." ckraju.net. Accessed 15 July 2020.
Rice, Jenny. *Distant Publics: Development Rhetoric and the Subject of Crisis*. U of Pittsburgh P, 2012.
Reinicke, Carmen. "This Is Why Apple, One of the World's Most Cash-Rich Companies, Just Sold $7 Billion of Debt." *Business Insider*, 5 Sept. 2019, https://markets.businessinsider.com/news/stocks/why-apple-sold-debt-despite-having-lots-of-cash-2019-9-1028503164#.
Riedner, Rachel C. "Where Are the Women? Rhetoric of Gendered Labor in University Committees" *Literacy in Composition Studies*, vol. 3, no. 1, 2015, pp. 122–30.
———. *Writing Neoliberal Values: Rhetorical Connectivities and Globalized Capitalism*. Palgrave, 2015.
Roberts, Dorothy E. "Is Race-Based Medicine Good for Us?: African American Approaches to Race, Biomedicine, and Equality." *Journal of Law, Medicine, and Ethics*, vol. 36, no. 3, 2008, pp. 537–45.
Robinson, Cedric J. *Black Marxism: The Making of the Black Radical Tradition*, 2nd edition. U of North Carolina P, 2000.
Robinson, James C. "Health Savings Accounts—The Ownership Society in Health Care." *The New England Journal of Medicine*, vol. 353, no. 12, 2005, pp. 1199–1202.
Robinson, John N., III. "Debt as Racial Capitalism." *Progressive International*, 13 Apr. 2021, https://progressive.international/blueprint/761166de-afa7-4b1f-9fd3-8cc64cdd6831-debt-as-racial-capitalism/en.
Roitman, Janet. *Fiscal Disobedience: An Anthropology of Economic Regulation in Central Africa*. Princeton UP, 2004.
Ross, Andrew. "Confronting the Creditor Class." *The Debt Age*, edited by Jeffrey R. Di Leo, Peter Hitchcock, and Sophia A. McClennen, Routledge, 2018, pp. 214–27.
Rosenthal, Caitlin. *Accounting for Slavery: Masters and Management*. Harvard UP, 2019.
Rothstein, Richard. *The Color of Law: A Forgotten History of How Our Government Segregated America*. Liveright, 2007.
Rothstein, Jesse, and Cecilia Elena Rouse. "Constrained After College: Student Loans and Early Career Occupational Choices." National Bureau of Economic Research, Working Paper, 2007, https://www.nber.org/papers/w13117.
Rowell, David, and Luke Connelly. "A History of the Term 'Moral Hazard.'" *Journal of Risk and Insurance*, vol. 79, no. 4, 2012, pp. 1051–75.
Royster, Jacqueline Jones. *Traces of a Stream: Literacy and Social Change Among African American Women*. U of Pittsburgh P, 2000.
Royster, Jacqueline Jones, and Gesa E. Kirsch. *Feminist Rhetorical Practices: New Horizons for Rhetoric, Composition, and Literacy Studies*. Southern Illinois UP, 2012.
Sangha, Jayden. "The City of Detroit Bankruptcy." *MunicipalBonds.com*, 18 Sept. 2019, https://www.municipalbonds.com/risk-management/city-of-detroit-bankruptcy/.
Sano-Franchini, Jennifer. "'It's Like Writing Yourself into a Codependent Relationship with Someone Who Doesn't Even Want You!' Emotional Labor, Intimacy, and the Academic Job Market in Rhetoric and Composition." *College Composition and Communication*, vol. 68, no. 1, 2016, pp. 98–124.
Sbragia, Alberta M. *Debt Wish: Entrepreneurial Cities, U.S. Federalism, and Economic Development*. U of Pittsburgh P, 1996.
Schell, Eileen E. "Gender, Rhetorics, and Globalization: Rethinking the Spaces and Locations of Feminist Rhetorics and Women's Rhetorics in Our Field." *Teaching Rhetorica: Theory, Pedagogy, Practice*, edited by Kate Ronald and Joy S. Ritchie, Boynton/Cook, 2006, pp. 160–74.

———. *Gypsy Academics and Mother-Teachers: Gender, Contingent Labor, and Writing Instruction.* Boynton/Cook Publishers, 1998.

———. Introduction. *Rhetorica in Motion: Feminist Rhetorical Methods and Methodologies,* edited by Eileen E. Schell and K. J. Rawson, U of Pittsburgh P, 2012, pp. 1–20.

Schell, Eileen E., and K. J. Rawson, editors. *Rhetorica in Motion: Feminist Rhetorical Methods and Methodologies.* U of Pittsburgh P, 2012.

Scott, J. Blake. *Risky Rhetoric: AIDS and the Cultural Practices of HIV Testing.* Southern Illinois UP, 2003.

———. "Tracking 'Translocal' Risks in Pharmaceutical Development: Novartis' Challenge of Indian Patent Law." *The Megarhetorics of Global Development,* edited by Rebecca Dingo and J. Blake Scott, U of Pittsburgh P, 2012, pp. 29–53.

Segal, Judy Z. *Health and the Rhetoric of Medicine.* Southern Illinois UP, 2005.

Shapiro, Thomas M. *Toxic Inequality: How America's Wealth Gap Destroys Mobility, Deepens the Racial Divide, and Threatens Our Future.* Basic, 2017.

Sharp-Hoskins, Kellie. "Rhetoric Future(s) and Accounting for Rhetorical Debt." *Peitho Journal,* vol. 21, no. 2, 2019, pp. 357–79.

Sharpe, Christina. *In the Wake: On Blackness and Being,* Duke UP, 2016.

Shiller, Robert J. *Narrative Economics: How Stories Go Viral and Drive Major Economic Events.* Princeton UP, 2019.

Siegfried, Kate. *Rhetoric of Exile: Black Proletarian Cartographies During the Cold War Era.* PhD dissertation, Texas A&M, 2021, https://oaktrust.library.tamu.edu/handle/1969.1/193127.

"The 1619 Project." *The New York Times,* 14 Aug. 2019, https://www.nytimes.com/interactive/2019/08/14/magazine/1619-america-slavery.html.

Stanford University Vaden Health Services. "How U.S. Health Insurance Works." https://vaden.stanford.edu/insurance/health-insurance-overview/how-us-health-insurance-works. Accessed 10 Dec. 2021.

Stanley, Jason. "The Emergency Manager: Strategic Racism, Technocracy, and the Poisoning of Flint's Children." *The Good Society,* vol. 25, no. 1, 2016, pp. 1–45.

Stephens, Rosemary A. Foreword. *The Blues: A History of the Blue Cross and Blue Shield System,* by John M. Cunningham Jr. and John Cunningham III, Northern Illinois UP, 1997, pp. vii–xii.

Stewart, Kathleen. *Ordinary Affects.* Duke UP, 2007.

———. "Precarity's Forms." *Cultural Anthropology,* vol. 27, no. 3, 2012, pp. 518–25.

Sweet, Elizabeth. "Debt-Related Financial Hardship and Health." *Health, Education, & Behavior,* vol. 48, no. 6, 2020, pp. 1–7.

Sweet, Elizabeth, Arijit Nandi, Emma Adam, and Thomas McDade. "The High Price of Debt: Household Financial Debt and Its Impact on Mental and Physical Health." *Social Science & Medicine,* vol. 91, 2013, pp. 94–100.

Tatham, Matt. "Student Loan Debt Climbs to $1.4 Trillion in 2019." *Experian,* 24 July 2019, https://www.experian.com/blogs/ask-experian/state-of-student-loan-debt/.

Taylor, Dorceta E. *Toxic Communities: Environmental Racism, Industrial Pollution, and Residential Mobility.* New York UP, 2014.

Temel, Judy Wesalo. *The Fundamentals of Municipal Bonds,* 5th ed. Bond Market Association, Wiley, 2001.

Trounstine, Jessica. *Segregation by Design: Local Politics and Inequality in American Cities.* Cambridge UP, 2018.

Turner, Susan M. "Texts and the Institutions of Municipal Government: The Power of Texts and the Public Process of Land Development." *Studies in Cultures, Organizations and Societies,* vol. 7, no. 2, 2002, pp. 297–325.

Turunen, Elina, and Heikki Hiilamo. "Health Effects of Indebtedness: A Systematic Review." *BMC Public Health*, vol. 14, 2014, pp. 1–8.

US Debt Clock.org. https://usdebtclock.org. Accessed 15 July 2020.

US Department of Education. "Over 323,000 Federal Student Loan Borrowers to Receive $5.8 Billion in Automatic Total and Permanent Disability Discharges." 19 Aug. 2021, https://www.ed.gov/news/press-releases/over-323000-federal-student-loan-borrowers-receive-58-billion-automatic-total-and-permanent-disability-discharges. Press release.

US Department of Labor. "Section 504." Rehabilitation Act of 1973. https://www.dol.gov/agencies/oasam/centers-offices/civil-rights-center/statutes/section-504-rehabilitation-act-of-1973. Accessed 5 Dec 2021.

US Securities and Exchange Commission (SEC). "Investor Bulletin: Municipal Bonds." 1 June 2012, https://www.sec.gov/oiea/investor-alerts-bulletins/investor-alerts-municipalbondshtm.html.

———. "Municipal Bonds." https://www.investor.gov/introduction-investing/investing-basics/investment-products/bonds-or-fixed-income-products-0. Accessed 31 July 2020.

Van Loon, Joost. *Risk and Technological Culture: Towards a Sociology of Virulence*. Routledge, 2002.

Vealey, Kyle P., and Alex Layne. "Of Complexity and Caution: Feminism, Object-Oriented Ontology, and the Practices of Scholarly Work." *Feminist Rhetorical Science Studies*, edited by Amanda K. Booher and Julie Jung, Southern Illinois UP, 2018, pp. 50–83.

Villanueva, Victor. "Toward A Political Economy of Rhetoric (Or a Rhetoric of Political Economy)." *Radical Relevance: Toward a Scholarship of the Whole Left*, edited by Laura Gray-Rosendale and Steven Rosendale, State U of New York P, 2005, pp. 57–67.

Washington, Harriet A. *Medical Apartheid: The Dark History of Medical Experimentation on Black Americans from Colonial Times to the Present*. Anchor Books, 2006.

Wanzer-Serrano, Darrel. "Rhetoric's Rac(e/ist) Problems." *Quarterly Journal of Speech*, vol. 105, no. 4, 2019, pp. 465–76.

Weisse, Kathleen Daly, Julie Jung, and Kellie Sharp-Hoskins. "Algorithmic Abstraction and the Racial Neoliberal Rhetorics of 23andMe." *Rhetoric Review*, vol. 40, no. 3, 2021, pp. 284–99.

The White House. "Fact Sheet: President Biden Announces Student Loan Relief for Borrowers Who It Need It Most." 24 Aug. 2022. https://www.whitehouse.gov/briefing-room/statements-releases/2022/08/24/fact-sheet-president-biden-announces-student-loan-relief-for-borrowers-who-need-it-most/. Press release.

Williams, Jeffrey J. "The Pedagogy of Debt." *College Literature*, vol. 33, no. 4, 2006, 155–69.

Williams, Miriam F. *From Black Codes to Codification: Removing the Veil from Regulatory Writing*. Baywood, 2020.

Wiltshire, Jaqueline, Keith Elder, Catarina Kiefe, and Jeroan J. Allison. "Medical Debt and Related Financial Consequences Among Older African American and White Adults." *American Journal of Public Health*, vol. 106, no. 6, 2016, pp. 1086–91.

Wingard, Jennifer. *Branded Bodies, Rhetoric, and the Neoliberal Nation-State*. Lexington, 2013.

Worsham, Lynn. "Going Postal: Pedagogic Violence and the Schooling of Emotion." *JAC*, vol. 18, no. 1, 1998, pp. 213–45.

Wright, Josh. "The Real Story on the $1.6 Trillion Student Loan Debt Crisis." *Boston Globe*, 3 Mar. 2020, https://www.bostonglobe.com/2020/03/03/opinion/real-story-16-trillion-student-loan-debt-crisis/.

Wynn, James, and G. Mitchell Reyes, editors. *Arguing with Numbers: The Intersections of Rhetoric and Mathematics*. Penn State UP, 2021.

Zaloom, Caitlin. *Indebted: How Families Make College Work at Any Cost*. Princeton UP, 2019.

Index

accounting
    critical accounting studies and scholarship, 15, 26, 27–28, 43
    for debt, 20
    debt reduced to, 158
    double-entry bookkeeping (DEB), 14–15, 169n11
    neutrality and dehumanization in, 13–14
    perspectives on methodologies for, 25–28
    and reparations for slavery, 161
    rhetorico-affective, 33–34
    standards and principles, 27–28
    See also rhetoric in debt, accounting for
actuarial science, 129–31, 132–33
Addo, Fenaba R., 80, 86
affect
    versus emotion, 170n9
    relationship between rhetoric, economics, and, 32–33, 35–42
    rhetorico-affective accounting, 33–34
affective labor, 160
Affordable Care Act (ACA), 124–25, 135, 143, 154
Ahmed, Sara, 36–37, 39, 40, 47–48, 50, 54, 73, 107
Aho, James Alfred, 14, 169n11
AIDS / HIV, risk associated with, 47
Akers, Beth, 60–61, 65
algorithmic abstraction, 119–20
American Medical Association (AMA), 130
Antico, Craig, 124
Apple, 171n10
Arbelaez, Jose J., 149
Arthur, Chris, 71–72, 73
Asen, Robert, 31
Ashton, Jerry, 124
auditors, 112
Aune, James Arnt, 29, 170n2
austerity measures, 112–13, 114, 158
Austin, Texas, 120–21, 122

"bad debt," 10–11, 146–47, 149, 158
Bangladeshi women, microfinance for, 169nn12–13

bankruptcy, municipal, 102, 112–15, 116, 118
Baum, Sandy, 64, 65, 70–71, 87
Bay, Charlotta, 43–44
Baylor's University Hospital, 128–29
Beck, Ulrich, 45–47, 48
behavior, debt repayment and standardization of, 38–39
Bennett, William J., 63
Bennett Hypothesis, 63
Berlant, Lauren, 26
Bernstein, Peter, 46
Beverungen, Armin, 63–64, 65
Bhattacharyya, Gargi, 4, 121, 123, 160–61
Biden-Harris Administration Student Debt Relief Plan, 171n1
Bielenberg, Jessica E., 148
Billings, B. Anthony, 111–12, 114–15
Black, Jason Edward, 97
Bohoslavsky, Juan Pablo, 55–56
Bonamici, Suzanne, 41
Bourdieu, Pierre, 75, 171n3
bricolage, feminist, 34–35
Brown, Wendy, 4, 31, 44
Burgard, Sarah A., 146
Burke, Kenneth, 27
Bush, George W., 136
Butler, Alexander, 100, 172n4
Butler, Judith, 48–49
Byrd, W. Michael, 134

capitalism
    as entangled with violent history, 11
    Lazzarato on, 167n5, 171n12
    racial, 31, 119
Caplan, Caren, 20–21
care work, 159–60
Carruthers, Bruce C., 15
Catasús, Bino, 43–44
Chakravartty, Paula, 45
Chaput, Catherine, 32–33, 36, 39, 47–48, 170n9
Chingos, Matthew M., 60–61, 65
Christie, Hazel, 77
Clayton, Linda A., 134

climate change, and municipal bond market, 109–10
climate refugees, 109
Cloud, Dana, 169n2
Coates, Te-Nahisi, 160, 161–62, 168n9
collections agencies, 149
college education
    gender and access to, 81–83
    middle-class narrative on, 57–58
    and national discourses of need for student loan debt, 61–63
    See also student loan debt
college graduation, 68–69, 79
college selectivity, 73–75
Colombini, Crystal Broch, 44, 171n11
colonial amnesia, 11–12
colonization, 59
Conley, Dalton, 67, 74, 78–79
contagion effect, 113–14
corporate bonds, 101, 171n10
COVID-19 pandemic, 57, 58, 101, 108–9, 124, 156
credit
    denial of, 156–57
    stickiness of, 45
    See also debt
credit score, 16, 17–18, 103–4
critical accounting studies and scholarship, 15, 26, 27–28, 43
Crotty, James, 112–13, 114
cultural capital, 76–77, 171n3
Cunningham, Robert III, 128
Cunningham, Robert M., 128

Darity, William A. Jr., 10–11, 75, 79–80, 168n8
Davis, Angela Y., 26
debt
    accounting for, 20
    alternative approaches to, 159–63
    assessment of use of, 54
    attachment of, to specific bodies and subjects, 48
    "bad," 10–11, 146–47, 149, 158
    cancellation of, 162–63
    conceptualizing rhetoric in, 3–5, 19–20
    cyclical patterns of, 145–46
    as entangled with rhetoric, 2
    fact of, 5–17, 24
    forgoing medical care in relation to, 146–47, 149–50
    "good," 10–11, 158
    as individual, moral, and volitional, 7–12, 18–19
    individual versus national, 8–9, 167n4
    materiality of, 26–27, 28
    moralization of, 7–12, 38–39, 54, 102–3, 115–18, 157–58
    numerical representations of, 25–26, 158, 169n11
    pedagogy of, 63–64, 73
    psychological consequences of, 37
    quantifiability of, 12–17
    as quantifiable, mathematical, and self-evident, 12–17
    relationship between health and, 148–49
    scales of, 51–52
    scholarship on rhetoric and, 4
    self-evidence of, 12–17
    and sharecropping, 168n9
    socially sanctioned versus disturbing, 21
    stickiness of, 36–42, 45
    and subjectivity, 90–93
    in US history, 59–60, 167n2
    of war, 59–60
    See also credit; medical debt; municipal bonds; rhetoric in debt, accounting for; school lunch debt; student loan debt
debt forgiveness, 85, 88, 124, 171n1
debt scholarship, interdisciplinary, 32–33, 35–42, 51
Deleuze, Gilles, 91, 163
Derrig, Richard A., 132–33
Detroit, Michigan, 114–19
DeVos, Betsy, 56–57
Dingo, Rebecca, 20, 41, 51
disabilities, 84–85
displacement, 121
dividuals, 91–92, 105–6
Dobkin, Carlos, 144–45
Dolmage, Jay, 84
"dominant pedagogy," 72
Donaldson, Cam, 130–31, 132, 135, 136, 138–39
double-entry bookkeeping (DEB), 14–15, 169n11
Dougal, Casey, 110
Douglas, Alexander X., 7–8
Duerringer, Christopher M., 4
Duster, Troy, 152
Dwyer, Rachel E., 68, 69–70, 81, 83, 87

economic crises
    deficit spending during, 60
    financial crisis (2008), 44–45, 78, 100
economic imaginary, 4, 94
economics
    insurance models and mainstream, 131–32
    orthodox and heterodox, 30–31

relationship between rhetoric, affect, and, 32–33, 35–42
relationship between rhetoric and, 29
as understood in relation to other forms of life, 4
Edbauer, Jenny, 37
Ehlers, Nadine, 134, 135, 152, 153–54, 155
Electronic Municipal Market Access (EMMA), 99, 106, 109
Emergency Manager Law(s), 115–16, 119
emotion
  versus affect, 170n9
  and affects of debt, 39
  cultural politics of, 54
  role in persuasive force of economic narratives, 36
emotional labor, 159–60
empirical proof, mathematics' separation from, 16
employment discrimination, 79–80
"empowered third world girl," 41–42
  See also microfinance
Enoch, Jessica, 82, 84
enthymematic analysis, 4, 7, 17–19
enthymeme, 5, 6, 7, 24
equivalencies, 13
Erie, Steven P., 96–97
Erie Canal, 94–95
Espeland, Wendy Nelson, 15
ethos, and financial literacy as individual possession, 43

FAFSA (Free Application for Federal Student Aid), 91–92, 171n1
Fauver, Larry, 100
federal government, purchases municipal bonds, 101
Federal Liquidity Facility, 101
feminist bricolage, 34–35, 52–53
feminist scholarship, transnational, 20–21
Ferreira da Silva, Denise, 45
FICO scores, 16, 17–18
financial crisis (2008), 44–45, 78, 100
financialization, 3, 12
financial literacy, 9–11, 42–45
  and Emergency Manager Laws, 116
  and gender, 83–84
  and Health Savings Accounts (HSAs), 141–43
  impossible expectations for, 85–86
  and municipal bonds, 103, 116
  negotiating health literacy and, 137–38, 141
  neoliberal requirements for performances of, 171n11
  and planned and unplanned medical costs, 143–46
  and race, 75–76
  and student loan debt, 69–73
financial literacy education, "public pedagogy" of, 71–73
Flores, Lisa, 32
Free Application for Federal Student Aid (FAFSA), 91–92, 171n1
Frees, Edward W., 132–33
Friedman, Milton, 110
Frost, Erin A., 34–35
Fuller, Mathew B., 63

Gao, Pengjie, 113–14
gender
  and "empowered third world girl," 42
  and microfinance, 169nn12–13
  in rhetoric studies, 32–33
  and student loan debt, 81–84
General Obligation (GO) Bonds, 100, 107–9, 111, 172n4
Georgiou, Omiros, 28
Gerard, Karen, 130–31, 132, 135, 136, 138–39
Ginsburg, Ruth Bader, 147
Goff, Robert, 124, 125
Goldrick-Rab, Sara, 62–63
"good debt," 10–11, 158
Grabill, Jeffrey T., 47
Graeber, David, 3, 7, 11, 12, 13, 162–63
Greene, Ronald Walter, 31, 169n2
Grewal, Inderpal, 20–21
Griggs, Jennifer J., 150
Guattari, Félix, 91
guilt, 8–9
  See also shame
Gupta, Arpit, 144

Haas, Angela M., 34–35
Haberman, Steven, 129
habitus, 75
Hamilton, Alexander, 94
Hamilton, Darrick, 10–11, 75, 79–80, 158, 168n8
Hanan, Joshua S., 4, 24, 94
Hannah-Jones, Nikole, 97
Harding, Sarah, 170n7
"hardship letters," 171n11
Harity, William A., 158
Harvey, David, 3, 12

190   INDEX

Haynes, Cynthia, 13
HBUCs (Historically Black Colleges and Universities), 110–11
health
  association of wealth and medical debt with, 150
  relationship between debt and, 148–49
health care
  evolution of American, 126–27
  forgoing, in relation to debt, 146–47, 149–50
  See also health insurance; medical debt
HealthCare.gov, 137–38
health insurance, 124–25
  and "bad debt," 147
  emergence of industry, 126, 128–30
  functioning of, 125, 126–27
  and health and financial literacies, 137–41
  HSAs as model for, 142–43
  and inequitable health outcomes along racial lines, 133–34
  "managed care" options for, 135–37, 141–43
  and personal responsibility, 134, 135
  and planned and unplanned medical costs, 143–46
  risk and issuance of, 47
  risk-sharing model of, 125–26
  viability of, 130–33
  See also medical debt
health literacy, 137–43, 151
Health Maintenance Organization Act (1973), 136
Health Maintenance Organizations (HMOs), 135–36
Health Savings Accounts (HSAs), 141–44
Herring, William Rodney, 4, 29, 33, 94
Hesford, Wendy S., 49, 50, 52
Hildreth, W. Bartley, 100, 172n3
Hinkson, Leslie R., 134, 135, 152, 153–54, 155
Historically Black Colleges and Universities (HBUCs), 110–11
HIV / AIDS, risk associated with, 47
Hodson, Randy, 68, 69–70, 81, 83
Hoedemaekers, Casper, 63–64, 65
Hoffman, Beatrix, 129–30
homelessness, 148
homo economicus, 4, 30, 36, 48, 158, 167n1
Houle, Jason N., 80, 86
housing discrimination, 78, 79–80, 120–21
Houston, Melvin, 111–12, 114–15
hypertension, and race-based medicine, 152

IFRS (International Financial Reporting Standards), 27, 28

income, correlation between student debt and, 68
indentured service, 11, 168n9
Indigenous land, 97–98, 168n9
individual, debt as, 7–12, 18–19
inequality
  in access to medical care, 133–34
  and municipal bonds, 96–99
  racial, 9, 88, 155, 168nn7–8
  and student loan debt, 67–68, 73–81, 86
infrastructure and development funding, 172n4
intergenerational wealth, 9, 78, 80
Issar, Siddhant, 32

Jackson, Brandon A., 86
Jackson, Matthew, 7
Johed, Gustav, 43–44
Joseph, Miranda, 2, 3, 14, 15, 26, 34, 35, 49, 83–84, 87–88, 89
Jung, Julie, 51, 52, 119–20

Kalousova, Lucie, 146
Karim, Lamia, 169nn12–13
Katz, Steven, 13, 14
Kimball, Justin Ford, 128, 129
Kirsch, Gesa E., 170n8
Knutson, Brian, 37
Konings, Martijn, 167n2
Krippner, Greta R., 3
Krugman, Paul, 167n4
Kundnani, Arun, 32

labor unions, 134
LaDuke, Winona, 153
Las Cruces, New Mexico, 107–9, 111
Lawrence, Robert S., 149
Layne, Alex, 52, 164, 170n7
Lazzarato, Maurizio
  on capitalism, 167n5, 171n12
  on creditor-debtor relationship, 6, 170nn4–5
  on debt and guilt, 8
  on debt and subjectivity, 90–91
  on debt cancellation, 163
  on debt repayment and behavior standardization, 38
  on effect of debt, 3
  on function of debt, 148
  homo economicus, 4, 30, 36, 48, 158, 167n1
  on MSRB Terms of Use, 105–6
  on relationship between neoliberalism, subjectivity, and affect, 34
Lea, Stephen E. G., 37
Lee, Chang, 113–14

Lee, Shawna J., 115–16
Levitt, Arthur, 99–100
Licona, Adela C., 49, 50
Lloyd, Jenna M., 133, 134, 147, 154
Longaker, Mark Garrett, 4, 29, 33

machinic subjection, 23, 91–93, 100, 109, 121, 123
Madison, James, 94
Manifest Destiny, 97
Mann, Horace, 61
Mantzari, Elisavet, 28
Marx, Karl, 13, 33, 90, 170n4
materiality of debt, 26–27, 28
maternity care, 143–44, 146
mathematics, 12–17
McCloskey, Deidre N., 29, 169n1
McCloud, Laura, 68, 69–70, 81, 83
McConnell, Michael W., 112, 114
McGee, Michael Calvin, 31
Medicaid, 125, 134–35, 150–51
"medical apartheid," 128, 133–34
medical debt, 124–28
    correlation between health and, 150
    defined, 125
    economic factors influencing, 145
    elimination of, 124
    forgoing medical care in relation to, 146–47, 149–50
    and homelessness, 148
    and personal responsibility, 153–54
    and planned and unplanned medical costs, 143–45
    and race, 150–51, 154
    statistics on, 167n2
    See also health insurance
medical hot spotting, 153–54
Medicare, 134, 150–51
Mendes de Leon, Carlos F., 150
mentoring relationships, 159–60
Mewse, Avril J., 37
Meyers, Glenn, 132–33
microfinance, 169nn12–13
    See also "empowered third world girl"
Millman, Marcia, 76–77, 171n3
Mills, Charles, 119
Moniz, Michelle H., 146
moral hazard, 131, 147
moralization of debt, 7–12, 38–39, 54, 102–3, 115–18, 157–58
moralization of health literacies, 143
Mortal, Sandra, 100
mortgage crisis (2008), 44–45, 78

mortgages, shame for, 42
Mullen, Ann L., 61–62, 74–75, 76, 82
municipal bankruptcy, 112–15, 116, 118
municipal bond insurance, 99
municipal bonds, 92–93, 122–23
    allocation of risk by and uses of, 107–11
    and development risk and rehabilitation, 119–22
    distribution of, 122–23
    emergence of contemporary market, 99–100
    history of, in United States, 94–100
    inequitable effects of, 96–99
    and infrastructure and development funding, 172n4
    low-risk reputation of, 100–103
    marking and shifting risk of, 111–13
    moralization of risk, 115–18
    perceiving and containing risk of, 113–15
    racialized risk of, 118–19
    ratings and determining risk of, 103–7, 111
    voting on, 118, 122, 172n5
Municipal Securities Rulemaking Board (MSRB), 99, 103–4, 105–7, 109
Munro, Moira, 77
Murphy, Dermot, 113–14
Murray, John E., 129, 130, 131

national debt, US, 8–9, 167n4
Nazi regime, 13–14
neoliberalism, 12, 15, 29–32, 63–64, 135, 167n5, 169n12, 170n5
Newcomb. Matthew J., 26
Newfield, Christopher, 68, 73–74, 77
Nietzsche, Friedrich, 38, 90
Noble, Safiya Umoja, 16

Obamacare (Patient Protection and Affordable Care Act [ACA]), 124–25, 135, 143
obligation, debt versus, 12
Ohlsson, Claess, 43
Oliver, Melvin L., 9, 76–78, 168nn7–8
Opel, Dawn S., 139–40
open futures, 78, 87
O'Toole, Thomas P., 149

Painter, Marcus, 109
Patient Protection and Affordable Care Act (ACA), 124–25, 135, 143, 154
Pearson, Robin, 131
Peck, Jamie, 106, 112, 118, 165
pedagogy of debt, 63–64, 73
personal responsibility, and health care, 135, 153–54

Pezzullo, Phaedra C., 153
Picker, Randal C., 112, 114
Prasad, Monica, 78
precariousness / precarity, 48–50
preexisting conditions, 47
pregnancy and maternity care, 143–44, 146
prescription drugs, and race-based medicine, 152
Price, Richard, 129
Prior, Paul, 140
public assistance, worthiness for, 38–39, 40–41
"public pedagogy" of financial literacy education, 71–73
punishment, for school lunch debt, 1–2

quantifiability of debt, 12–17
Quattrone, Paolo, 169n11

race
 and affect and stickiness of debt, 39–40
 and development risk and rehabilitation, 120–21
 and financial literacy, 44, 75–76
 and gendered performance of financial literacy, 83–84
 and homelessness due to medical debt, 148
 and impact of subprime mortgage crisis, 44–45
 and inequitable access to health care, 133–34
 and inequitable effects of municipal bonds, 96–98
 and inverse relationship between medical care and medical debt, 154
 "medical apartheid," 128, 133–34
 and medical debt, 150–51
 and municipal bond risk, 115–16, 118–19
 in rhetoric studies, 31–32
 and student loan debt, 68, 73–81, 86
 and wealth gap, 88, 168n8
race-based medicine, 151–52, 154
racial capitalism, 31, 119
racial domination, 32
racial inequality, 9, 88, 155, 168nn7–8
racial justice, 3–4, 9–11
Raffer, Kunibert, 55–56
railroads, 95, 99
Raju, Chandra Kant, 16
Reagan, Ronald, 40
relations, serving as conditions for possibility of debt, 50–51
reparations for slavery, 160–62
Reynolds, John R., 86

rhetoric
 conceptualizing, in debt, 3–5, 19–20
 debt as entangled with, 2
 relationship between economics, affect, and, 32–33, 35–42
 relationship between economics and, 29
 scholarship on debt and, 4
 rhetoric in debt, accounting for, 24–25, 158–59, 164–66
 accounting for "financial literacy," 42–45
 accounting for relations serving as conditions for possibility of debt, 50–51
 accounting for risk, 45–50
 accounting methodologies and contextualization of, 25–28
 methodology via feminist bricolage, 34–35, 52–53
 relationship between economics, affect, and rhetoric, 35–42
 rhetorico-affective accounting, 33–34
 scales of debt, 51–52
 scholarship on rhetoric and economics and groundwork for, 29–33
rhetoric studies
 gender in, 32–33
 race in, 31–32
Rhodes, Steven, 115, 116
Rice, Jenny, 120–21, 122
Riedner, Rachel, 20, 36, 170n3
RIP Medical Debt, 124
risk
 and accounting for rhetoric in debt, 45–50
 associated with HIV / AIDS, 47
 health insurance as sharing of, 125–26, 127
 See also municipal bonds
risk sharing / risk contagion, 113–14
risk society, 46–47
Roberts, Dorothy, 151–52
Robinson, Cedric, 31
Robinson, James, 141, 142–43
Robinson, JohnnIII, 3–4
Roitman, Janet, 21
Rosenthal, Caitlin, 14, 161
Ross, Andrew, 9, 73
Rothstein, Richard, 98, 122
Royster, Jacqueline Jones, 35, 170n8

Samanez-Larkin, Gregory R., 37
Sano-Franchini, Jennifer, 170n3
Sbragia, Alberta, 94, 95, 96, 118, 172n2
scales of debt, 51–52

school lunch debt, 1–2, 19
Scott, J. Blake, 47, 48, 54
Securities and Exchange Commission (SEC), 99–100, 101
security, risk and, 48
Segal, Judy Z., 145–46
segregation, housing, 120–21
　See also housing discrimination
self-evidence of debt, 12–17
sensation, 170n9
service industries, 160
shame, 39–41, 44–45
　See also guilt
Shapiro, Thomas M., 9, 76–78, 88, 168nn7–8
sharecropping, 168n9
　See also indentured service
Sharpe, Christina, 14, 169n10
Shiller, Robert J., 20, 36
Sibbett, Trevor A., 129
sickness funds, 126, 129
　See also health insurance
Simmons, W. Michelle, 47
Simon, Daniel, 80, 86
slavery and slave trade, 11, 14, 59, 97, 160–62, 169n10
social class
　and college selectivity, 74–75
　Greene on, 169n2
　and student loan debt, 67–68, 78–79
social contract, 119
social subjection, 91, 92
sovereign debt crises, 55–56
Stanley, Jason, 116, 119
Stephens, Rosemary A., 126
Stewart, Kathleen, 49
Stuart, James E., 128
student loan debt, 54–55, 84–88, 89–90
　"crisis" of, in United States, 55–58, 88
　defaulting on, 69–70
　defining terms of, 65–66
　as dependent on normative intergenerational relationships, 167n6
　disabilities and access to and discharge of, 84–85
　forgiveness of, 85, 88, 124, 171n1
　and gender, 81–84
　identifying new metrics for, 67–70
　national discourses of need for, 59–64
　posting financial literacy as solution to problems associated with, 70–73
　and race, 68, 73–81, 86
　and social and machinic subjection to emergence of rhetoric in debt, 91–92
　See also FAFSA (Free Application for Federal Student Aid)
subjectivity, 90–93
subprime mortgage crisis (2008), 44–45, 78, 100
Supplemental Nutrition Assistance Program (SNAP), 40–41
Sweet, Elizabeth, 146, 148–49

Taft, Robert, 134, 135
tax preferences, 78
Tax Reform Act (1986), 172n3
Temel, Judy Wesalo, 104, 172n4
"Terms of Use," 105–7, 123
territorial expansion, 97
Teston, Christa, 49, 50
"third world girl, empowered," 41–42
　See also microfinance
toxic exposures, 153
transnational feminist scholarship, 20–21
transportation, and municipal debt in US, 94–95
Trump, Donald, 56–57
trust, risk and, 48
Turner, Susan M., 121–22

unionization, 134
United States
　debt in history of, 59–60, 167n2
　history of municipal debt in, 94–100
　national debt of, 8–9, 167n4
University of Texas, 120–21
unstated premises, surfacing, 19–21
urban development, 119–22
urban renewal, 120–21

Van Loon, Joost, 45, 46
Vealey, Kyle P., 52, 164, 170n7
Veldman, Jeroen, 63–64, 65
Volz, William H., 111–12, 114–15
voting, on municipal bond issuance, 118, 122, 172n5
voting-rights laws, 98

Walcott, Rinaldo, 153
Wanzer-Serrano, Darrel, 32
war, debts of, 59–60
Washington, Harriet A., 128, 133–34, 151
wealth
　association of, with health metrics, 150
　intergenerational, 9, 78, 80
　municipal bonds and accumulation of, 103

wealth gap, 88, 168n8
　See also inequality
Weisse, Kathleen Daly, 119–20
"Welfare Queen," 40
westward expansion, 97
Williams, Jeffrey, 64, 65
Williams, Miriam F., 98
Wiltshire, Jaqueline, 150–51
Wingard, Jennifer, 20, 36
World War II, deficit spending during, 60
Worsham, Lynn, 32, 71–72, 170n3

worthiness
　and "empowered third world girl," 41–42
　for public assistance, 38–39, 40–41
Wrapson, Wendy, 37
Wright, Josh, 69

Zaloom, Caitlin, 57, 62, 67–68, 78, 87, 91, 92, 167n6, 171n1
"zones of death," 153
Zong, 169n10
Zorn, C. Kurt, 100, 172n3

www.ingramcontent.com/pod-product-compliance
Lightning Source LLC
Chambersburg PA
CBHW022057290426
44109CB00014B/1132